ARC
LIBRARY

Beyond the Closet

Beyond the Closet

THE TRANSFORMATION OF GAY AND LESBIAN LIFE

Steven Seidman

ROUTLEDGE NEW YORK AND LONDON

Published in 2002 by
Routledge
29 West 35th Street
New York, NY 10001
www.routledge-ny.com

Published in Great Britain by
Routledge
11 New Fetter Lane
London EC4P 4EE
www.routledge.co.uk

Routledge is an imprint of the Taylor & Francis Group.

Library of Congress Cataloging-in-Publication Data

Seidman, Steven.
Beyond the closet : the transformation of gay and lesbian life / by Steven Seidman.
p. cm.
Includes bibliographical references and index.
ISBN 0-415-93206-8 (HB : alk. paper)
1. Homosexuality. 2. Gays—Identity. 3. Lesbians—Identity. I. Title.
HQ76.25 .S485 2002
306.76'6—dc21 2002009214

For Lou

CONTENTS

ACKNOWLEDGMENTS

I have benefited greatly from the comments of Jeff Alexander, Steven Epstein, Josh Gamson, Linda Nicholson, Arlene Stein, Jeff Weeks, Kath Weston, Ken Plummer, Henning Bech, Patricia Clough, Roger Friedland, Judy Stacey, Chyrs Ingraham, Richard Lachmann, Jim Zethka, Chet Meeks, Francie Traschen, Nancy Fisher, and James Dean. In particular, Linda Nicholson and Lou Rose read each chapter and offered helpful and always encouraging comments. I am very lucky to have these two wonderful people in my life.

This book began in 1996. Over the years I have had the good fortune to present my ideas to varied audiences. I am especially grateful to the students and faculty at the University of Victoria, the State University of New York at Albany and Buffalo, the University of California, Santa Barbara, the Center for Lesbian and Gay Studies at City University of New York, the Havens Center at the University of Wisconsin-Madison, the New School for Social Research, the Universities of Chicago, Hawaii, Akron, and Kentucky, Rice University, and colleagues in Amsterdam, Gert Hekma and Jan Willem Duyvendak in particular. Special thanks to the Great Barrington Theory group, where I initially presented some of these ideas.

I do not know how to thank my editor, Ilene Kalish. She read every line of every chapter, offering remarkably wise and often pointed advise that, despite being cranky at times, I almost always followed. Thank you, Ilene.

INTRODUCTION

In March 2001, *New York* magazine published a special issue, "Gay Life Now." The portrait that emerges spotlights one overriding theme: gay life now is not what it was just a decade or so ago. The culture critic, Daniel Mendelsohn, set the tone of the issue.

> Twenty years ago . . . my gay friends and I would have made the time to watch anything that promised a gay sensibility, gay subplots, gay characters. . . . That's how hungry we were to see ourselves reflected in . . . network TV—to feel that media validation, to feel that we were visible. . . . Twenty years later, there are so many gay films . . . , gay books, gay plays, gay TV characters and subplots, and now gay TV shows, that you wouldn't be able to keep up with them if you wanted to.[1]

Mendelsohn is not pleased with the portrayal of gay men as either straight-looking-and-acting or as buffoonlike jesters (respectively Will and Jack of *Will and Grace*), while lesbians remain conspicuously absent. Still, he is stunningly surprised by the sheer magnitude of change over the last two decades. "Times have clearly changed."

Gay visibility in television and popular culture is not viewed as exceptional, but speaks to broader changes in the social status of lesbians and gay men. True, gays can't marry or serve in the military, and are still vulnerable to being fired, harassed, and assaulted. Yet Jesse Green provocatively declares that "the war for acceptance is practically won." Further, "We have . . . moved forthrightly into the larger world . . .as power brokers, opinion-makers. . . . If you look at the past 30 years—the past ten especially—you have to conclude that while losing almost all the battles, we have won the war. . . . Most of us feel surer, safer, more integrally American than anyone ever dreamed possible in 1970."[2] While the writer protests that it is mostly white middle-class men who are invited to have a place at the table, we are assured that the table is getting bigger all the time.

To further assess the state of gay life in America, *New York* magazine conducted a poll of straight, gay, and lesbian New Yorkers. The survey uncovered "landslide-levels of acceptance. . . . Most straight people are not only very comfortable with gays but are socially and professionally intimate with them as well. . . . Straight New Yorkers are broadly accepting of gays in positions of responsibility and public leadership. . . . And they take gay relationships seriously." Further, 80 percent of straight New Yorkers would be comfortable with an openly gay police officer, 70 percent with an openly gay doctor, and 65 percent with an openly gay elementary school teacher; 58 percent of straight New Yorkers think gays should be able to marry.[3]

New York is not America. Still, *New York* magazine got one thing right: the place of gays in America has changed significantly.

THE DEBATE OVER "GAY LIFE NOW"

While there is little disagreement that gay life in America is changing, there is little agreement about what this means.[4] For some observers, social integration is the defining trend. Gays are being incorporated into "mainstream" society; there is a slow and uneven but steady march toward social acceptance and equality. Accordingly, many gays can now choose how to be gay and how to relate to the larger society. And many are said to be choosing a conventional life of marriage, raising a family, building a career, and owning a home, options that were until recently unavailable to most gay Americans. Speaking of these mainstreaming trends, Michelangelo Signorile, editor of *The Advocate* and author of *Queer in America* and the best-selling *Life Outside,* writes, "As more people come out of the closet, they create more choice about how to be gay or lesbian. . . . Many are . . . living their lives as most other Americans do."[5]

Bruce Bawer, conservative culture critic and author of *A Place at the Table*, also thinks that integration and mainstreaming is the dominant trend. "Today individuals have more freedom. . . . Things have improved. . . . People are more enlightened."[6] And not only are gays coming out in record numbers, they are no longer leaving their hometowns to establish separate identities and lives in urban enclaves. Instead, gays "are choosing to be part of the American mainstream."[7] Bawer recognizes that gays still suffer prejudice and that some individuals will reasonably choose to retreat into silence or live double lives. However, efforts by old-styled liberationists to either romanticize gays' outsider status or mobilize their deep-seated rage against what they imagine to be an oppressive system is an obstacle to continued progress. The vast majority of gays want to "live ordinary middle class lives." And the best path to social acceptance is to educate the public about the common human bonds between homosexuals and heterosexuals. "America is basically a tolerant nation in which a misunderstood and persecuted minority's best chance lies not in sowing antagonism but in attempting to sow understanding. . . . Mainstream gays . . . must help heterosexuals to recognize . . . the common humanity, common backgrounds, and common values that they share with most homosexuals."[8]

But even supporters of mainstreaming concede that progress is slow and uneven. Andrew Sullivan, the controversial author of *Virtually Normal,* comments that "fear and loathing of homosexuals is still a powerful force in the culture."[9] And, he points out, "homosexuals are still systemically discriminated against *by the state* in the military, in law and in marriage rights."[10] Sullivan insists, though, that the old pact that tolerated homosexuals so long as they were private and hidden from respectable society is being renegotiated. "The old public-private distinction . . . in which homosexuals committed sexual acts in private and concealed this from public view . . . disappears and a new public-private distinction emerges: [today] homosexuals claim publicly that they are gay."[11] Sullivan speaks optimistically of a "fitful process of assimilation."[12]

Not all observers are so positive about the present and hopeful about the future. Some agree that gay integration is a leading social trend, but they are disapproving. In his spirited polemic *The Rise and Fall of Gay Culture*, Daniel Harris criticizes the lesbian and gay movement for aspiring to assimilate into what he describes as a media- and business-driven, socially homogenizing American culture. While acknowledging the personal costs of being an outsider, Harris laments the decline of a gay sensibility that has been a key source of cultural innovation in America. He argues that "assimilation . . . has profound ramifications for the country's cultural life, which will be deprived of a major source of artistic and intellectual energy as homosexuals are finally integrated."[13]

Still other critics take issue with the claim that integration and equality is the chief trend today. In her weighty polemic against assimilationism, Urvashi Vaid, the prominent activist and author of *Virtual Equality*, "exposes" the illusion of progress.

> The irony of gay and lesbian mainstreaming is that more than fifty years of active effort to challenge homophobia and heterosexism have yielded us not freedom but "virtual equality." . . . Gay and lesbian people possess some of the trappings of full equality but are denied all of its benefits. . . . We are at once members of the traditional family. . . but are treated as if we are aliens to the family as an institution. We participate daily in every community, culture, profession . . . but we are forced to deny that we exist. . . . Gay men and lesbians work alongside their heterosexual counterparts in every job . . . but the condition for keeping these jobs is pretending not to be gay or lesbian. We pay taxes, yet our government denies gay people its public embrace, access to its programs, and its protection. . . . [In short], I believe that the notion that homosexuality has been mainstreamed is an illusion.[14]

Vaid does not deny that some gays, mostly white, middle class, and urban, have benefited from legal reform and a softening of homophobia. But the vast majority of lesbians and gay men still feel compelled to take refuge in the closet. Vaid speaks of "the other gay America. . . . It is the one in which most of our people live, dominated by fear, permeated by discrimination, violence, and shame. A place where people are still governed primarily by the fear of disclosure of their sexual orientation."[15]

The radical activist and academic queer writer Michael Warner similarly doubts the new triumphalist view of the gay movement. "At a time when homophobic initiatives are gaining ground at local, state, and federal levels, when even the movement to repeal sodomy statutes has all but stalled, the assumption of inevitable progress toward equal rights for everyone should give us pause." Indeed, Warner believes that the few successes of a right's-oriented movement in the 1980s and 1990s have come to a virtual standstill as it encountered a stone wall of hardcore homophobia and heterosexual domination. "The military service campaign has resulted in a higher rate of military discharges for homosexuality. . . . The marriage campaign resulted in the Defense of Marriage Act. . . . Both the military policy and DOMA . . . sanction homophobia as national policy. Both exemplify an overreaching confidence in progress that has led to results that . . . are regressive."[16]

Critics like Vaid and Warner advocate the renewal of the radical activism of gay liberationism. While they support reforming laws and attitudes to permit gays greater open participation in the mainstream, straight America itself needs to be changed to enhance the freedom of all its citizens. Institutions such as marriage and the family, and a culture organized around dichotomous gender identities and an ideal of heterosexual love and romance, are oppressive to many gay—and straight—citizens.

These varied perspectives frame the outlines of the debate now taking place regarding the social and political meaning of the changing status of gays in America. Each side has, I think, both grasped and missed something fundamental about the present.

Perspectives that spotlight expanding individual choice and social integration are compelling because they speak to real, dramatic developments in gay life. And they rightly understand that many lesbian and gay Americans desire little more than to be treated as ordinary citizens with the same rights, respect, and opportunities as their straight counterparts. However, I share the view with those on the left side of the debate that gay inequality is deeply rooted in American society. A movement aimed at gaining equal rights and respect for a social minority leaves heterosexual dominance intact. For example, extending civil rights to lesbians and gay men doesn't alter a gender order that favors men and heterosexuals; it doesn't challenge a culture that makes heterosexuality the norm and ideal. Accordingly, I favor a movement that broadens its agenda beyond seeking equal rights for sexual minorities to addressing wider patterns of sexual and social injustice. At the same time, the very real and significant improvement in gay people's lives that have been made possible by recent social reforms should not be discounted. Integration is not, as Vaid declares, an "illusion." And, if champions of mainstreaming accept too quickly the virtues of assimilating into America as it is, some critics on the left too easily surrender to a romanticism that imagines America as fundamentally repressive and gays as potential revolutionaries.

Gay life *is* today very different than it was just a decade or two ago. Gay Americans today have more choices about how to live, and their lives often look more like those of conventional heterosexuals than those of the closeted homosexuals of the recent past. Still, heterosexuals enjoy a privileged, superior social status that is secured by the state, social institutions, and popular culture. Gay life today is defined by a contradiction: *many individuals can choose to live beyond the closet but they must still live and participate in a world where most institutions maintain heterosexual domination.*

THE DISAPPEARING CLOSET

Between 1996 and 1998, I interviewed thirty individuals of different races, classes, genders, and generations. What they were all supposed to share was the experience of being in the closet. I wanted to understand the psychological and social texture of the closet. I was especially interested in the emotional and social costs of passing and how a sense of self and social belonging is fashioned under such conditions. To find closeted individuals I placed ads in local and regional gay newspapers and newsletters. Some of these individuals referred me to friends and acquaintances.

When I began my research I was convinced that the closet was still the defining reality for most gay Americans. I considered my own experience to be atypical. I am a gay man whose life is more or less like those of my straight friends and colleagues. I reasoned, though, that I was part of a somewhat unique academic social world, a large university, that is much more tolerant and respectful of social differences than the rest of America.

I was prepared to tell a story of the closet as a condition of social oppression. In particular, I wanted to focus on the way heterosexual domination is sustained by shaping the psychology of closeted individuals, though I didn't like the widespread image of gays as passive victims. I realized that I needed to show that the closet means different things to people depending on their age, income, gender, sense of self, and the strength of their homo- and heterosexual feelings. I knew from experience that some closeted individuals fashion satisfying lives, while others suffer tragically. I was also uncomfortable with the notion that coming out is liberating. Coming out feels good and surely makes more choices possible. However, I also believed that simply coming out does not rid us of feelings of shame and guilt, and that visibility alone does not threaten heterosexual privilege. In short, I wanted to offer a more complex view of the experience of being in the closet.

What I heard was unexpected. While many of the individuals I interviewed described themselves as closeted, their current lives didn't fit what I take to be as the defining feature of the closet. The closet, I reasoned, is about an individual's having to make life-shaping decisions in order to pass. The individuals I interviewed described *past* lives that were closeted. However, as they talked about their present lives it became clear that, except for a few individuals, they were not making decisions about love, work, friends, and social activities to avoid exposure or suspicion. Almost all of the individuals I interviewed spoke of concealing their homosexuality in specific situations or with particular individuals. This episodic pattern of concealment should not be confused, as many of my interviewees did, with the closet. There is a huge difference between concealing from an uncle or a client and marrying or avoiding certain occupations in order to pretend to be straight. The former may be a source of anxiety and discomfort, but the latter potentially shapes a whole way of life. If the concept of the closet is to be useful in understanding gay life, it should describe a "life-shaping" social pattern.

Homosexuality is so fateful for the individual precisely because the closet involves fashioning a public life at odds with private feelings and one's core sense of self. If there were no need to be closeted, homosexuality might still be a source of disrespect and disadvantage. However, the realities of the closet force individuals to make a momentous choice: a life of passing or a struggle to come out. Either way, the closet makes homosexuality a potentially life-shaping condition. Also, and importantly, the fact that the closet is about individuals making decisions about love, work, residence, and friends in order to conceal an important part of who they are suggests that it is more than an inconvenience or minor nuisance; it is a condition of social oppression. Closeted individuals suffer systematic forms of disadvantage and disrespect. Accordingly, the closet is not simply a product of individual ignorance and discrete acts of prejudice and discrimination, but is created by the actions of the government, the criminal justice system, families, and popular and scientific culture. In short, the closet refers to a state of gay oppression produced by a condition of heterosexual domination.

No one, surely not myself, can seriously maintain that the realities of homophobia and heterosexism are in the past. Some facts are indisputable. According to the Uniform Crime Reports, hate crimes against gays have increased almost fourfold between 1991 and 1998; since the "Don't ask, don't tell" policy was installed in 1994, the number of lesbians and gay men discharged from the military has risen by almost 70 percent; while the number of pro-gay bills introduced into state legislatures increased steadily in the mid-1990s (for example, 41 in 1995,

128 in 1997), so too has the number of anti-gay measures (64 in 1995, 120 in 1997). And let's not forget that families, schools, the military, and churches, not to mention the Boy Scouts, remain minefields for many gay Americans. Sadly, the closet remains a reality for too many lesbians and gay men.

Still, my research suggests that many gay Americans today live outside the social framework of the closet. These individuals approach their homosexuality as a natural, good part of themselves; they have integrated it into their daily lives; they have lovers and partners; they are out with some coworkers, kin, and friends, and openly participate in mainstream social life. If I am right, many of the chief ways that gay life has been understood in post-Stonewall culture are no longer accurate; for example, in terms of a narrative of coming out or as a story of migration to gay ghettoes. In particular, individuals approach sexual identity differently as the closet disappears.

SEXUAL IDENTITY

Identities refer to the way we think of ourselves and the self image we publicly project.[17] No doubt our identities are related to how we feel about ourselves and to our character or personality; as such, the image we publicly fashion might feel like a spontaneous expression of who we really are. Yet we can project an identity only through acting purposefully. The decisions we make about the way we dress, walk, and talk, the language we use and how we use it, who we associate with, and where and with whom we live make a statement about who we are. These practices announce to the world something about our gender, sexuality, parental status, social class, ethnic identity, and countless other markers of identity. In other words, we fashion identities by drawing on a culture that already associates identities with certain behaviors, places, and things.

Identities are complex. We don't have just one and in the course of our lives we can alter—add or subtract—identities. We make choices about which identity or identities to make into a core part of our self-definition and which will be treated as "threads" or secondary.

If an identity such as being a wife is considered "core," it will shape an individual's decisions about friends, residence, social activities, and employment. A core identity will be a key part of one's public presentation; it will carry over to diverse situations and remain part of varied social roles. It will be a chief way you want friends, coworkers, acquaintances, and kin to see and respond to you. For example, if being Jewish is a core identity, an individual will fashion a public self that consistently signals this identity by means of clothes, language, social activities, and friends. Decisions about partners or lovers, work, residence, and donations of time and money will likely be shaped by a core identity. By contrast, approaching identity as a thread suggests that an identity is important or self-defining in only some situations. While we may have only one or two core identities, we have many identity threads. For example, when I'm at home my identity as a parent may be paramount but at work it's my identity as a professor that matters; while as an active member of the gay community it is being gay that is crucial.

Not all identities are chosen or easily managed. There may be social pressure to approach certain identities as core ones; other individuals may disregard your wish to make this or that identity into a core or a thread. For example, for many people, race and gender function as a core identity. If you're black, others will likely assume and react as if this racial identity is primary regardless of your wishes.

During what we might call the heyday of the closet era, between roughly 1950 and 1980, some closeted individuals downplayed their homosexuality as an identity. They managed what was publicly considered a deviant identity by defining homosexuality as a secondary part of themselves, something akin to a peculiar appetite or an unusual sexual impulse. Yet for some individuals the sheer magnitude of energy and focus spent managing this stigmatized identity, and the fact that avoiding suspicion and exposure sometimes shaped a whole way of life, meant that homosexuality functioned as a sort of hidden core identity.

For individuals who decided to come out during this period of heightened public homophobia, the intensity of the struggle for acceptance of the self, and the anticipation that disclosure would likely bring a major lifestyle change, pressured some individuals to make homosexuality a focus of their lives. The pervasiveness of public fear and loathing of homosexuals that sustained the closet made coming out a deliberate, intense life drama. It is hardly surprising that many of these individuals would come to define their homosexuality as a core identity. Also, during these years many individuals migrated to urban centers and built protective subcultures. Becoming a part of these enclaves often meant fashioning a life around a core gay identity, as one became integrated into the dense social networks of an exclusive outsider world.

To the extent that the closet has less of a role in shaping gay life, the dynamics of identity change somewhat. As the lives of at least some gays look more like those of straights, as gays no longer feel compelled to migrate to urban enclaves to feel secure and respected, gay identity is often approached in ways similar to heterosexual identity—as a thread. However, it is a thread of a minority rather than a dominant majority—more like being a Muslim-American than like being a Protestant American. Given gays' historically embattled status, individuals will often be deliberate in publicly asserting a gay identity in order to make a personal statement of pride or a political statement. Many people continue to claim a core gay identity, despite the lessening of public acts of homophobia and social repression. Today, individuals may choose to adopt a core gay identity as a lifestyle or for political reasons. For example, individuals may migrate to urban subcultures and fashion lives around being gay, but less to escape a claustrophobic, hostile social milieu than to find kindred spirits who share particular lifestyle choices.

It occurred to me, as my research progressed, that as some of us are living more openly and freely, heterosexuals are now routinely exposed to positive images of being gay and to actual gay individuals. I wondered whether straight Americans might alter the way they approach sexual identity. I decided to interview mostly younger folk, roughly age seventeen to early twenties. I figured that any change in the culture of heterosexual identity would be easier to detect in younger people.

I found contradictory patterns. On the one hand, as straight individuals viewed gays as normal, some reported being less attached to or less assertive of a heterosexual identity. These individuals told me that they do not act to avoid gays or any suspicion of being gay by deliberately flagging a heterosexual identity. They have deemphasized heterosexuality as an identity and some have said they no longer consider sexuality an important marker of identity. They prefer to identify themselves and others in nonsexual ways; for example, in terms of gender, social values, occupation, or as just "people." On the other hand, some individuals respond to the new gay visibility by becoming more purposeful about being seen as heterosexual. I was particularly interested in those individuals who said they view gays as ordinary people. Many of these individuals told me that they want to be recognized as straight. Some said that it's because that's who they are. Perhaps that's true, but it's also the case that claiming a heterosexual identity confers real social and cultural privileges.

The heightened sense of identity among heterosexuals and their deliberateness about asserting a heterosexual identity is, I think, something new. In the era of the closet, everyone was simply assumed to be straight; to be sure, individuals also projected a straight identity by being homophobic or gender conventional. Today, as it becomes less acceptable to be publicly homophobic, and as many gays and straights look and act alike, some individuals are deliberate in presenting a public heterosexual identity.

HETEROSEXUAL DOMINANCE

I work in one of the most liberal institutions in America, a research university, in one of the most liberal states in the nation, New York. Among colleagues and administrators, I feel respected as an individual and as a scholar who studies and writes about gay life. I have never experienced anything remotely close to discrimination or disrespect—at least not for reasons of sexual orientation. Still, my institution does not offer domestic partnership benefits for same-sex partners; gays are not included in the university policy of promoting respect for social diversity; there has never been any effort to hire openly gay professors;

and except for myself and a handful of faculty who teach women's studies and English, I know of no faculty that includes lesbian and gay scholarship as part of his or her regular course offerings. In short, the personal aspects of my work life are "virtually normal," but my public status is that of a second-class citizen.

If gay life is freer and more open for many of us today, it is not because heterosexual dominance has ended. Discriminatory social policies and laws continue to organize American institutional life. Still, there has been something of a shift, at least in emphasis, in the way that heterosexual privilege is enforced. In many social settings, homophobic and blatantly repressive institutional practices are losing legitimacy as gays are seen as ordinary, "normal" human beings deserving rights and respect. We have cautiously been invited to join the community of Americans, but so far the invitation has not extended beyond tolerance of a minority; heterosexual dominance has not been seriously challenged. How is it that gays can be viewed as normal but are still unequal?[18]

To understand changes in patterns of heterosexual dominance, I decided to look at commercial films. Since the early 1960s, homosexuals have regularly appeared on the screen. However, the dramatic rise in their visibility since the 1990s makes film useful for charting shifts in how homosexuality is understood and regulated.

After analyzing almost fifty films that appeared between 1960 and 2000, I've concluded that for most of these years heterosexual dominance worked by polluting homosexuality. The homosexual was viewed as such a despicable and disgusting figure that no one would want to openly declare herself a homosexual. Conversely, the heterosexual was defined as a pure and ideal status. Moreover, to the extent that homosexuals were imagined as predators, child molesters, disease spreaders, or cultural subversives, the state and other social institutions were given a broad social mandate to protect respectable citizens by purging America of any visible signs of homosexuality. This culture of homosexual pollution contributed significantly to creating the conditions that we have come to call "the closet."

Until the mid-1990s, the image of the polluted homosexual dominated the screen. Then there was a striking change: the rise of the "normal gay." In films such as *Philadelphia*, *In and Out*, *The Object of My Affection*, *As Good as It Gets*, and *My Best Friend's Wedding*, gays step forward as "normal" human beings. Normality carries ambiguous political meaning. The status of normality means that gays are just like any other citizens. We have the same needs, feelings, commitments, loyalties, and aspirations as straight Americans. Accordingly, we deserve the same rights and respect. But normal also carries another normative sense: the normal gay is expected to exhibit specific kinds of traits and behaviors. He is supposed to be gender conventional, well adjusted, and integrated into mainstream society; she is committed to home, family, career, and nation.

This claim to normality justifies social integration but only for normal-looking and acting gays and lesbians. Moreover, to the extent that the normal gay aspires only to be a full-fledged citizen or to be accepted into America as is, her integration does not challenge heterosexual dominance. The politics of the normal gay involves minority rights, not the end of heterosexual privilege.

THE POLITICS OF SEXUAL CITIZENSHIP

The closet was not only a response to a culture that polluted and scandalized homosexuality. Stigma and the shame it induced would surely create ambivalence around being seen as homosexual, but they would not necessarily keep homosexuals silent and secretive. If many gay individuals chose to organize public heterosexual lives, it was in no small part because of a government that waged a war against homosexuals. From the 1950s onward, the state enacted laws and policies that persecuted and prosecuted homosexuals. If exposure risked public disgrace and the loss of job and family, is it any wonder that many individuals opted for a closeted life?

Throughout most of American history homosexuals were not the targets of state control. From the beginning of the republic through much of the nineteenth century, homosexuality was not viewed as the basis for a distinct self-identity, and homosexual behavior was not the focus of specific laws. Homosexual behavior was outlawed as an act of "sodomy," which referred to a wide range of nonmarital, nonprocreative acts. This changed in the late nineteenth and early twentieth centuries as a variety of powerful social groups enlisted the state to battle what they saw as the spread of vice, divorce, and sexual and gender deviance. The state became heavily involved in regulating the intimate affairs of its citizens. Still, it wasn't until the 1950s and 1960s that the government mobilized its considerable resources and authority to crack down on homosexuals. At this point, the closet became the defining reality of gay life in America.

Homosexual repression and pollution was met with political resistance. From the beginning, the modern gay movement has been divided between a rights-oriented assimilationist and a liberationist agenda. Both wings of the movement made dismantling the closet a chief political aim. Except for a short period in the early 1970s and a brief flourish in the late 1980s and early 1990s (ACT UP and Queer Nation), a rights agenda has dominated the chief organizations of the gay movement. Its aim, roughly speaking, is to bring gays into the circle of citizenship and social respectability.

The rights-oriented movement has had many successes. Repressive laws have been repealed or now go unenforced; and positive rights have been established in many municipalities, workplaces, and institutions of all sorts. These social gains have made it possible for many of us to organize fairly routine personal and public lives. And, as many of us have come to feel a strong sense of self-integrity and social entitlement, mainstream gay politics has responded by shifting its agenda from gaining tolerance (decriminalization) to achieving civil and political equality. In this regard, it is not accidental that battles around gay marriage and gays in the military have gained prominence. There cannot be real equality without equal marital and military rights.

As the rights wing of the gay movement moved forward confidently, as there developed multimillion-dollar national organizations battling for our rights, the voices of some critics have also grown sharper and louder. Liberationism didn't, after all, expire in the mid-1970s or the mid-1990s. It survived on the margins, in the culture of academics, artists, writers, and some activists. And, as the rights movement has helped gays gain a footing in the social mainstream, liberationists have expressed concerns. While some critics wrongly interpret the struggle for rights as a desire to mimic straight life, liberationists have also understood, in a way that rights advocates have not, that heterosexual dominance is deeply rooted in the institutions and culture of American society. Gaining equal rights, including the right to marry and serve in the military, will not bring about full social equality. Without challenging a culture of advertising, television, film, music, literature, and news that makes heterosexuality the norm and the ideal, there cannot be social equality. Until our public schools hire openly gay teachers and administrators, and incorporate the teaching of gay lives, families, culture, and politics into the curriculum, there may be tolerance but not social equality. Until our workplaces celebrate events such as Coming Out Day and the anniversary of Stonewall, until companies advertise to attract gay consumers, promote openly gay employees to managerial and supervisory positions, encourage gay employees to bring their partners and dates to work-related social events, and offer the full range of health and other social benefits to gay employees, civic equality will remain an unrealized promise. We need a movement that broadens rights activism to include an agenda of across-the-board institutional equality and cultural justice.[19]

The struggle for gay equality should not be isolated from other social and sexual conflicts. From lesbian feminists and gay liberationists to queer activists, a liberationist tradition has sought to broaden our thinking about the politics of sexuality. They invite us to view the politics of sexual identity as part of a larger network of sexual and social conflicts.

From a liberationist perspective, bringing gays into the circle of good sexual citizens would still leave in place a sexual order that unnecessarily restricts the range of desires, behaviors, and relationships that are considered acceptable and worthy of value and social support. In other words, the idea of a good sexual citizen is associated with specific sexual-gender norms—what we might call a notion of "normal sexuality." Only sexual desires and acts that are viewed as normal are acceptable. Behaviors between consenting adults that fall outside the boundaries of normal sexuality may be labeled "abnormal," "diseased," or "unhealthy"; individuals who engage in these behaviors may be perceived as sick, immoral, and socially dangerous.

My sense is that, despite some dissent and conflict, there is a dominant culture that associates normal sexuality with sex that is exclusively between adults, that conforms to dichotomous gender norms, that is private, tender, caring, genitally centered, and linked to love, marriage, and monogamy. There is then a wide range of consensual adult practices that are potentially vulnerable to stigma and social punishment; for example, rough or S/M (sadomasochistic) sex, "casual" sex, multiple-partner sex, group and fetishistic sex, and commercial and public sex. Individuals who engage in some of these acts will be scandalized as "bad citizens"; demands will be heard to use repressive or therapeutic interventions to protect good citizens from contamination—that is, being seduced, molested, or infected by disease-carrying sexual deviants.

The gay movement should not ignore this broader sexual political context. Like it or not, a movement seeking gay equality inevitably supports or challenges a wide network of sexual control. Obviously, it challenges the outsider status of gays. But, to the extent that this movement appeals to a narrow set of sexual norms associated with the good citizen to justify its claim for rights and respect, it reinforces the outsider status of many sexual agents who engage in consensual, victimless practices. In fact, as the "normal gay" is integrated as a good citizen, other sexual outsiders may stand in for the homosexual as representing the "bad" or dangerous sexual citizen. Polluting specific sexual citizens as "bad" and dangerous (for example, sex workers, libertines, sexually aggressive women, sexually-active youth, pregnant young women) establishes certain sexual acts or lifestyles (commercial sex, multiple-partner sex, youthful sexuality) as unacceptable; those who engage in these acts risk public disgrace or worse. Bringing gays into the fold of the good citizen may not then bring about expanded choice for all citizens. It may evoke fears of disorder, and this may bring about the tightening of sexual control for all citizens.

Liberationists remind gays that there are many types of outsiders. There are outsiders among insiders (for example, straights whose desires run to the nonconventional) and insiders among outsiders (gays who are thoroughly straight-looking-and-acting). So, yes, gays need and deserve equal rights and full, across-the-board social equality. But there are battles around sexual regulation that need to be waged beyond gay rights and equality. Liberationist voices need to be heard.

A MULTICULTURAL AMERICA

Gays' changing social status is connected to the making of America as a multicultural nation. The United States is becoming a society that is more socially diverse than it has been at any other time in its history. And, for many of its citizens, respecting and valuing group differences is a key part of this nation's identity.

Today, many Americans see themselves as national citizens but also as members of particular cultural communities. We are proud to be American but also to be women, African American, Chinese, Irish, Catholic, Muslim, Latino/a, gay, or part of a disabled community. And we don't confine our differences to private life; we assert our group identities in social and political life. We bring our differences into the cultural and institutional arena and expect them to be respected.

Outsider groups, including gays, have benefited from this multicultural remaking of America. For example, Americans are today expected to initially withhold judgment when encountering individuals who are culturally different. We are encouraged to consider varied points of view on sexuality, family, politics, education, and faith. For individuals and groups who are marginal or who have been outside of what is considered "the mainstream," a multicultural national ideal makes it possible for them to at least get a public hearing. In a multicultural society, public space, however cramped and marginal, is created for outsider groups to make their case to be respected as part of the spectrum of legitimate social difference.

At a deeper level, as a national culture takes shape that values group differences, there is occurring something of a shift from "absolutist" to "pragmatic" types of moral reasoning. The former makes judgments on the basis of transcendent worldviews. For example, divorce might be criticized because it violates a fixed, absolute norm of permanent marriage established by religion, tradition, or natural-law thinking. By contrast, a pragmatic approach offers loose guidelines in making judgments; it acknowledges that there can be varied legitimate moral points of view and that these should be reckoned with. This approach encourages a more situation-specific style of moral decision making; individual needs, purposes, and possible social consequences should be considered. Judgments about the ethics of divorce should weigh issues of individual well-being and public welfare and perhaps involve some sort of calculus of advantage and disadvantage. Absolutist thinking is not so much declining as making room for pragmatic moral styles.

A pragmatic moral culture encourages gay integration. If an identity or way of life can be deemed worthy of social respect because it promotes personal and social well-being, and cannot be shown to have clear social harm, gays need only make the case that homosexuality is both victimless and, like heterosexuality, essential to personal happiness. To the extent that a pragmatic moral style gains a social footing, those who aim to deny gays' rights and respect by relying on absolutist arguments (for example, that homosexuality is a sin or disease) may be put on the defensive, as they are accused of intolerance, authoritarianism, or cultural backwardness.

Changes in America's moral culture pressure institutions to accommodate group differences. In the past few decades, we've seen institutions make real efforts to incorporate people of color, women, ethnic minorities, the disabled, and gays. In each case, though, social accommodation has meant tolerance, not full social equality.

Group differences are recognized but understood as products of prejudice and discrimination. Inequalities are to be remedied by education and the establishment of equal rights and opportunity. In effect, complex cultural communities such as those of blacks, the deaf, or gays are viewed as temporary social adaptations to intolerance. Individual members of these groups are assumed to share core national values, beliefs, and social goals. As outsiders are tolerated and integrated into the social mainstream, their participation in these particular cultural communities is expected to weaken. These ethnic-like identities will become merely personal or symbolic, if they do not entirely disappear. At least that's the expectation and hope. In this view of a multicultural America, group differences are recognized, but integration through legal rights and identity normalization leaves the dominant social norms and hierarchies in place.

For example, confronted with the women's movement the state and other social institutions responded by narrowing its agenda to one of granting women's formal equality. As men and women become equal national citizens or bearers of equal rights as workers, family members, and political citizens, gender differences other than those that relate to rights, equal opportunity, and respect are understood as personal. However, many in the women's movement claim that there are important differences in social values and outlook between men and women; these differences have mostly been ignored by our institutions.

The way multiculturalism currently works in the United States leaves in place the dominant social groups and social norms. A social order that is disproportionately shaped by the interests of, say, men, whites, the abled, or straights is not seriously threatened by enfranchizing gays, women or blacks. Still, integrating outsider groups such as these improves the quality of their lives and may have important unintended consequences. For example, the state, pressured by various groups, has passed a great deal of legislation that expands individual control over bodily, sexual, and intimate expression. Thus, the legalization of abortion in *Roe v. Wade* and a wave of legislation aimed at protecting women from sexual harassment and violence has expanded women's capacity to make sexual-intimate choices. Appealing to an ideal of sexual autonomy that is implicit in this legislation, women may claim a right to remain single, to be single parents, or to choose other women as their partners.

Although this liberal state practice promotes tolerance, it has considerable limits and can be stalled or reversed. In general, as the agenda of social movements has shifted from abstract civil rights to actual institutional equality, the state has retreated from an agenda of promoting diversity. Thus, as gay marriage became a national issue after the Hawaii Court of Appeals case, the U.S. Congress passed, with the overwhelming support of the Democrats and the president, the Defense of Marriage Act, which restricted marriage to heterosexuals. Nevertheless, to the extent that the state endorses the right of individuals to control their own bodies and sexual expression, gays can appeal to this principle to make demands for tolerance and equality.

OVERVIEW

Gay life has changed considerably in the past few decades. Social perspectives that focus on coming out of the closet, the championing of a core gay identity and gay pride, and the migration to gay urban enclaves are less descriptive of gay life today than they were years ago. Many of us live beyond the closet. We have remained part of our families of origin and sometimes have created new families; we are open at work and with our friends, and we live wherever our lives feel right. We feel a deep sense of entitlement to have the same opportunities in love, work, and social life as any other citizen. We demand equality—full, across-the-board equality. We are not, needless to say, getting everything we want. In particular, institutions from the government to our schools and families often barely manage tolerance. The multicultural remaking of contemporary America virtually ensures our integration, but not our equality. As we are gaining a foothold in the social mainstream, there are rumblings of discontent within gay communities. Differences of all sorts are surfacing, and liberationists are pushing for a politics that focuses on expanding sexual choice beyond that of tolerating straight-looking-and-acting gays.

In chapter 1, I argue that the closet was shaped in postwar America primarily by two events: the making of a national culture of homosexual pollution and state-driven social repression. The closet is an accommodation to a society that makes heterosexuality compulsory. To be in the closest means making potentially life-shaping decisions in order to manage a public heterosexual identity. It is a condition of social oppression, but gays are not just victims. We negotiate this restrictive social space; sometimes we fashion good-enough lives. Moreover, closeted lives vary considerably depending upon social factors such as age, class, race, gender, ability or disability, regional location, and political culture. I illustrate the negotiated, varied texture of the closet through a series of case studies.

Chapter 2 provides snapshots of life outside the closet. There are of course a dizzying variety of postcloseted patterns. But many individuals who chose to live openly feel an emphatic sense of self-integrity and entitlement to a good, satisfying life. These individuals want and expect the same range of choices, opportunities, rights, and duties as any other American. This sense of entitlement is the psychological force driving individuals out of the closet to demand social equality. Through case studies, I try to sketch something of the psychosocial texture of gay life after the closet.

Of course, our demands for equal rights and respect are not always well received. In our workplace we often find tolerance and even support among coworkers, but its laws, policies, and practices may lack even basic protections. This also seems to be changing, especially in big corporations, unions, and the professions.

In chapter 3, I consider how gays are received in their families. Many of us who have stepped outside the closet have decided to stay inside our families. How do families react to this unprecedented reality of openly gay kin? The good news is that many families are accommodating, even if not cheerfully and often with a good deal of stress and pain for all concerned. The bad news is that tolerance, not acceptance and equal treatment, is still the rule. And for gays whose kin have fundamentalist convictions, accommodation is tougher—a lot tougher.

Interviews with young straight Americans are encouraging. Younger people seem more accepting. In part this reflects a much more libertarian approach to personal life than that of older folks; also, if my interviews are at all indicative of social trends, younger people are exposed to both images of gays and actual gay people in ways that were not the case for previous generations. Finally, chapter 3 explores the implications of gay integration for the way straights approach their own sexual identity. Using case studies, I show that some straight individuals downplay the importance of sexual orientation in their own and others' social identity; others have made being straight into a core, purposefully fashioned and managed social identity.

In chapter 4, I turn from private to public life. If gays are stepping out it's in part because of the weakening of a culture of homosexual pollution. Whatever individual Americans may feel or think, it has become less acceptable to publicly express blatantly homophobic views. Through a study of Hollywood films, I document a shift from images of the polluted homosexual, which dominated the screen from 1960 through the 1980s, to the "normal gay." Gays are today not only routinely on the screen, and sometimes in blockbuster hits, but they are often portrayed as normal, good citizens. The normal gay, however, deserves integration but doesn't necessarily challenge heterosexual privilege. She just wants to be part of the American family, to blend in to America, as is. Tolerance, not equality, is the rule in public culture.

Gay integration, both as a reality and a moral view, is relatively new. In the days of the closet, gays were integrated but only on the condition of remaining invisible and silent. If they are integrated and open today, if they are accorded a "virtually normal" status, I wondered how this might impact on the regulation of straight Americans. In the final section of this chapter, I examine the ways films depict straight sexuality. I found a tightening of regulation; there is less tolerance for sexual variation among heterosexuals. I believe this is related to fears of social disorder that accompany gays' social integration.

In chapter 5, I argue that the state no longer sustains the closet. A thumbnail sketch of the history of sex laws shows that the state has retreated from the criminalizing and persecution of homosexuals. Laws and court cases since World War II reveal a fairly steady, if uneven, trend toward sexual liberalization. Gays are being integrated into the national community as visible citizens—more as tolerated minorities than equal citizens. The Defense of Marriage Act and the "Don't ask, don't tell" military policy speak powerfully to gays' unequal social status.

The battle over the politics of citizenship is also occurring within the gay movement. There is a long-standing division between rights-oriented and liberationist agendas; each has different ideas of sexual citizenship and justice. The former has triumphed, but its agenda has expanded, in part under the influence of liberationist critics. Today, tolerance is no longer enough; gays want inclusion, but as equals. Buoyed by their gains, and pressured by liberationists, the gay movement is slowly, if unevenly, expanding its political scope to fighting for full social equality—in the state, in schools, health-care systems, businesses, churches, and families. Still, liberationists are right to push the movement to broaden its agenda to one of sexual justice.

In the conclusion, I reiterate my main point: gays' place in America has changed; struggles around tolerance, equality, and justice will not subside. Gay equality has become an issue of social justice for many Americans. Underlying gays' changing social and moral status is the multicultural remaking of national identity. Not only is social diversity a prominent reality today, but a national identity is forming that makes respect for varied cultural communities and identities a core value, a source of national pride, and a guiding moral definition of being an American. To date, the dominant form of multiculturalism has sought to integrate gays into the national community without granting them full equality. The battle of gay Americans for equality is the same struggle that is being waged by women, people of color, the disabled, and native Americans; it is a struggle over the meaning of a multicultural America.

CHAPTER ONE

In the Closet

Heterosexual domination may have a long history, but the closet does not.[1] As I use the term, the closet will refer to a life-shaping pattern of homosexual concealment. To be in the closet means that individuals hide their homosexuality in the most important areas of life, with family, friends, and at work. Individuals may marry or avoid certain jobs in order to avoid suspicion and exposure. It is the power of the closet to shape the core of an individual's life that has made homosexuality into a significant personal, social, and political drama in twentieth-century America.

The closet may have existed prior to the 1950s, but it was only in the postwar years that it became a fact of life for many gay people.[2] At this time, there occurred a heightened level of *deliberateness and aggressiveness* in enforcing heterosexual dominance. A national campaign against homosexuality grew to an almost feverish pitch in the 1950s and 1960s. Observes Allan Berube, author of *Coming Out under Fire*,

> [Gays came] under heavy attack during the postwar decade. . . . When arrested in gay bar raids, most people pleaded guilty, fretful of publicly exposing their homosexuality during a trial. . . . Legally barred from many forms of private and government employment, from serving their country, from expressing their opinions in newspapers and magazines, from gathering in bars

and other public places as homosexuals, and from leading sexual lives, gay men and women were denied civil liberties. . . . Such conditions led to stifled anger, fear, isolation, and helplessness."[3]

The attack on gays accompanied their social visibility. After the war years, many gay individuals moved to cities where they expected to find other people like themselves and at least enough tolerance to put together something like a gay life. My sense is that gay visibility was less the cause than the justification of an anti-gay campaign. A growing public homosexual menace was invoked to fuel an atmosphere of social panic and a hateful politic. But why the panic around homosexuality?

Despite popular images of domestic tranquility on television and in the movies, the 1950s and early 1960s was a period of great anxiety for many Americans.[4] There was a feeling of change in the air that evoked new hopes as well as new dangers. For example, as the war ended America emerged as a true superpower. However, it now faced what many considered to be a growing Soviet threat. Hysteria around the red scare narrowed social tolerance. Dissent and nonconventional lifestyles were associated with political subversion. Communists and homosexuals were sometimes viewed as parallel threats to "the American way of life." As invisible, corrupting forces seducing youth, spreading perversion and moral laxity, and weakening our national will, communists and homosexuals were to be identified and ruthlessly suppressed. And ruthlessly suppressed they were.[5]

Moreover, though the war was over and America was victorious, this nation was changing in ways that were troubling to many of its citizens. For example, women now had some real choices. Their social independence during the war gave many women a sense of having options; some wanted only to return to being wives and mothers, but others wished to pursue a career or remain single. Set against the happy homemaker on television shows such as *I Love Lucy*, *Leave It to Beaver*, and *Ozzie and Harriet* was the "new woman" in *Cosmopolitan* or Helen Gurly Brown's *Sex and the Single Girl*. The *Cosmo* girl may have been heterosexual, but she was also educated, career-minded, and sexy.

Men were also restless. During the war they had been exposed to different types of people, places, and ideas. While many men wanted little more than a job, wife, and a home, the world they returned to offered them many choices—a bounty of well-paying jobs, free higher education, and "good" women who did not necessarily believe that sex had to lead to marriage. Hugh Hefner's playboy lifestyle may not have expressed men's actual lives, but it tapped into a reality and a wish for expanded sexual choice.

It was not just adults who were restless. There was a growing population of young people who were becoming downright unruly. The popularity of rock 'n' roll expressed something of their restless spirit. Many young people wished to fashion lives that expressed their individual desires and wants rather than the social scripts of their parents and society. The panic over "juvenile delinquents" and "loose girls" expressed Americans' fears that the family, church, and neighborhood community had lost control of their youth.

So, while changes in the postwar period created a sense of expanded choice for many Americans, it also stirred up fears of disorder and social breakdown. Many citizens looked to the government and cultural institutions like television and magazines such as *The Reader's Digest* to be reassured about what this nation stood for. On the global front, protecting what came to be thought of as "the American way of life" meant flexing our military muscle to ward off the communist threat. On the domestic front, moral order was thought to require stable families—and such families were to be built on the exclusive foundation of heterosexuality, marriage, monogamy, and traditional dichotomous gender roles. In this context, the homosexual stepped forward as a menacing figure, invoked to defend a narrow ideal of respectable heterosexuality. In popular culture and in the psychiatric establishment, the homosexual came to symbolize a threat to marriage, the family, and civilization itself; he or she was imagined as predatory, seductive, corrupting, promiscuous, and a gender deviant. The moral message of this campaign against homosexuality was clear: anyone who challenges dominant sexual and gender norms risks homosexual stigma and social disgrace. The homosexual was not alone in symbolizing social disorder and deviance; there was also the "loose woman," "the delinquent," and "the sex offender." All these menacing figures served to reinforce a narrow norm of the respectable sexual citizen—heterosexual, married, monogamous, gender conventional, and family oriented.

By the end of the 1960s, the idea of a rigid division between the pure heterosexual and the polluted, dangerous homosexual began to take hold in American culture. The state and other institutions were given the moral charge to protect America from the homosexual menace. Gay men and lesbians were to be excluded from openly participating in respectable society. They were demonized, and any trace of them in public was to be repressed. The world of the closet was created.

THE CLOSET AS SOCIAL OPPRESSION

Not all instances of homosexual concealment should be described by the term *the closet*. Consider Lenny (b. 1935), one of the people I interviewed.

Lenny was keenly aware of his homosexuality as a young person. However, he was not clear about what these feelings meant. Growing up in a small town in the 1940s and early 1950s, he was not exposed to any explicit ideas about homosexuality. He never heard the term used in his family, among peers, or in the popular media. Throughout adolescence and even as a young adult, he thought of his homosexuality as a discrete feeling or impulse that could be isolated and managed. His homosexuality did not figure in the way that he defined himself.

Heterosexuality and marriage was so deeply ingrained in the world of his kin and peers that it was never doubted or questioned. Lenny grew up wanting to marry, to have a family, and to be part of a respectable heterosexual society. These heterosexual longings were deeply felt; they were real feelings and wants.

Lenny didn't anguish over his homosexuality through his adolescence and early adulthood. He knew that these feelings were not acceptable and he kept them hidden. He never entertained the idea of a life organized around his homosexuality. Until he was well into his forties (in the 1970s), he had never known an openly gay individual; he had never read about homosexuality; and he doesn't recall having been exposed to images of the homosexual in the movies or on television. Through the 1950s and 1960s, Lenny never knew there were gay political organizations such as the Mattachine Society, a small, secretive organization that focused on educating the public. Lenny felt little pressure to think of his homosexuality as an identity, and there was virtually no social encouragement for him to live an openly gay life.

Lenny eventually married. Even today, after a gay movement has vilified the closet and championed the idea of a proud, public gay self, Lenny doesn't view his straight life as a strategy to pass. "I married because that's what I wanted to do. I wanted that kind of a life." He still enjoys a heterosexual way of life. Lenny doesn't buy into the view that his straight life is a lie or is inauthentic. Lenny's life, at least through early adulthood, should not be described as "in the closet."

If the concept of the closet is to be sociologically useful, it should not be used casually to cover any and all acts of homosexual concealment. The closet is a historically specific social pattern. This concept makes sense only if there is also the idea of homosexuality as a core identity. Viewed as an identity, homosexuality cannot be isolated and minimized as a discrete feeling or impulse; choosing to organize a public heterosexual life would create a feeling of betraying one's true self. The closet may make a respectable social status possible but at a high price: living a lie. Not surprisingly, the closet is often likened to "a prison," "an apartheid," "a coffin-world," or to "lives led in the shadows."[6] It is said to emasculate the self by repressing the very passions that give life richness and vitality. Listen to Paul Monette, author of the award-winning memoir *Becoming a Man*: "Until I was 25, I was the only man I knew who had no [life] story at all. I'd long since accepted the fact that nothing had ever happened to me and nothing ever would. That's how the closet feels, once you've made your nest in it and learned to call it home." Monette's struggle for an authentic self is narrated as a war against the closet, which he variously describes as an "internal exile," an "imprisonment," and as "the gutting of all our passions till we are a bunch of eunuchs."[7]

In short, the closet is about social oppression. Among its defining features are the following. First, to be in the closet means that individuals act to conceal who they are from those that matter most in their lives: family, friends, and sometimes spouses and children. Being in the closet will shape the psychological and social core of an individual's life. Second, the closet is about social isolation. Individuals are often isolated from other homosexually oriented individuals and are often emotionally distant from the people they are closest to—kin and friends.[8] Third, secrecy and isolation are sustained by feelings of shame, guilt, and fear. The closeted individual often internalizes society's hatred of homosexuals; if he or she manages to weaken the grip of shame, the fear of public disgrace and worse enforces secrecy and isolation. Finally, secrecy, isolation, shame, and fear pressure individuals to conduct a life involving much deception and duplicity.[9] To be in the closet is, then, to suffer systematic harm—to lack basic rights and a spectrum of opportunities and social benefits; to be denied respect and a feeling of social belonging; and more than likely to forfeit the kinds of intimate companionship and love that make personal happiness possible.

This notion of the closet makes sense only in relation to another concept: *heterosexual domination*.[10] The closet is a way of adjusting to a society that aggressively enforces heterosexuality as the preferred way of life. In the era of the closet, heterosexual dominance works not only by championing a norm of heterosexuality but also by demonizing homosexuality. The making of a culture of homosexual pollution is basic to the creation of the closet. Enforcing the exclusion of homosexuals from public life also involves aggressive institutional repression. Homosexuals are suppressed by means of laws, policing practices, civic disenfranchisement, and harassment and violence. The state has been a driving force in the making of the closet. To the extent that heterosexual privilege is enforced by keeping homosexuals silent and invisible, we can speak of a condition of heterosexual domination.

The closet does not, however, create passive victims. Too often, critics emphasize only the way the closet victimizes and strips the individual of any sense of integrity and purposefulness. But closeted individuals remain active, deliberate agents. They make decisions about their lives, forge meaningful social ties, and may manage somewhat satisfying work and intimate lives, even if under strained circumstances.

Passing is not a simple, effortless act; it's not just about denial or suppression. The closeted individual closely monitors his or her speech, emotional expression, and behavior in order to avoid unwanted suspicion. The sexual meaning of the things (for example, clothes, furniture) and acts (for example, styles of walking, talking, posture) of daily life must be carefully read in order to skillfully fashion a convincing public heterosexual identity. For closeted individuals, daily life acquires a heightened sense of theatricality or performative deliberateness. The discrete, local practices of "sexual identity management" that is the stuff of the closet reveals something of the workings of heterosexual domination but also of how gays negotiate this social terrain.

Accommodating to the closet is only part of the story. Rebellion is the other. For individuals to rebel against the closet they must be seen as active, thoughtful, and risk-taking agents. Passive victims do not rebel; they surrender to things as they are. To reject the closet, individuals must view the disadvantages and indignities of the closet as illegitimate and changeable. They must have the inner resources and moral conviction to contest heterosexual domination. As sociologists have put it, rebellion is propelled less by utter despair and victimization than by "relative deprivation." Individuals rebel when social disadvantages feel unjust but changeable—which is to say, when they don't feel only like victims.

Finally, it is perhaps more correct to speak of multiple closets. The experience and social pattern of being in the closet vary considerably depending on factors such as age, class, gender, race, ability or disability, region, religion, and nationality. In this chapter I convey something of the negotiated and varied texture of the closet through a series of case studies. These examples are not intended to capture the full spectrum of closet experiences, but to show something of its oppressive, negotiated, and varied character.

THE CLOSET BEFORE STONEWALL: LENNY'S STORY

We've already been introduced to Lenny. He grew up in a small town in Massachusetts at a time when few Americans were exposed to clear ideas about homosexuality. Lenny understood that his attraction to men had to be kept secret; no one had to tell him. Heterosexuality pervaded and organized his world. His family, friends, popular music, and peer culture conveyed a simple truth: heterosexuality was the right way to live. There was no need to aggressively enforce heterosexual dominance.

At the age of twenty-two (in 1957), Lenny had his first homosexual experience. It happened in the navy. It was hard for Lenny to forget the pleasure associated with that encounter. Confused and fearful, Lenny initially suppressed his homosexuality. He thought of these feelings as a strange, disturbing part of himself that needed to be controlled. Lenny didn't define himself as a homosexual; this notion was alien to him. He moved forward in his life. He did what was expected of him, which was also what he learned to want. He married and had a family. Lenny and his wife are still married and living in the town he grew up in.

However, between the 1950s, when Lenny was coming of age, and the 1970s, America had changed. Homosexuals were now a part of public life; they were in the news and from time to time the topic of homosexuality surfaced in conversations among family members and peers. His approach to homosexuality also began to change. Lenny learned that his attraction to men was more than a minor impulse; it meant, at least in the eyes of others, that he was a homosexual, something nobody wanted to be.

Lenny's fear of exposure intensified. "I had a wife and a child, and I certainly didn't want anybody to know about it. I had too much to lose. I enjoyed married life. I enjoyed what it gave me by way of security, home, family, children, relatives, and friends." Lenny stepped into the closet and has remained there. "No one knows about my homosexuality—not family, friends, or neighbors. I never thought about telling anybody. I won't tell anybody."

Although closeted, Lenny no longer represses his homosexual feelings. His initial homosexual encounter stirred up passions and pleasures he had not felt with women. He decided to find safe ways to have sex with men. He minimized the risk of exposure by separating these experiences from the rest of his life—geographically, emotionally, and socially. His work allows him to travel, and during his trips he has sex with men. Lenny enjoys homosexual sex and considers it natural and normal, though he is convinced that others don't see it this way. Accordingly, being closeted is, for Lenny, not about denying his homosexuality but regulating it.

Managing his homosexuality means minimizing its importance. Despite a culture that views homosexuality as an identity, he continues to think of it as merely a sexual feeling or impulse. Lenny keeps these feelings separate from the rest of his emotional and social life. Although he acts on these desires, they lack any deeper meaning for his sense of identity. Lenny understands his homosexuality as a sexual impulse that can be psychologically compartmentalized.

Socially speaking, managing his homosexuality involves a twofold practice. On the one hand, Lenny has to successfully perform a public heterosexual identity. Being married and a father makes this easy, he says. On the other hand, he must avoid homosexual suspicion. Lenny says that his marital and parental status, along with a conventional masculine gender status, makes passing relatively effortless.

Yet as Lenny described his daily life it was obvious that avoiding homosexual suspicion involves considerable effort and focus. Fear of exposure is almost constant. "I am always concerned that somehow, some way, I will be found out. I am always suspicious that somebody might pick up something." Accordingly, daily life must be deliberately and carefully managed. For example, Lenny is silent in the face of homophobic comments by family, friends, or coworkers; he will never defend gay or lesbian people for fear of arousing suspicion. He not only avoids the company of openly gay people but will not associate with people who might be suspected of being homosexual. Lenny is especially mindful to avoid staring at men for fear of being noticed. In order to reduce the risk of exposure, Lenny travels about fifty miles from his hometown at least once a week to have sex with men. In fact, he went into his present business in part because it made such travel possible without raising suspicion. Still, fear accompanies these homosexual episodes; he worries that someone will recognize him. Lenny wrestles with feelings of guilt for betraying his wife's trust.

Although safe in a marriage and family where suspicion is greatly minimized, homosexual suspicion is never absent from Lenny's world. For example, he believes that his brother might suspect him. "He may suspect. Any time I say that I've met a male friend, he wants to know if he's married." Also, Lenny is very tolerant toward people who are different. "I'm not prejudiced or bigoted at all . . . and my brother knows that." Lenny thinks that his brother might interpret his tolerant social attitudes as a sign of homosexuality. Moreover, Lenny himself is suspicious of others. He says, "I know of a man who embroiders or crochets and right away I think, 'He's gay.'" Gender nonconformity is for Lenny, and, as we'll see, for all those I interviewed, the most telling sign of a gay identity.

For the most part, Lenny says that he likes his life. He enjoys marriage and family life. His standing as a valued part of the community means a lot to him. His business has brought him great success and satisfaction. Yet Lenny is aware that he pays a price for a heterosexually organized life. "Being in the closet limits my life. I have to put constraints on myself." When asked what it feels like to conceal his homosexuality, he says that it's "confining." Lenny may wish that this aspect of his life was different but he won't change, because he enjoys a conventional heterosexual life and fears social rejection. "I'll never come out to anybody. I'm going to keep it closeted."

Lenny's decision to be closeted as a condition of maintaining a respectable social status works, in part, because he is a man of his generation. There were few alternatives to heterosexuality for many men and women born in Lenny's time and circumstances. Heterosexuality was simply taken for granted. This was, moreover, a generation that often looked longingly to a peaceful, secure, and happy heterosexual domestic life in the wake of World War II and the Korean War. It was also a generation in which self-satisfaction was tightly linked to social approval. An individual's personal goals often overlapped with social expectations. The tension between self-fulfillment and social approval was heightened in subsequent generations. Indeed, by the 1960s and 1970s the heterosexual dream of marriage and the family as havens of love and intimacy was tarnished by public revelations of the dark side of family life—violence, abuse, divorce, abortions, and gender conflict. Moreover, the baby boomer generation came of age in the midst of the rise of a proud and assertive gay movement. In short, Lenny's choices are indicative of a world that is passing—a world where doing what was expected was self-fulfilling, where heterosexuality was taken for granted, and where heterosexuals and homosexuals were rigidly segregated with little or no intermingling. In this world, passing as straight was relatively easy for men and women who were married, had families, were gender conventional, and avoided homosexual associations. This world is still a part of America, but it is less so. Today, self-fulfillment is defined more in terms of subjective satisfaction than gaining social approval. Individuals have more choice about intimate lifestyle. And the texture of life in the closet has also changed.

SOCIAL CLASS AND THE CLOSET: BILL'S STORY

Bill (b. 1958) is a baby boomer. Like Lenny, he grew up in a small town. Bill recalls feeling sexual desire for boys at an early age. "I probably started thinking about my homosexuality around the time I was ten. I guess it was when other boys were becoming interested in girls and dating and I wasn't. That's when I started to see that I've got to hide who I am and I've got to pretend that I like girls." Unlike Lenny, Bill remembers being exposed to an public culture of homophobia. Family and friends referred to homosexuals in demeaning ways. Bill was very religious and quickly learned from his church minister that "God hates homosexuals." Born a generation later than Lenny, Bill grew up in a culture that not only viewed heterosexuality as an ideal, but also aggressively enforced its compulsory status by defiling the homosexual.

Bill felt overwhelming pressure to be heterosexual. His parents encouraged dating and expected him to marry and have a family. Kin, friends, church, and the media likewise celebrated an adult life organized around heterosexuality. For virtually all Americans born after 1950, there was a clear, often explicit expectation that adults should marry and raise a family.

Bill didn't want to disappoint those who mattered to him. While being socialized into an ideal of heterosexuality motivated him to adopt a public heterosexual identity, fear drove Bill into the closet. "Fear is the biggest thing. Fear of the people that might find out, fear of what will happen if they did." Fear, for Bill, translated into an anxiety that he would lose his family, livelihood, and the respect of his community.

The closet provided Bill with a strategy to resolve the conflict between social expectations and his homosexuality. He decided to present a consistently heterosexual public identity. This entailed managing his homosexual feelings and negotiating a public identity that avoided suspicion. From the standpoint of being in the closet, Bill experienced social life as filled with risk, a world where others read the sexual meaning of his behavior. To navigate this scary world, Bill had to learn the skills to successfully project a heterosexual identity.

High school was a frightening time. The term *fag* circulated as the ultimate put-down. "It was the worst thing to call somebody a faggot, even though kids didn't always know what it was." Bill knew what it meant and he saw how individuals were shamed and shabbily treated if suspected of being gay.

Bill, and almost everyone I interviewed, experienced high school as a seamless homophobic social environment. One man I interviewed, Ralph (b. 1962), avoided any behavior that might even remotely raise suspicion. For example, he decided against pursuing cooking and dance in favor of "wood-shopping." And, despite considerable athletic talent and his coach's encouragement to pursue gymnastics, Ralph feared exposure. "In the men's locker room I was panic stricken every time we had to take off our clothes. I was afraid of being aroused by whoever was standing next to me." Pressured by his parents, he joined the library club. This made him very nervous because he feared that his classmates would interpret his bookishness as a sign of being gay. For Ralph, high school meant isolation and surviving by establishing social distance. "Very few people noticed me. I stayed to myself and didn't even like to go outside."

Bill's strategy of passing in high school was different from Ralph's. Bill was more social. His friends mattered a great deal to him. The problem was they all dated; so, Bill followed suit. "I pretended to be interested in girls. I dated and I think these were attempts to hide the fact that I was gay." Bill eventually found a girlfriend, whom he later married. Still, Bill vigilantly monitored his behavior to avoid suspicion. He gradually turned to drugs and drinking to sustain a sexually active heterosexual relationship, even though his desires pulled in the opposite direction. Managing his sexuality also involved maintaining silence in the face of homophobic comments that were pervasive in school culture. Gradually, Bill grew distant from family and many friends, as he feared exposure.

After high school, Bill worked as a middle-level manager. He was very careful. His boss "was very heterosexual. He talked loudly and repeatedly about heterosexual sex. I felt really compelled to conceal." Bill learned to fit into a heterosexual world by accommodating to others' expectations. "I'm like a chameleon. I was attuned to how others felt about gays and would adjust." Bill learned to pass by mastering a public heterosexual persona.

Despite having a girlfriend, Bill couldn't escape an almost paralyzing fear of exposure. His demeanor presented a seamless masculine self. He speaks of "straightening" up his appearance. "I was very practiced in walking very straight and very military-like." Ultimately, anxieties of exposure drove Bill to join the marines. "I thought that if I was in the marines nobody would suspect, that maybe they could teach me to be more masculine."

After the marines, Bill married. All of his friends "knew that I was married and I let them assume things. I was afraid of them finding out. I was scared about it." Bill explains his decision to get married.

> I don't think anybody really wants to be homosexual. Who wants to be subjected to the jokes, the harassment, the beatings, the

> condemnation, having to live your life as an actor? I know I didn't want to be. I knew I was homosexual from the time I was six. I wanted to be whatever normal was. I wanted a family, children. I bought the lie that if I met the right girl that the sexual attraction would be there or develop. If I loved her, it would work. I just didn't think a homosexual life was possible.

Bill married in part because he wanted the life promised by marriage—a companion, family, and social approval. He also married to avoid suspicion. Several people I interviewed were convinced that being a single adult would raise suspicion. Mike, another baby boomer, felt that staying single amounted to virtually coming out. "I knew that I was gay before I married. I was afraid not to be married. I was afraid of what it might indicate if I didn't get married. It felt like I'd be forced to come out. How could I keep hiding, being single? I was just terrified of not being married."

Bill married despite the absence of sexual attraction. "I kept waiting for the sexual attraction to come but it never did. As a result, when we had sex I had to fantasize about men." Throughout his marriage Bill struggled with his homosexual longings. He tried to suppress them. "I wanted to be faithful to my wife." He turned to alchohol. "I drank to not deal with the [homosexual] feelings, to not feel."

From childhood to his coming out in his mid-thirties, Bill relied on several strategies to sustain the closet. At the heart of the closet was self-control. At times, this meant that Bill simply had to suppress any homosexual feeling. "I didn't act on it at all for many years." At other times, Bill threw himself into work and his marriage to control his homosexuality. "I channeled my energies into work and our marriage. I wanted a family, a house. I just worked and worked. I was so closeted." Even after he was married, Bill describes a life of intense self-control to a point of self-estrangement. "I've always been aware of what I say and how I act, how I hold my cigarette, how I laugh, I mean anything. When I was living in the closet, I had a mask that I presented to anybody. It was tailored to the person or people that I was around. I didn't know who I was really." Self-control meant carefully regulating his behavior. Bill dressed to avoid homosexual suspicion. "I didn't wear anything that looked like it could be gay." Finally, self-control involved social distance. Bill had few friends after high school, and they were kept at arm's length to avoid possible exposure. Although his family was close, Bill kept aloof from his parents. "I couldn't be as open to them as I wanted to be."

In Bill's closet world, everyone potentially suspected. Despite his considerable efforts to avoid suspicion, including marriage, enlisting in the marines, and a seamless masculine self-presentation, Bill believed that his wife suspected. Perhaps, he thinks, she interpreted his lack of sexual passion symptomatically. Bill believes that his parents suspected as well. Asked why, Bill referred to a cluster of behaviors that might signal homosexuality. "The people I hung around with, the way I dressed, and [after marriage] the absence of a girl in my life." Bill thought that his mother suspected because he didn't date after his divorce. Bill threw himself into work and parenting in part to avoid suspicion. "I was hoping that my mother would figure that I didn't have time for a relationship, but I think that's when she started to question [my sexual identity]." In this world of pervasive suspicion, Bill began to suspect others. For example, he wondered about his father. "I always had an idea that he might be gay. He was very gentle. He tried real hard to get everybody to like him, and everybody did."

Bill described his closet world in theatrical terms. "My whole life until recently has been being the actor, pretending I'm somebody I'm not." Invoking the image of the actor to describe his life tellingly acknowledges that Bill had in fact acquired considerable social skill in order to succeed at passing. Of course, this heterosexual identity performance meant, as he says, living an inauthentic life. Bill passed successfully, but to do so he married, had children, joined the marines, became dependent on alcohol, and distanced himself from his own inner life as well as from family and friends. In short, the closet was a way to accommodate being the bearer of a polluted identity but at a considerable psychic and social cost.

Managing homosexuality was somewhat different for Lenny and Bill in part because of their age difference. Lenny came of age in the 1950s and in a small town in the northeast where homosexuals were never seen or talked about; still, he somehow knew it was a defiled status. He accommodated, as did many in his generation, by fashioning a conventional heterosexual life interrupted by furtive homosexual episodes. Bill's coming of age paralleled the rise of a nationally organized gay movement. Heterosexual privilege could no longer be sustained by simply taking heterosexuality for granted. America responded to this new homosexual assertiveness with an aggressive strategy of cultural pollution and social repression. Bill grew up hearing only disparaging remarks about homosexuality from his family, peers, minister, and in newspapers and the movies. Still, as Bill reached adulthood he was aware that there were public spaces (for example, bars and community centers) where being gay was accepted. Bill initially managed these conflicting social currents by fashioning his own closet pattern. However, in contrast to Lenny, Bill eventually decided to live an open, integrated gay life.

Despite their generational differences, it is important to note that Lenny and Bill share a similar class position. They grew up in working-class families and neighborhoods. Their fathers worked in local factories and their siblings and kin were blue-collar workers, clerks, secretaries, and receptionists. No one in their families went to college. Boys were expected to work after high school.

Homosexuality presented a real symbolic and economic threat to Lenny and Bill. In their working-class culture, family was the cornerstone of life. Getting married and having a family was expected and celebrated. Men were expected to present a more or less seamless masculine self. Homosexuality threatened humiliation—for themselves and their families. Exposure risked isolation from their kin and their blue-collar community of kin, peers, and neighbors.

Their fear of exposure was also economically based. The financial interdependence between the individual and family is central to working-class life. For example, as a wage earner Bill was economically independent. Yet he was aware that his material well-being was never secure. Growing up, he had seen adults lose jobs as industry migrated from his hometown. He saw kin sustaining their own when brothers, cousins, aunts, and uncles were out of work for long periods of time.

Bill considered his family a potential source of material support; he also expected that at some point his family would ask for his financial help.

Class shapes closet patterns.[11] The extent of economic interdependence between the individual and his or her family varies between blue- and white-collar workers. This class difference shapes how individuals manage their homosexuality.

For the middle class, economic independence is valued and expected. This provides a material base for coming out and organizing a public gay life. At a minimum, middle-class individuals have options. They can move to avoid exposure; they can afford to establish a workable double life; and they can sustain themselves if estranged from their families. Moreover, because of the high value placed on individualism, middle-class individuals anticipate a considerable disengagement from their family and the community they were brought up in. They can also expect a relatively smooth integration into a middle-class gay life as compensation for any estrangement from family and friends resulting from coming out.

For working-class individuals, economic interdependence with kin is a lifelong expectation. Exiting the closet as a working-class lesbian or gay man carries serious economic risks—for themselves and their kin. Blue-collar workers expect that at some point they will either turn to kin for economic help or their family will turn to them. Additionally, estrangement from kin carries the threat of losing a primary source of community. There is no anticipation of an immediate compensation for lost community because of the middle-class character of the gay institutionalized world.

The closet is not, then, the same experience for all individuals. To understand its workings, we have to pay close attention to age and social class.

RACE AND THE CLOSET: ROBERT'S STORY

Bill's and Lenny's strong economic ties to their families made exiting the closet difficult and potentially more risky than for the economically independent middle class. But their white racial status made it relatively easy for them to identify as gay. The gay world—at least the institutionalized world of bars, social and political organizations, and cultural institutions (newspapers, magazines, publishers, theater groups)—was and still is overwhelmingly white. Moreover, American public cultures, both white and nonwhite, associate being gay with being white. Accordingly, race is a key factor shaping the dynamics of homosexuality, including the closet.

Generalizations are risky. The few interviews I conducted with people of color, and the paucity of relevant social research, gives a somewhat speculative cast to my comments. Still, the evidence suggests what we would expect: race matters.[12]

To illustrate, consider the implications for blacks of an overwhelmingly white gay community. No matter how accepting some individuals may be, blacks often feel like outsiders in the gay community. The culture, the leadership, the organizations, and the political agenda of the institutionalized gay world have been and remain dominated by whites. Blacks often report encountering an inhospitable gay world, one that until recently participated in the racism of straight America. For example, through the early 1990s, black men tell of being carded at gay bars or objectified as exotic sexual selves; black women describe being silenced or ignored in decisions about social events and politics. Despite a deliberate commitment to a multicultural gay community, blacks continue to feel that they have to negotiate a somewhat foreign social terrain.

White privilege in the gay world means that blacks manage their homosexuality somewhat differently than whites. Whites may come out to an unfriendly world of kin and friends, but they anticipate an easy integration into a gay world that will affirm their sense of self and offer an alternative type of community. By contrast, if blacks exit from the closet they expect a struggle for acceptance not only in the straight but also in the gay world. To state the contrast sharply, whites expect a trade-off when they come out: estrangement from the straight world in exchange for social integration and acceptance in the gay community. Blacks do not expect such compensation for their anticipated disapproval and diminished status in the straight world. Given their more ambivalent relationship to the gay community, blacks may be more likely than their white counterparts to manage their homosexuality within the framework of the closet.

If an inhospitable or at least uncertain reception in the gay world gives pause to blacks as they consider coming out, so too does the central role that a race-based community plays in their lives. Many blacks have a fundamental personal and social investment in maintaining integration into a race-based community. This community offers protection and material sustenance in the face of the bodily and economic threats of racism; it provides a positive culture of racial pride and solidarity. Maintaining strong ties with kin and a race-based community is a cornerstone of black identity in a way that is obviously not true for whites. If whites grow up with a sense of racial entitlement and a feeling that it is their America, many blacks experience and expect an inhospitable reception in the larger society. Experience and kin have taught them that their personal and social well-being depends on maintaining solidarity with a black community. For many blacks, America is two nations, and it's only in the black world that they feel a sense of integrity and social belonging.

In short, blacks—straight or gay—are heavily invested in their racial identity and in their membership in the black community in a way that is generally not true of whites. Coming out, then, risks not merely estrangement from kin and community but potentially the loss of a secure sense of identity and social belonging. In other words, leaving the closet threatens social isolation from both the straight and gay worlds. It risks being cast adrift in a society that does not recognize or value being black and gay; it jeopardizes a secure sense of belonging and protection (physical and economic) in exchange for an outsider status.

If a white privileged society creates pressures for blacks to sustain primary lifetime ties to their racial community, the latter pressures individuals to maintain the primacy of their racial identity. And if the individual turns out to be gay, the black community has often demanded that this identity be kept private as a condition of acceptance.

Whites, like blacks, can expect a mixed reception in the straight world. For example, an organized anti-gay opposition led by a white-dominated Christian Right has focused largely on the white gay population. However, at least since the mid-1980s, there is also considerable support for gay rights and respect from "white" elite institutions and public figures—from newspaper editors to intellectuals, writers, and church and political figures. Until fairly recently, black gay men and women could not count on much, if any, support from the elite community. The dominant institutions and leadership in black communities have been routinely indifferent, if not hostile, to gays. This is a repeated motif in the stories black gay men and women tell of coming of age in the 1980s and 1990s. The late artist and activist Marlon Riggs commented bitterly on the degraded status of black gay men in black communities:

> The terrain black gay men navigate in the quest for self and social identity is, to the say the least, hostile. What disturbs—no enrages me, is not so much the obstacles set before me by whites . . . but by my so-called brothers. . . .
>
> I am a Negro faggot, if I believe what movies, TV, and rap music say of me. . . . Because of my sexuality, I cannot be black. A strong, proud, "Afrocentric" black man is resolutely heterosexual. . . . My sexual difference is considered of no value; indeed it's a testament to weakness. . . . Hence, I remain a sissy, punk, faggot. . . . I am game . . . to be used, joked about, put down, beaten, slapped, and bashed, not just by illiterate homophobic thugs in the night, but by black American culture's best and brightest. . . . I believe [that] black America's pervasive cultural homophobia is the desperate need for a convenient Other within the community, yet not truly of the community, an Other to which blame for the chronic identity crises afflicting the black male psyche can be readily displaced.[13]

I am not saying that black communities are more homophobic than other racial or ethic communities. After all, anti-gay movements have largely been affairs of white people—led by whites and largely addressing white publics. Furthermore, there is at least anecdotal evidence suggesting informal tolerance toward gays in black communities. However, tolerance often gives way to aggressive homophobia if being gay is made into a public identity and a political cause. And, as Riggs and many others have insisted, this informal culture of tolerance has often coexisted with an elite culture that has been routinely hostile to gays.[14] This has begun to change in the last decade as academics and public figures like Jessie Jackson and Mayor Willy Brown, public intellectuals like Angela Davis, bell hooks, Cornel West, and Henry Louis Gates, and writers like Alice Walker and Toni Morrison, have stepped forward as advocates of gay rights.

If there has been weak institutional support for gays in black communities it is in part because of an underdeveloped black gay culture. While public gay cultures were established in many towns and cities across the country during the post-Stonewall period, this has rarely been the case in black communities. There has been individual- and kin-based support, and informal networks and sometimes bars or baths have evolved that cater to blacks, but there are few public social and political organizations, or groups in black communities. Even in Harlem, where one researcher has argued that there is considerable tolerance and integration of gays, there is no community center, no political club or organization, and no openly-gay leader among Harlem's political elite.[15] Indeed, only in the last decade, as more and more black gay men and women have exited the closet, have loosely formed organizations been created to represent their interests within both gay and straight communities.[16]

The absence, at least until recently, of a politically assertive public gay and straight culture supporting black gay men and women has made the wager of coming out risky and potentially too costly for many individuals. Moreover, as black communities have continued to struggle with a sense of being under assault by racism, poverty, and family instability, tolerance for a public gay life is shaky. The closet presents a credible option, especially if, as some evidence suggests, a more relaxed or flexible closet pattern than that experienced by Lenny or Bill is possible in many black communities. Moreover, as black gay networks developed in the 1980s and 1990s, some blacks now have an alternative to the closet. However, to the extent that these networks remain small and institutionally insecure, establishing an independent gay life remains much more difficult for many blacks than for whites.

Some of these dynamics and dilemmas of being black and gay in America surface in Robert's story. His is a story of a black gay man trying to navigate between a black world that is not seen as particularly hostile nor especially friendly and a somewhat welcoming white-dominated gay world but one that doesn't feel quite like home. In the end, Robert tries to forge a satisfying life by becoming part of a small, fragile black gay world that is not solidly part of a gay or a black community.

Robert was born in 1974 and came of age in the 1990s, when gays were experiencing more personal freedom. He grew up in a large, close, middle-class family in Brooklyn. He was aware of his homosexuality as a child. He accepted these feelings as a natural part of himself. Still, he kept his homosexuality a secret through his teen and early adult years. Unlike Lenny and Bill, Robert's chief closet strategy did not involve a deliberate projection of a public heterosexual identity that included marriage or a hypermasculine self-presentation. Robert sought to avoid suspicion by maintaining a rigid separation between a gay and straight world.

Anticipation of disapproval and rejection underpins Robert's emotional and social distancing from the straight world. Fear prevented Robert from disclosing to his family as a young person. Fear also shaped his public school experience. Although he grew up in a predominantly black community in Brooklyn, Robert went to high school in what he described as a small all-white town in upstate New York. He lived in an almost constant state of fear during these years. Negotiating his racial difference was hard enough. The prospect of being viewed as sexually deviant terrified him. Robert managed by maintaining social distance. He avoided any contact with classmates that might be suspected of being gay. He remained silent in the face of an openly homophobic school culture. Robert tried to fit in by lying about having a girlfriend back home. Despite excelling in sports and enjoying athletics, Robert refused to participate in any school team sports. He was afraid that he'd "get a hard-on in the shower."

Robert spoke of feeling like he was "the only gay person in the world." Isolated and terrified of exposure, Robert felt suicidal throughout his high school years. Exercising extreme self-control and social isolation, which entailed the vigilant monitoring of his feelings, self-presentation, and behavior, was how he got by. "I mostly kept to myself. I had few friends and didn't get involved in school life. I could never be relaxed. I always feared someone would find out. I never let anyone get to know me."

After high school, Robert joined the navy, where exposure would have meant a discharge as well as social disgrace. He managed to pass by being a loner and by excessive drinking during his years in the service.

After leaving the navy, Robert worked as an electrician in Los Angeles. Away from home, economically independent, and in a liberal social environment, Robert began to participate in gay life. He dated and soon had a boyfriend.

Robert did not, however, disclose his sexual identity to any of his coworkers. He preferred to keep personal matters out of his work life. Although his coworkers often talked about their boyfriends, girlfriends, marriages, and children, Robert never shared any of his personal life. Robert remained aloof. Although he worked at this job for six years, he did not become friends with any of his coworkers. In order to sustain social distance, Robert avoided any meaningful social ties with his coworkers. As a result of being closeted, Robert's workplace experience resembled the impersonal, dehumanizing world that Karl Marx and Max Weber described in their chilling portraits of modern industrial life.

At the age of twenty-three, Robert came out to his mother, who told his father and his siblings. Robert has never discussed specific aspects of his gay life with any family member. They all know, but it's not talked about. Robert interprets the absence of hostile behavior and rejection on the part of his family as indicating acceptance. Asked why he keeps his gay life separate from his family, Robert says that his homosexuality is personal and doesn't need to be shared. Accordingly, his family knew nothing of his boyfriend or any other aspect of his personal life. Much to his regret, but hardly surprising, Robert speaks of a weakening of his family bond. Today, he's not close to his mother or anyone in his family. His visits with his family are infrequent and lack the emotional spontaneity and richness of past family interactions. For these reasons, Robert has not told his family that he is HIV positive.

Several years ago, Robert moved back east. However, still wanting to sustain social distance from his family, he resides in a midsized city in the northeast. He chose this place in part because it has a sizable gay community. His initial visit to the gay community center was telling of his strained, distant relationship to the white gay world. "I went to the community center . . . to see who else in this community is like myself. And I really didn't find anybody . . . because most of the gay community was what it is, it seems to be white. So, I just accepted that to be what gay culture was."

Cheap housing led Robert to live in a predominantly black neighborhood. His contacts with his neighbors are formal and lack emotional depth. In fact, he has never come out to any straight black person, aside from his mother. Robert says matter-of-factly that no black person ever asked him if he was gay. He admits, though, that many blacks disparage being gay. "Many blacks think . . . it's already dangerous out there for a black man, why would you want to add another danger to your life? Besides, being gay was viewed for a long time as equivalent to having AIDS. So, most of the conversations [among blacks] about being gay . . . is about having sex and death. Because they perceive the lifestyle as being very painful . . . not many people are going to be accepting of the lifestyle."

Robert eventually found a small network of black gay men and women. This network is the emotional and social focus of his life.

Today, Robert's life is divided between a gay and a straight world. The former provides emotional and social sustenance; the latter is a somewhat risky terrain he navigates to do what he has to do. He speaks, as is typical of those speaking from a closeted standpoint, of a heterosexual dictatorship. Robert's closetedness entails such a narrowing of his world that intimate expression and bonding are possible only within a very small social circle. His closet world is not built on pretense (as was true of Bill), but a fear and distrust so deeply felt that his social distancing has cost him his family, meaningful ties to a black community, a satisfying work life, and has resulted in a pervasive loneliness.

From Lenny's generation to Robert's, the psychosocial texture of the closet has changed considerably. For Lenny and many of his generation, the closet often meant a double life: a conventional public heterosexual life and a secretive homosexual life. By contrast, coming of age in the 1990s, Robert never married. But if Robert rejected strategies involving deception and disguise, he still lives a double life. Like many individuals who are closeted today, he is both part of a gay world and maintains a clear separation from the straight world. The nongay world remains a world of risk and danger. Roberts avoids suspicion and potential conflict by organizing a life of extreme self-control; sadly, he has paid a steep price for passing.

GENDER AND THE CLOSET: RENEE'S STORY

Despite their age, class, and race differences, Lenny, Bill, and Robert relied heavily on being more or less conventionally masculine men to avoid suspicion. Fortunately, a masculine self-presentation and social roles expressed their spontaneous sense of themselves. However, not all lesbians and gay men can manage a conventional gender presentation so effortlessly. For some individuals, their sense of self can be poignantly at odds with gender norms. If these individuals are to avoid coming out, they must find ways to be gender nonconventional without eliciting suspicion.

These remarks highlight an obvious point: managing gender has been and still is at the heart of managing sexual identity. This is true for men and women. To the extent that men and masculinity are socially privileged, however, the dynamics of managing gender and sexual identity are somewhat different for men and women.[17]

For men, exhibiting the conventional signs of masculinity confers social authority and privilege. Although factors such as class, ethnicity, or ableness create inequalities among men, their masculinity establishes them as a privileged group in relation to women. Masculine men are also presumed to be heterosexual. Of course, if men fail to exhibit those behaviors that serve as conventional markers of masculinity, their dominant status is threatened. And if men depart considerably from masculine norms, they risk losing the privileges associated with being a man and being heterosexual. For men whose inner sense of self is emphatically feminine, passing presents a huge challenge because of the scarcity of acceptable social identities and roles for feminine men. Accordingly, gay men who wish to successfully pass must effectively manage a routine performance of masculinity. But—and here's the key point—when gay men pass by means of exhibiting a conventional masculine persona they share fully in men's gender privilege. Closeted gay men are given the same support straight men receive to conform to masculine gender roles and can claim its considerable social benefits.

For women, the gender managing of sexual identity is somewhat different. Although a conventional feminine self-presentation confers a status as normal and straight, it also positions women as subordinate to men. Respectable women are expected to take up social identities and roles that are consistent with feminine gender expectations. In contemporary America, these roles do not carry the authority, status, and material advantage of masculine roles. Women who wish to assume the social roles and claim the privileges associated with masculine men risk disapproval and may forfeit the benefits of being a normal woman. Lesbians who wish to pass but also to appropriate masculine roles that confer authority and material advantage risk exposure. This is a dilemma that men don't experience. Men who claim masculine power are rewarded as men, and as presumptively straight; women who claim the same privileges associated with masculinity are gender rebels and risk stigma and social harm.

One way that lesbians manage this dilemma is to take on social roles that may be considered masculine (for example, as an athlete, a member of the military service, an office manager) but are viewed as marginally legitimate for straight women. Although there are such roles, they are few and are not free of risk. The story of Renee illustrates this particular closet strategy.

Renee describes herself as a masculine woman. She was born in

1970 and grew up in a small southern town. Her Baptist family and community did not accept homosexuality. Growing up, she became aware of her strong feelings for women while learning that others considered homosexuality to be immoral. She was confused about what these feelings meant for her sense of self. She decided to keep them secret. "I was brought up hearing the statement that you can grow up to be anything you want except a faggot. And it was engrained in me that this was not an accepted lifestyle. It was sinful and it was a way that God was telling you that your life is not good." Renee "feared rejection. I mean, nobody wants to be rejected." Exposure would put her at risk of losing her family "emotionally and financially. . . . The biggest thing that I feared was they wouldn't love me anymore because it was so engrained that this [homosexuality] was not an acceptable lifestyle."

It was not only the homophobia of her family and community that worried Renee. The world of her kin, neighbors, and church was heterosexual—it was both the reality and the unquestioned ideal. Renee was expected to marry and have a family. "My father talked all the time about how much he was looking forward to walking me down the aisle and that I should have lots of children so that they could have lots of grandchildren." Renee retreated into the closet to avoid social rejection and to manage the conflict between what was expected of her and her desires.

Because Renee is not a feminine woman, the closet has been a difficult adjustment. As long as she can remember, Renee felt more comfortable as part of a masculine male culture. As a young person, she was thought of as a tomboy. She says that in the town where she grew up in the 1970s and early 1980s, the tomboy did not evoke homosexual suspicion. Girls could be tomboys but only, as she came to learn, as a young person. The same masculine self-presentation in an adult would evoke suspicion.

In high school, the sexual meaning of her masculine self-presentation became more ambiguous. Renee thinks that the absence of a public language of homosexual identification in her school allowed her to mostly avoid suspicion. In this small southern town, even in the late

1980s, her classmates were only vaguely aware of homosexuals and a culture of homosexual signs. They had absorbed a culture that understood the tomboy as a legitimate role for masculine women. Yet with her gender nonconformity she could not entirely avoid suspicion. "I think I did a better job at concealing it from myself than I did anyone else." For example, she remembers that her father made her wear her hair long in high school. She wasn't allowed to cut it. She believes that her parents had some inkling of her sexual identity. "I know they had suspicions. My father used to ask my mother all the time why I'm hanging around always with girls, why I'm not dating boys, why I'm more concerned with hiking and sports."

By the late 1980s, adults like her parents were aware of homosexuality and would sometimes interpret behavior in terms of its sexual meaning. Moreover, Renee was now reading her own behavior symptomatically, and her masculinity was frightening. Renee tried to avoid public suspicion. She began to date men. She even went to the prom. "I went to the prom and did all the high school things I was supposed to, even though I had absolutely no desire to go."

Renee felt that a masculine-gendered self was basic to who she was. It could not be denied or changed, but perhaps its social meaning could be managed. As the tomboy identification lost credibility in high school, she tried to fashion a public identity as an athlete. Renee thought that participating in school sports might minimize suspicion or at least create ambiguity around the sexual meaning of her masculine presentation. It was as if being identified as a female athlete, like her earlier identity as a tomboy, would allow Renee to safely express her masculinity. In short, as Renee moved closer to an adult world, it was harder to control the social meaning of her masculine self-presentation; it became difficult to avoid being read, by herself and others, as a lesbian.

In a last-ditch effort to find a legitimate social role for her masculinity, Renee joined the military. She encountered a fairly open network of lesbians. She came to accept herself as a lesbian in the course of her military duty.

She believes that today people look at her and see a lesbian.

"There's no doubt in my mind that because of my masculine way of dress and look that this signals to people that I am a lesbian. . . .The way I walk, dress wear my hair. . . . I look like a dyke." Renee feels the weight of a society that collapses gender and sexual nonconformity. Indeed, since Renee believes that her masculinity expresses something basic to who she is, the choice she confronted was stark: to be spontaneous and honest, and therefore to be read as a lesbian; or to pass, which would require a considerable effort at refashioning her public persona. Because gender nonconventionality was at the core of her sense of self, the closet proved a tough accommodation. For a time, the availability of social roles for masculine but presumed straight women (tomboy, athlete, soldier) allowed Renee to avoid exposure. However, as she became an adult civilian, the lack of such roles put pressure on her to either escalate gender management in order to pass or come out. Renee eventually came out.

While there are no unambiguous markers of sexual identity in contemporary America, gender has served as perhaps the chief sign. Masculine men and feminine women are typically assumed to be heterosexual. Emphatically feminine men and masculine women would likely surrender this presumption. As one twenty-four-year-old gay man told me, "You assume straight men are more masculine, a little rough looking, hair's not perfect. So when you see a guy whose dress is perfect, the hair's perfect, everything is, you know, picture perfect, that's gay." Managing gender presentation has then been at the heart of managing sexual identity. To the extent, moreover, that gender is thickly coded, passing may entail considerable effort. Describing herself as having a forceful, take-charge personality as well as preferring a no-makeup, jeans-and-sweatshirt look, Rachel, a forty-three-year-old lesbian, says that passing required a virtual makeover of her public self. She groomed and dressed in a self-consciously feminine style and crafted a public persona that deemphasized her masculine personality. "I try to look and act very feminine so people won't look at me or take notice."

Gender is not, however, an unambiguous sign of sexual identity. Albert is a twenty-six-year-old gay black man. His soft and high-pitched voice and the meticulous attention he pays to grooming and dress could have marked him as gay during high school. However, Albert thinks that his high profile as an athlete and the absence of explicit homosexual disclosure created ambiguity around his sexual identity. Being black reinforced uncertainty about the sexual meaning of his gender nonconformity. "A lot of people see being gay as a white issue."

The indeterminate character of a homosexual sign system is in sharp contrast to the way racial and gender identities are socially coded. In the United States, race is in most instances unambiguously conveyed by skin color. And gender is so thickly coded by the sexed body and by our behaviors that it's almost impossible to avoid publicly flagging a clear gender identity.[18] Sexual identity, however, is thinly and ambiguously coded. In the age of the closet, there were efforts to thicken the code by identifying specific behaviors as marking heterosexual and homosexual identities. In particular, gender served as a master code of sexual identity, but it remained somewhat ambiguous as a sexual signifier. A prolonged single status, a lack of interest in the opposite sex, a steady gaze at a person of the same sex, or a fastidiousness about grooming (men) or the lack thereof (women) have also functioned as part of a historically specific grammar of sexual identity.

NEITHER VICTIMS NOR HEROES

The closet is a condition of social oppression. To be in the closet is to live with shame, guilt, and fear. Individuals carefully manage daily life in order to avoid suspicion. Some individuals may make life-shaping decisions about love and intimacy, or work and friends, that are motivated by the wish to avoid detection. The closet makes integration possible but at a considerable personal cost: passionless marriages, loveless lives, estrangement from family and peers, and, sometimes, a paralyzing isolation that leaves individuals depressed and suicidal.

The closet didn't just happen. The aggressive enforcement of heterosexuality as an identity and way of life produced it. Specifically, the closet took shape in response to a culture that polluted homosexuality and policed behavior by stigmatizing gender nonconformity as a sign of homosexuality. And, through the repressive (censoring, criminalizing, and disenfranchising) practices of the state, the homosexual was driven from public life. By the 1950s the closet had become the defining reality for many gay Americans.

The closet is a strategy of accommodating to heterosexual domination. Individuals choose the closet to manage what is considered a deviant identity; it makes possible social respect and integration, even if it may cost the individual his or her sense of personal integrity and well-being. There is enormous variation in closet patterns.

Age is crucial. Lenny was in some ways emblematic of his generation. He felt that he had no realistic alternative to living a heterosexual life. His social world of kin, peers, neighbors, and popular culture was so thoroughly heterosexual that there was apparently little need to make its compulsory status explicit. But it wasn't only that Lenny did what he was expected to do; the deeply ingrained heterosexual character of his world shaped his needs; living a heterosexual life was in a sense what he learned to want. Lenny never felt that he was living an inauthentic life; he wanted to be married, to have a family, and to be a good citizen in his community.

Lenny's heterosexuality felt almost "spontaneous," but not quite. After his passion for men was awakened by a chance homosexual experience, Lenny realized that he would pay a price for his heterosexual life. The closet cost Lenny in ways he didn't always acknowledge. He lived with an almost constant anxiety of exposure. This drove him to exercise exacting self-control, which, in turn, inhibited emotional spontaneity and openness; a certain psychological tightness was evident in Lenny's demeanor and talk.

Ironically, the closet was perhaps an easier accommodation for Lenny than it was for many individuals coming of age after Stonewall. Although the rise of a national movement that championed a proud and public gay identity made life considerably better, it also intensified individuals' inner struggles. Homosexuality was no longer viewed as simply a desire or an impulse, but the core of a social identity. The decision to be in or out of the closet became a matter of considerable moral weight, as the very authenticity and integrity of the individual was now at stake. Adding to the growing moral and emotional weightiness surrounding the closet, more and more Americans were becoming aware of homosexuality and skilled at reading signs of sexual identity. Accordingly, the closet became the focus of a highly deliberate, intense personal drama.

This shift in the emotional, moral, and social texture of the closet after Stonewall is evident in the stories of Bill, Robert, and Renee. Like Lenny, they each grew up in a world organized around heterosexuality. But there was a well-organized visible movement and gay subcultures in many cities that celebrated being gay as good. Despite the weight of society pressuring them to live heterosexually, the decision to live as a "heterosexual" wasn't a foregone conclusion. Individuals coming of age after the 1970s had a sense of choice that was for all practical purposes absent for Lenny. But the flip side was that choosing to be closeted was likely much more anguished and difficult for these later generations than it was for Lenny's. Being in the closet was now associated with living a false, inauthentic life.

Remember the depth and intensity of Bill's struggle with his homosexuality. From roughly the age of ten, Bill lived with a constant, deeply felt fear of exposure. Fear drove him to marry, join the military, and to discipline his body to present a seamless masculinity and heterosexuality. Eventually, Bill's life reached a breaking point. A loveless, passionless marriage, excessive drinking and drug use, and feelings of inner despair prompted him to make big changes in his life. He got divorced, filed for joint custody of his son, and came out to his family and to his hometown as he was interviewed by his town newspaper on being gay and Christian.

Bill's closet pattern almost mirrors the public's stereotype of this condition. The closeted homosexual who in his private and public life expresses an ideal of heterosexuality—married, gender conventional, a parent. Who could suspect Bill? But Bill's masterful performance disguised a life spiraling toward despair and rage.

Many gays still marry and have families in order to pass. However, as the 1970s rolled into the 1980s and 1990s, many individuals chose adaptive strategies that permitted them greater freedom to explore being gay. Robert was one such individual.

By the time Robert came of age in the mid-1990s, Stonewall was already decades old. Many gays were out and were demanding respect and rights; and more and more straight Americans were publicly supporting the cause of gay justice. But this was less true in the black community. There was no Stonewall in black America. Until the mid-1990s, there were few black gay organizations and few straight black allies publicly defending gays.

Robert was born and raised as part of a black community, but he came out to only one straight black person—his mother. His conventional masculine self-presentation made passing relatively easy. No one suspected him. But Robert paid a price. His relationships with kin, church, friends, and neighbors suffered; his ties to the black community were either severed or became shallow.

Robert's relationship to the straight white community was not much different. No one knew, but Robert's isolation among whites didn't matter to him. He didn't have the kind of personal investment in the white world that he had in the black community. He did, however, look to a predominantly white gay world to recover a sense of social belonging. Although he didn't find community in the white gay world, he did eventually become a part of a small circle of black gay men and women. This small island of a community is the only place where Robert feels he belongs. Unfortunately, it is an unstable social network—it's small (Robert mentioned five to eight regulars), and individual participation is usually quite limited and often ends as people find partners or their career or family pulls them in other directions.

Renee retreated into the closet once she began to realize she was a lesbian. It was not an easy accommodation. She was a gender bender of sorts. Renee felt a very strong inner masculine sense of self; she loves sports, is a forceful and assertive person, and enjoys hanging with the boys. To successfully be in the closet, she would have to suppress this core part of herself. She couldn't and wouldn't do this. Instead, Renee tried to find social roles that permitted women to be masculine without raising suspicions—for example, as an athlete, a soldier, a hospital emergency worker. Fear and anxiety were always present. As Renee reached her thirties, her single status and decision to not date men, along with her masculine self-presentation, made the closet an almost impossible accommodation. Her gender nonconformity was, she believed, often interpreted as revealing a lesbian identity. Renee eventually came out—sort of. She did what many gays did in the era of the closet: she established a separate gay life far away from the people she grew up with, who knew little of her "other life."

Stonewall likely had the effect of driving many individuals deeply into the closet. Indeed, many homosexuals who came of age in the 1950s and early 1960s thought that this new social assertiveness and visibility would bring about greater social repression; it would also create considerable turmoil for many homosexuals who had managed a more or less comfortable social adjustment in the closet. They were in some ways right. While the closet doors may have tightened for some, they were loosened, even unhinged, for many others. "Out of the closet" became the slogan of the new gay liberationist movement.

The closet is an unstable social condition. While its purpose is to keep homosexuals silent and invisible, its very creation causes a heightened public awareness of homosexuality. Laws criminalizing homosexuality, police harassing and arresting homosexuals, and newspapers publishing their names in order to shame them have the effect of both enforcing heterosexual domination and heightening public awareness of the pervasive presence of homosexuals. The closet may expel real, living homosexuals from visible public life, but it makes this sexual personage into a haunting symbolic presence.[19] The status of the closeted homosexual as both omnipresent but unseen shapes a culture of homosexual suspicion. In principle, no one is to be spared. No matter how impeccable an individual's heterosexual credentials, he or she is not entirely free of suspicion. A flawless heterosexual presentation may, after all, be taken as masking a latent homosexual self.

The closet has another ironic effect. It creates a heightened self-awareness on the part of homosexually oriented individuals. The social pressure to methodically conceal rivets attention precisely on that which is proscribed: homosexuality. For some closeted individuals, homosexuality becomes a core self-identity as daily life centers on either avoiding suspicion of homosexuality or coming out. And the fashioning of homosexuality into a core social identity makes rebellion against the closet possible—and likely. At an individual level, rebellion often meant coming out, affirming a gay self, and becoming part of a gay community. At a political level, a movement took shape—gay liberationism and lesbian feminism—that challenged the institutional and cultural supports of the closet; that is, the culture of pollution and the state-backed policy of repression. This movement has, by all accounts, been enormously successful even if so many battles have been lost and so many remain to be waged.

The era of the closet is hardly over. Yet the present is a world apart from that of just one or two decades ago. The universe of the butch, the queen, the normal straight, the culture of camp, the seamless and open homophobic culture, and uniform state and institutional repression are taking on the character of a historical era. The closet has not disappeared, but there are today more people choosing to live beyond the closet.

CHAPTER TWO

Gay and Lesbian Life after the Closet

"I'll never come out," Lenny insisted in our initial interview in 1996. True to his word, he hasn't, at least as of May 2000, when we had a follow-up conversation. While he regrets the lack of passion in his marriage and suffers some guilt for having sex with men, it is more than compensated for by the satisfaction he feels as a husband, father, and respected member of his community.

Bill's story unfolded differently. His marriage ended in the mid-1980s. It lacked more than passion. It lacked the kind of intimacy he needed to feel loved and to love: the intimacy of a man. The end of his marriage triggered a decision to reconsider the place of homosexuality in his life.

Bill stepped out of the closet. Initially, he came out in the gay world of bars; he slowly became part of a tight-knit circle of friends. This social network encouraged him to come out to his mother and eventually to his entire family, friends, coworkers, ex-wife, his son, and, after agreeing to be interviewed by a local newspaper, to his entire hometown.

It would be a mistake to interpret Lenny's biography as a story of his failure of nerve while reading Bill's life as a heroic tale of the triumph of freedom over fear. The different paths of Lenny and Bill are not simply stories of individual personalities; and they should not be read as tales of moral character. Between Lenny's and Bill's coming of age, there was a sea change in the place of gays in America. Their individual stories express something of the difference in being gay before and after Stonewall.

For Lenny and many of his generation, homosexuality was approached as a shameful or guilt-ridden impulse to be kept private. In Lenny's day-to-day reality, heterosexuality was the right and only way to organize personal life. There were few options for Americans who became adults in the 1950s. Heterosexuality was simply taken for granted. For individuals like Lenny who grew up and lived in small to midsized towns, there was hardly an awareness of homosexuality. True, the 1950s witnessed the rise of new political organizations such as the Mattachine Society and the Daughters of Bilitis. However, these groups were small and highly secretive, and they barely registered on the screen of public opinion. Lenny had never heard of these organizations and was not exposed to any public images of homosexuality until well into the 1960s. And if Lenny had come out in the 1950s or 1960s, he would have faced a wall of intolerance extending outward from his family to his peers and coworkers. Risk and danger were what Lenny, and many of his generation, anticipated if their homosexuality was exposed.

Despite growing up in a blue-collar town like Lenny's, Bill came of age in a different era. By the 1980s, gays were a visible part of the public world. Gay institutions and organizations were established not only in urban centers but in small and mid-sized cities like Utica, Albany, and Syracuse, in New York. Gays were on television, in the movies, and in the news and newspapers. A national movement gave gays a public face and voice.[1] Moreover, if the 1950s culture that Lenny absorbed expected individuals to follow rigid social scripts, American culture in the 1980s valued self-expression, authenticity, and individual and group difference. This social world made coming out a virtual ethical duty—"to be true to oneself."

Lenny's world is disappearing. Of course, many individuals, sadly but understandably, choose to be in the closet. Still, the closet is today not what it was for Lenny. America has changed. There's no longer the blanket silence around homosexuality and gays are no longer invisible; and while there is still a great deal of intolerance, we have newspaper editors, writers, politicians, celebrities, and rabbis and ministers who publicly support gay rights. In short, contemporary America is a much more welcoming environment in which to be publicly gay.[2]

Bill's life is more typical of gay life today. Many gay Americans have organized lives beyond the closet. For many of us, our lives bear a closer resemblance to those of conventional heterosexuals than to those of closeted homosexuals. Indeed, for the first time in the postwar period many gay men and women arrive at adulthood with the experience of the closet as a part of their past; many of us live a large portion of adulthood as openly gay.[3] For many of us, gay life today is as different from gay life for the Stonewall generation as their lives were different from the generation of the 1950s. To be sure, the chief narrative themes of the Stonewall era such as coming out of the closet, gay pride, and migrating to gay enclaves still resonate with many lesbians and gay men. Yet listening to the stories of those living outside of the closet, I heard a somewhat different inflection, a voice that was at ease with being gay and confident in its demand for a respected place in America. At the root of this voice is an *emphatic sense of personal integrity and an unshakeable feeling of entitlement—a right to love, to intimate well-being, to equal opportunities, and to respect.*

SNAPSHOTS OF LIFE OUTSIDE

For individuals who live beyond the closet, the core areas of their lives—family, love, friendship, and work—are not decisively shaped by the need to pass. These individuals are not making life-shaping decisions to avoid exposure or suspicion. They may still conceal their sexuality from some people or in some situations and they may still struggle with shame and fear. However, their caution around coming out will not drive them into a closeted life. For these individuals, gay life today is a world apart from that of past generations. If my research speaks to broad social trends, the choice for many gays today is no longer between denial or living a double life. Rather, gays struggle with defining the meaning and place of being gay in lives that allow for considerable personal choice while navigating a public world that continues to pose risks.[4]

Karen

Karen was the first person I interviewed. It was 1996. We met at a McDonald's. She had responded to an ad I put in a local gay newsletter soliciting people to interview about being closeted.

Karen was in her early forties. She is white, working class, and was raised and still lives in a a small rural town outside of Troy, New York. Karen has struggled with thyroid problems which have often kept her out of work. She lives alone and has been single for her entire adult life. Although she lacks a formal education beyond high school, she prides herself on being a keen reader. I anticipated a difficult interview. I was a little anxious, and she seemed guarded. I was mistaken. Karen proved to be very forthcoming and won me over with her frankness and intelligence.

Until 1994, just two years before I interviewed her, Karen thought of herself as straight. She'd had only two or three sexual experiences with men and these lacked passion. She worried that she might be asexual. This bothered her enough to see a doctor, who thought her passionlessness was a symptom of her thyroid problem. Karen never suspected that a desire for women might explain her lack of desire for men. She was simply not aware of any sexual feelings for women.

This changed in 1994. Karen was working at a social service agency. She became friendly with Linda, a coworker. Karen remembers how she felt being around Linda. "Whenever I was around her I would tingle all over and my heart would be thumping. . . . I initially dealt with it by telling myself I must be pretty hard up to get so excited by her. I needed to get laid by a man." At the time, Karen was on medication that had the effect of diminishing her sexual drive. She felt almost sexless. As Karen's health improved to the point of ending medication, her sex drive returned and jolted her into a new sexual awareness. "Right about this time I was nearly forty, horny as hell, and finally found myself thinking, 'Why can't I find a man that makes me feel the way Linda did?' It was at that moment that I then asked myself, 'Who said it has to be a man?' Precisely at that moment a lightbulb went off in my head and I became consciously aware that I was sexually attracted to her [Linda] and had been for five years."

Almost immediately, Karen began to think of herself as a lesbian. There was no protracted struggle of self-acceptance. Karen felt that the closet was not really an option. "I'm not very good at being in the closet. On the very first day [of becoming aware of her sexual feelings] I decided to identify. My first reaction to myself was, 'How are you going to do this? . . . You can't hide, you'll have a nervous breakdown. You're not the kind of person who can be totally closeted.'"

Coming out frightened her. "It was very hard for the first six months after I started to identify as a lesbian. It completely changes your perspective on all of your experiences in life. . . . For several months my life felt upside down. I had diarrhea for a month."

Karen wasn't sure who to turn to. Unlike Lenny, she felt that she had to come out. At the time she was seeing a counselor but was reluctant to tell him. She feared rejection by someone she had come to like and on whom she felt emotionally dependent. She worried that he would be angry at her for deceiving him. "I felt that he would look at me differently." Eventually she did come out to him, and "he actually turned out to be absolutely great about it. . . . He was extremely accepting."

Karen decided to come out to one or two of the lesbians she came to know while working at the social service agency. It felt safe. "I was being pretty conservative about who I was going to tell. . . . Even now, my guidelines about coming out to people are, um, I question my motives, why is it important for me to tell them, what will be different if I tell them. [At this point] I never came out to anyone who was straight."

I knew Karen was anxious about coming out to straight people, but I wanted to know more about this fear. After all, she voiced no sense of shame or guilt about being a lesbian and, without any risk of losing her livelihood and lacking close personal ties to anyone at the agency, I wondered what the caution meant. In her typically clear and thoughtful way, Karen voiced her main concern. "Two things I think kept me from coming out [to straight people]. One, I figured they didn't know what it was like to be gay, and secondly . . . I came in [to the social service agency] identifying as heterosexual. So here we are changing identity in midcourse, so to speak and I didn't know if I wanted to do that."

Karen knew that she had to come out to her family, which included her elderly parents, an older sister, and a younger brother. They all lived near Karen. She saw them frequently and described her family as tight-knit and close.

Karen decided to come out to her brother. She explained that he had casually mentioned some sexual experiences with men when he was in prison. Karen expected a supportive response. Instead, he was angry and disapproving. Her brother is still not supportive but he no longer voices disapproval. Karen is convinced that he is in denial about his own homosexuality. Still, this experience gave her reason to pause.

Fear stopped her from quickly coming out to the rest of her family. I asked Karen what she had anticipated. "I thought my mother would go off the deep end. . . . I expected my sister to make fun of me." Even though Karen gradually realized that her brother had mentioned her coming out to the rest of the family, nobody said anything. She believed they knew, but it wasn't talked about. In the meantime, Karen had accepted herself and wanted to share this information. In many respects, discovering that she's a lesbian was a great relief. For the first time in her life, Karen had a clear sexual identity. "I was confused for so long. I didn't have an identity. I thought that I was straight, but it wasn't fulfilling and I didn't know why." Karen wanted to share this newfound sense of self with her family.

Her mother's anticipated rejection filled Karen with dread. She decided to come out to her sister first. "I first told my sister. . . . She's not generally a very supportive person." Karen was again surprised, but this time pleasantly. "She said to me . . . that she still loved me, and it didn't make any difference, and that she wasn't going to view me any differently." Emboldened by this experience, Karen came out to her mother. Her mother's reaction was far from what she expected. "The first thing that she said to me was, "Why did you wait to tell me? Why didn't you tell me before?'" Her mother was accepting, and her support has never wavered.

Today, Karen is out to all of her family—including some cousins, aunts, uncles, nephews, and nieces. She is not out to her father. "We don't tell him anything important." Being "out" means that they know she is a lesbian. It's been explicitly said and is talked about as part of her everyday talk about her life. Being out also means that she talks to them about the lesbian aspects of her life in a way that, she says, is no different than if she were straight. They know about her dates and her participation in the gay community, and she routinely talks about news events that speak to gay life. "I can talk about everything that's going on. . . in an open way."

Karen is similarly forthcoming about the lesbian aspects of her life with friends. Typical of many of us who live beyond the closet, her friends are a mix of straight and gay individuals. They all know that she's a lesbian. For example, Karen's closest friend is a straight woman. Karen was nervous about coming out to her. "I was afraid she would freak out and not want to be friends with me." In fact, they've become a lot closer. "Her and I have a lot in common even though she's straight. She actually helped me a lot with this issue. . . . She's a white, straight female in a serious committed relationship with a black male. So there's a situation where family and society does not want to accept who she loves. . . . The parallels were, like, really pretty significant."

Karen came out to other people as she thought it to be appropriate. For example, she disclosed to her gynecologist. Karen remembers this coming-out event. During a routine visit, her physician asked what form of birth control she was using. Karen responded that she doesn't have sex with men. Similarly, when a male friend asked her out for a date, Karen told him that she doesn't date men.

Karen doesn't feel the need to tell everyone. Store clerks, service providers, and casual acquaintances do not need to know. This issue of who she tells and why is something she struggles with. She knows that it's often confusing to disentangle homophobic from other reasons to come out. For example, Karen initially felt that her neighbors did not need to know. "I want my home to be my private place." However, in the course of the interview Karen acknowleged that she was anxious about what her neighbors would think if butch-looking women visited. Karen eventually confronted her lingering sense of shame. "I will be attracted to whoever I'm attracted to. You can't let that stop you," she told herelf. In general, Karen says, "if I don't know people well, there's no reason for them to know." And, "I don't feel like I need to explain it [being a lesbian] unless they want to ask."

As she became more self-accepting and open about her sexual identity, Karen got involved in the gay community. She would sometimes volunteer at commmunity events. And, through reading gay books and closely following news about gays in the local and national media, Karen feels a sense of gay identification and integration. "There really is a gay culture. . . . Gay people talk about gay stuff." Today, Karen feels she has both a clear sexual identity and a sense of social belonging. This has given her a feeling of "normality," something she had rarely experienced in the past.

Her life today is no longer focused on coming out. She's already out to those that matter—family, close friends, and the gay community. Establishing a relationship is her primary concern. "Coming out is not a big issue for me. I think I've got the door open and I'm standing right outside the door and looking out. . . . Today, the big issue is relationships. . . . You know it's about people's morals and sense of commitment. . . . It's the whole social thing. Of course, it's the same thing in the straight world."

Karen recognizes, however, that the issue of coming out is not over. Decisions about coming out will have to be made throughout her life. Moreover, she also has to deal with her mother's coming out about her to relatives and friends. "My mother definitely went into the closet. She ain't discussing it with nobody." Karen will not come out to her mother's friends or kin unless her mother approves. "I wouldn't tell them. I'll stay in the closet. . . . I don't want to overwhelm my mother. I don't want to rush her, because I understand what the process [of coming out] was for me. It's not something you can rush. I want to let her go at her own pace. I see her going through what I went through in the beginning." Karen worries less about her own coming-out decisions than those of her mother, siblings, or friends.

Karen's coming-out story is not the typical post-Stonewall narrative. There was no prolonged and anguished struggle for self-acceptance, no protracted closeted period, no migration to an urban gay enclave, and her coming out was not met with a wall of rejection and hostility. In fact, once she became aware of her attraction to women, she quickly came out to herself and celebrated her new sexual identity with her kin and friends. With Karen we are in a world apart from Lenny—the world after the closet.

Gordon

Gordon is ten years Karen's junior. He was born in 1970, which means he came of age as an adult in the late 1980s and early 1990s. While there may be only a ten-year difference between them, coming of age in the mid- to late 1970s, as Karen did, is almost a world apart from reaching adulthood in the 1990s. At the time of the interview, Gordon was in his mid-thirties. He grew up in Brooklyn. He has a bachelor's degree and works for the State of New York in a mid-level white-collar job.

I felt it was important to interview gay people of color who had come out and stayed out. I knew it would not be easy to find such individuals. Frankly, I knew very few gay people of color and the few I knew were either academics or activists. I wanted to interview individuals who were less absorbed in gay life. I learned of a newly formed organization for black gay men and women in Albany. I attended a meeting and introduced myself. I talked about my research, and several people, Gordon among them, agreed to be interviewed.

Gordon is a solidly built, husky sort of guy. So I was initially taken aback by his soft-spoken demeanor and the gentleness, even vulnerability, that comes through in what he says and how it's said. Gordon is immediately disarming and likeable. We interviewed at his apartment in a mixed-race, mixed-class part of Albany. Just before the interview, he introduced me to his lover, a white man.

I knew that the interview needed to be angled somewhat differently than I had initially intended. I wanted to know how this black man from a predominantly black neighborhood ended up living with a white man and participating in an organization for black gays. In his calm way, Gordon told his story.

"I always identified as gay. There was never really a time that I didn't identify as gay. I just never really was out like I am today." Always identified as gay? I pressed Gordon to explain. "[When I was a boy] I always had feelings for [other] little boys. . . . I thought it was bad. Nobody told me otherwise."

Gordon grew up learning that a good boy should not be thinking about sex, let alone homosexuality. He quickly came to understand that his homosexual feelings were dangerous. He heard the terms *faggot* and *sissy* growing up, and knew they could mean him. His grandmother once called him a sissy for wearing "girl's" sandals. His sister's angry response to this accusation made it clear that this was not what he wanted to be called. "I put it away. I didn't think about it." And Gordon "put it away" all through high school. This became harder as his attraction to men intensified. His efforts at concealment became more deliberate and the risks of exposure more frightening. "I didn't want people to know. . . . People were mean to gay kids."

Unlike Lenny, as Gordon grew into a young adult he became aware that his grandmother, sister, and peers were not the only people who had opinions about homosexuality. Newspapers, magazines, and books exposed him to positive, prideful images of being gay. He learned that there were gay communities with their own organizations and culture. And he came to know other gay people.

Gordon's life began to change when he went to college. For the first time, he was away from home and among mostly white people. This proved to be freeing for him. He began to have sex with men and eventually found a lover. Although he had by this time accepted his homosexuality as natural, he still kept it kind of hidden. "I didn't advertise it. I still didn't want people to know." This was in the late 1980s. Gordon's life was somewhere between a double life and an integrated, open one. He was still emotionally and financially dependent on his family and greatly feared their rejection.

Gordon was raised by his mother in an almost exclusively black community. He has one sister. His mother is part of a large family with many brothers and sisters, a grandmother, uncles, aunts, cousins, nieces, and nephews. Gordon is very close to his mother. Today, his immediate family—mother, father, sister, and grandmother—knows he's gay. He remains close to them.

During a summer break from college, his mother found a letter from his lover. She was upset. "She was very angry and very confused and very hurt. And she made it very clear that this was something wrong and needed to be dealt with right away." She thought it was a phase or some kind of adolescent acting-out. She blamed the absence of his father for his homosexuality and suggested therapy. Mixed with her religious-based disapproval was a sober social assessment. "It's hard enough being a black man in this world, now you want to add this to it." Much to Gordon's dismay, the relationship became strained. She refused to talk about it, and Gordon didn't press the issue.

A visit from her and his uncle and aunt to his college proved to be a turning point. Gordon introduced them to his lover, and to his surprise his mother liked him. From that time forward, she became decidely more accepting, and their relationship returned to its previous closeness. "We don't talk a whole lot about the homosexuality thing, but then again we never did talk about personal things like that." Still, Gordon introduces his dates and lovers to his mother and he will talk now and again about the gay aspects of his life. She has been supportive of him and his lovers once it became clear that this is who he is and that he can be happy.

Coming out was and still is hard. "I think it's always hard to come out even though you'd been gay for years. It's a hard thing to do." Watching and listening to Gordon, I believe that his discomfit about coming out related more to his personality than feelings of shame or anticipated social risk. As a somewhat shy, sensitive man the emotional risks of revealing himself and exposing strong feelings is likely very difficult for Gordon. This sense of Gordon was conveyed as he talked about coming out at work. It turns out that he rarely comes out to coworkers directly, but neither does he pretend to be straight. Coming out, Gordon says, would not pose any risks in terms of his job or collegial respect. Still, he feels that unless someone asks him directly there is no reason to come out. He is not close with any of his coworkers. Gordon is convinced that they all know anyway. Gordon's previous lover worked in an adjacent office. They often socialized at work. When his lover got sick and died of AIDS, his coworkers, including his boss, learned of this and were very supportive. His boss visited Gordon's lover in the hospital and attended the funeral. Gordon's decision to not come out directly to coworkers is not about being closeted. Rather, it speaks to his personality and to a struggle, common among those living outside the closet, of figuring out when and how to come out after you've already made being gay a routine, ordinary part of your personal life.

There was another factor that made coming out hard: Gordon is black. He grew up in an almost all-black community, went to an all-black high school, and was heavily involved in a local black church. He sang in the choir, attended Baptist services regularly, and looked up to his minister as a sort of father figure.

Gordon reluctantly admitted that coming out in this community has not been easy. "Everyone was seen as straight. . . . Being gay was like foreign . . . a white thing." Comments from his kin and peers made it crystal clear that being openly gay would make him the target of ridicule and perhaps harassment. After Gordon came out in college, he returned to his old neighborhood to visit his family, but remained aloof from old friends and neighbors.

Gordon felt that he had to decide whether to be openly gay, which for all practical purposes meant severing his ties to the black community, or sustaining such ties but at the cost of being closeted. "You can't have the best of both worlds. . . . I chose the gay world because I felt it was more comfortable to deal with my sexuality and check people on their racism. It's easier than coming out in an all-straight black community. I had to weigh which of the two were going to be harder. And I had to go with what people are going to be more accepting."

To live as an openly gay individual, Gordon had to greatly weaken his identification and ties to the straight black community. After graduating from college, he moved to Albany. He decided to fashion a life around being an open, proud gay man. He wanted, however, to establish some kind of connection to the black community. After his gay life was more or less settled, he reached out to some politically oriented blacks, but "their response . . . told me that it wasn't worth the bother. They didn't really want to deal with issues associated with homosexuality or being black and gay." Although his previous lover was a black man, Gordon was unable to create any strong personal ties with straight black men or women. "It's because of my homosexual lifestyle."

Gordon's decision to fashion a life around being gay was not an easy one. He grew up as black identified and considers himself a proud black man. And Gordon found in his kin, the black church, and his peers a rich sense of community that he needed. Moreover, "I was a stranger to everything in the gay world." Gordon had never participated in organized gay life, and "most of the gay community was white." He felt guarded, and worried about whether there was a place for him in this community.

But gay life had changed considerably between the early 1970s and the mid-1990s. Feminism, the political activism of people of color, and AIDS activism had shaped a culture that valued social diversity. Differences among gays, especially relating to race, gender, and disability, were now to be respected and represented in gay organizations. In fact, by the time Gordon turned to the gay community in the mid-1990s, there was already a short history of efforts to organize gay people of color. Gordon located kindred folk and soon found a place in the gay world that felt right. Most of his close friends are black and gay. He is part of a community within a community. If it's not the dense community of his upbringing, it's still a home.

Today, Gordon strongly identifies as gay—"that's who I see myself as being." Unlike Karen, Gordon's life is in some ways less integrated; it's divided into three fairly distinct spheres. He describes a comfortable work life in a largely straight white workplace; he feels respected and liked but different as a gay man. He has not established any close personal ties at work. At the end of the workday, Gordon drives home to a racially mixed neighborhood where he shares an apartment with a white man. Gordon admits of no discomfiture; he has not experienced any harassment, but neither has he forged personal ties with anyone in the neighborhood. While work and home are satisfying, Gordon looks to his small circle of black gay men and women to lift his life to a higher plane. In this personal sphere, Gordon finds his deeper sense of self affirmed and feels a true sense of belonging. Despite this social fragmentation, Gordon has organized a stable, fairly conventional life that allows for love, deep friendships, work satisfaction, and a sense of community. The closet is not a focus of his life. Today, Gordon's worries are about "racism in the gay and lesbian commnity" and HIV-AIDS, the disease that took his first lover's life.

Clara

As the interviews piled up, I was realizing that the closet was not the pervasive reality that I had expected it to be. Instead, for the people I interviewed, it was more a phase or a part of people's past. My own life was not as exceptional as I had thought. If my research speaks to larger social trends, many gay individuals are living adult lives beyond the closet. They may be managing their sexual identity in specific situations or with specific individuals, but they are not marrying, dating, or otherwise deliberately organizing a life aimed at passing as straight.

As I was unexpectedly encountering the disappearance of the closet, the horrors of the lives of many gay youths were gaining public attention. While the brutal death of Matthew Shepard made national headlines, activists and scholars were documenting a steady stream of incidents of hate crimes and anti-gay violence. And researchers were uncovering a world of despair and rage among gay youths who often struggled with a hostile school and family environment.[5] The world of gay youth looked a lot like the world of the closet. I was keenly aware of this because one of my doctoral students, Melinda Miceli, was studying gays in high school.[6] I had read some of her interviews, which were often quite moving. But the concept of the closet did not seem like a suitable way to understand their lives. These kids were often self-accepting; many of them had been exposed to positive, affirmative views of being gay in the media and often through participation in local gay organizations. Many of their difficulties stemmed from being financially and emotionally dependent on their families and schools—two of the most unfriendly environments for gay people. Melinda uncovered more than just confusion and desperation; these kids often found one another and could look to an established gay community for a sense of belonging.

I was intrigued. What is the place of the closet in the lives of today's gay youths? I decided to interview individuals who came of age as adults after the mid-1990s—a period I consider to be a watershed in gay life. I wanted to grasp something of the lives of young gays who were poised to enter an adult world. I thought that this generation, born just after 1980, was the first to come of age in a social setting decidely more friendly than any previous one. This was a generation that from a young age saw gays on television, in the movies, and in the newspapers and heard public figures, from celebrities to presidents, defend gays as part of America. This was, as well, a generation whose parents were baby boomers (my generation). Whatever else baby boomers are, we grew up in one of the most liberal periods in American history; a national visible gay movement and culture forced us to confront and sometimes clarify our views on gays.

Clara's is just one story. As you'll see, it's unlikely that you could describe it as typical. Still, something of the sensibility of this generation and those living beyond the closet is vividly presented in her story. In particular, what comes through in Clara's story is a strong feeling of self-worth and integrity as a gay person; this gives her a sense of entitlement to equal rights, to a public voice and presence, and to social respect. This sense of integrity and entitlement is at the heart of a post-closeted gay sensibility. It drives gays into the outside world.

At the time of the interview, Clara was a freshmen at an all-girl's college. She was eighteen years old and a lesbian. Her father is Jamaican and her mother is African American. Her parents were separated when she was a child. Clara mostly lived with her mother in a Washington, D.C., suburb, but also spent time with her father in Harlem.

At the time of the interview, Clara lived in a campus dorm; her dormmates are all straight, mostly white. Clara is not political. Her life revolves around her family, a network of friends, male and female, straight and gay, and her current lover. She is "out" to all of these people. Indeed, as we'll see, her lesbian life is conducted in a strikingly open and unapolegetic way.

Her family consists of her parents, many uncles and aunts, two older sisters, a nephew, niece, and brother-in-law. Everybody in her family knows she is gay, and at least some of them know a lot about her gay life. "I talk about everything with my mother and my sisters and one brother because he's who I see the most and they know my lover and everything like that. So they know just about everything."

I asked Clara to describe her coming-out experience. She recalls feeling attracted to girls at a very young age. "I was having feelings for females when I was in the third grade, but I thought it was because I was so tomboyish. I thought they just looked cute . . . because they had on dresses. . . . But then, as I got older and saw boys got into girls, I got into girls too." Clara came out when she was fourteen. She had no doubt that she was a lesbian. She had "read a lot of books . . . life-story type of books about lesbians and coming out." She understood that being attracted to women made her a lesbian; having absorbed the positive images in coming-out stories, she accepted herself as a lesbian with apparently little inner anguish. It was, as she repeatedly said, "just normal for me."

She initially came out to her mother, then to the rest of her family and friends. Despite narrating her coming out in a strikingly matter-of-fact way, some underlying anxieties surfaced in the course of the interview. Her mother was, and still is, her closest friend. Her acceptance meant a lot to Clara. She worried that her mother might reject her. "The worst thing that could have happened . . . was that she wouldn't accept it . . . that she would put me out or she would be like, 'Well I don't want any of you dykes around my house.'" Clara didn't expect this reaction, but "I always expect the worst."

In fact, her mother was accepting. "My mom didn't have a problem with it. . . . My mother was just like, let's talk about it." Her father's response was different. "My dad really took it the hardest, because Island [Jamaican] men don't feel cool about it. So he had the biggest problem with it, but it didn't matter to me, 'cause I just told him to be telling him. I wasn't telling him for approval."

The rest of her family was accepting. "They were okay with it." With her sister and brother she talks about her lesbian life, including her girlfriend.

Clara thinks that one reason her family has been so accepting was that her older sister had come out a year or so earlier. Additionally, her mother is forty-three and shares the broadly liberal attitudes toward personal life of many in her generation. Also, as a single parent Clara's mother is all too aware that lives and loves come in many shapes and forms.

Clara subsequently came out to her friends. She is part of a tight-knit friendship circle. She considers them family. Her friends, it turned out, were also coming to terms with their sexual identity, and many of them also came to identify as lesbian. Coming out to her closest friend was hard because she was straight. "The only person I didn't tell initially or was kind of scared about telling was my best friend. I kind of had a crush on her, and me and her had been friends since second grade. If she rejected me I didn't want her to reject my friendship, too. So, I just, like, gave myself enough time to be able to deal with whatever was coming."

Clara decided to not directly and indiscriminately come out to her high school classmates. "People that weren't my closest friends I didn't tell because I felt it was none of their business." However, she "never did anything to hide it . . . from others." She was aware of the risks of being out in high school. She acknowledged that some classmates teased her when they learned of her sexual identity. Clara's sense of self-assuredness protected her from feeling hurt. "I didn't care, you know. It was like, you all have to deal with it, not me. . . . I just didn't pay them any attention." Still, I wondered what it meant that she had a boyfriend during high school. She explained. "Well, I had a boyfriend for three years, but that's because I really wanted to be with him. It took so much time to learn somebody else so I just stayed with him." Clara eventually left him for a girl. While I am not persuaded that Clara's narrative of easy self-acceptance is the whole story, her actions speak to a life beyond the closet.

When she moved to go to college in 1997 she had to deal with coming out again. She lived in a college dorm and shared a room with two other girls, who were straight. I wondered how Clara came out and how her dormmates had reacted. Clara explained, "They kind of all found out at the same time because we were all in our room one night and we were eating pizza and they were like, "'Wow, this boy he's so cute,' and I was like [showing them a photo], 'That's my girlfriend.' I just said it and kept eating because it's just normal to me and they were like, 'Oh my god, I don't believe it.'" Her dormmates accepted her. "Everything stayed the same."

Clara knew that this news would spread rapidly through the college. Asked about how others on campus reacted, Clara described an incident. "Some girls were going to a fraternity party and asked me to join them." Clara responded, "I'm not going and they were like, 'Why?' And, I'm like, 'I don't do dick.' And, they were like, 'Oh my God, what do you mean?' I was like, 'I'm a lesbian.' And, they were like, 'What! . . . You say it like you're so normal,' and I'm like, 'It is the norm for me, you know. It's not normal to you, but it's normal to me.'" Clara says that she has not experienced any problems in coming out to classmates. She talks with her classmates and dormmates the way they talk to her. If they talk about boys, she talks about girls. Their only surprise is that Clara doesn't look and act like the stereotypical man-hating, masculine woman.

Clara does not go out of her way to indiscriminately tell people that she is a lesbian. She just acts in spontaneous, ordinary ways, and sometimes that means she will come out. For example, Clara describes coming out to her dentist. "He knows because when I went to get my teeth checked and all that, my girlfriend came with me. It wasn't like I sat down and told him, but he asked who she was and I was like, 'Oh, that's my girlfriend.'" I asked how he reacted. "He was like, 'Oh, how's she doing?' He's so nice. . . . Every now and then he'll ask about her."

Clara feels no need to come out to people she doesn't know or isn't close to. For example, she'll hold hands with her lover in public, but this is not about grabbing attention or making a statement; "it's just normal for me. I would do it with my boyfriend, so it's no different than the fact that it's a woman." Clara doesn't dress or act in ways that might signal her sexual identity. While she sometimes wears buttons or has a gay rainbow flag on her car, it's more about being expressive or about style and attitude than about coming out. "I'll get a button and I'll put it on . . . because I think it's nice. Not because I want somebody, you know, everybody to see it like that." I asked why she doesn't try to signal her sexual identity when she's out in public. She wants to choose who she tells and when; mostly, disclosure is considered important when it's a matter of establishing friendship and intimacy. "I feel like if I wanted them in my business I would just be like, 'Hey, I'm gay.' I don't do that; that's not me." Clara insists that choosing not to come out to people she's not close to is not about passing or being closeted. "I'm not trying to pass as a heterosexual, because if it ever came up, I would say something about it. . . . I would be like, 'Yeah, you know, I'm gay.'"

Coming out for Clara is not about making some kind of political statement but about accepting who you are. "I didn't come out to make a political statement. . . . I think first you have to, like, really accept it yourself, because a lot of people don't accept it so they think something's wrong with them, so they don't tell anybody. When you accept it yourself, when you're like, 'Okay, I'm gay, I'm comfortable with it,' then it's easier to come out to others." Coming out to others is about respect. "I really want people to respect the fact that I'm gay."

Clara realizes that, for reasons having to do with her personality and her family, coming out for her has been much easier than for many people. She knows that some people are in the closet; some of her friends have struggled long and hard for self-acceptance; and she knows that not everybody's family and friends are as accepting as her own. In fact, her girfriend has not had an easy time of coming out to her family. As we'll see in the next chapter, Marcia's mother was and still is, some four years after she initially came out, disapproving and sometimes hostile.

Although struggling with the closet has not been part of her life, "being a lesbian is not easy in this world." And, while she has choices that were mostly unavailable to gay people just two decades ago, Clara must still deal with the prejudices and discomfort of many people. She tires at times of dealing with the hassles and strains of an often intolerant straight world. She would like someday to start a family and to just be who she is without the stares, guarded comments, and sense of threat that is at times present.

Clara's preference to live in a gay-friendly place is a far cry from Robert's closeted view of the world as divided between a public straight and a private gay world. "I've never ever thought about it like that," says Clara. She navigates daily life as an open lesbian. The public world is not just a straight world; it may be straight dominated, but it is a world where she participates and feels she belongs.

Clara is probably not typical of her generation and is surely not typical of gays today. But I think she gives expression to something of the sensibility of a generation living beyond the closet. At the heart of this sensibility is a feeling of self-worth and moral integrity and a sense of deserving the same respect and rights as any other citizen. This feeling of personal integrity underpins a strong sense of entitlement. Gay people should be free to make choices about intimacy and career without having to consider social prejudice and discrimination. This sense of self-integrity and entitlement translates into a political demand for social equality.

OUT AT WORK

Despite her sense of freedom and self-assuredness, Clara anticipates that she will need to be more guarded when she enters the workforce. "I'm not going to be so loose about it, because you do have to watch who you say something to, and that's not . . . like going back in the closet. I just feel like it's protecting your job, your career. You know not everybody has to know, and when they find out that could cause a problem." Clara understands that stepping out into the public world of work as an adult who has to be self-supporting, who wishes to have a family, and who has career aspirations introduces a host of new challenges to being gay and out.

The anguish and turmoil many of us feel around coming out to family and friends is a real source of suffering. Yet the private world is one of strong personal ties, a world of love, caring, and intense emotional connection. These ties may be weakened or even temporarily suspended, but they will not be easily broken or permanently severed. By contrast, the public world of work, government, and school is not sustained by strong personal ties. It is not a sphere of love and emotional solidarity, but rather is organized around formal rules, social roles, and a spirit of impersonality and professionalism.

How do gays who live outside the closet in their private lives negotiate public life? I focus on the world of work.[7]

After graduating from high school, Clara's girlfriend, Marcia (b. 1978), took a job as a house counselor for developmentally disabled adults. Her coming out was not easy. While she avoided a protracted closeted period, her mother was stubbornly disapproving. Just one year after coming out to herself, family, and friends, Marcia had to deal with managing her sexual identity at work. The risks were considerable; she was living away from her family and was self-supporting.

Marcia decided that she would not deliberately try to pass with her coworkers and boss. "I don't hide it. . . . When I went in [to work] someone asked if I had a boyfriend and I was, 'No, no, I'm gay.'" Marcia's decision to be casual and open about her sexual identity was made a little easier after she learned that two coworkers were also lesbians and were out.

Although "pretty much everybody knows at work that I'm gay," Marcia does not disclose to everyone and varies how much information about her personal life she shares. Several considerations guide her decisions to come out.

Marcia considers the timing of disclosure in order to try to avoid stereotypical reactions. "If I tell a person that I'm queer immediately, then they don't really know who I am." In this regard, she has been cautious about coming out to a new employee. "I get the feeling from him that I need to wait a little. . . . He needs to know me because he seems like the type of person who's going to judge me [based solely] on my sexual identity. I don't want people seeing me and thinking, 'Oh she's a lesbian' . . . and don't even think about the type of person I am."

In deciding whether to come out at work, Marcia also considers the level of intimacy that is socially appropriate and that she wants with different coworkers. There is one coworker "that I kind of bonded with. . . . I can talk about anything to her. She tells me about her boyfriend, and I tell her about my girlfriend." If Marcia lacks a personal relationship with a coworker, she considers her lesbian identity and life to be "none of their business." For example, "I don't think my boss needs to come up to me and be, 'So how's your girlfriend?' I really do like to keep my personal home life away from work."

There is an additional factor that Marcia considers: fear of the consequences of coming out. With friends and peers, an individual can often minimize or end contact with people who are not respectful. In work life, barring harassment or violent behavior, an individual either manages disrespectful behavior or finds another job. For many of us the latter is not a realistic option. It might take only one or two openly prejudiced coworkers to make work stressful. Moreover, many workplace environments lack laws and social policies to protect gays against discrimination and harassment. Accordingly, work life for many gays has an air of risk and insecurity that is absent for straight wage earners. In many work situations, gays can be fired, denied raises and promotion, and harrassed based on nothing more than perceived sexual identity—and they may have little or no legal redress.

Marcia doesn't worry about being fired, but she believes that she must be cautious in the work world because, at bottom, tolerance, not acceptance, is what she expects. In this regard, Marcia won't bring her lover to social events at work, such as the Christmas party. "There's a difference, I think, between being out and being with someone. I think there's more of a threat if the person is with somebody, than just being out and alone. . . . There's another lesbian couple that I work with and . . . one time they made the mistake of working together. She [my boss] really got on their ass and made them separate working environments. . . . I think it had to do with the fact that it was two women who were a couple working together." Marcia thinks that "they tolerate it, but . . . most of them [coworkers] don't like it."

For all these reasons, Marcia feels pressure to publicly manage her sexual identity. She does not consider herself in the closet at work. "If

I want to be an assistant manager, then I kind of need to not lie and say I'm hetero, but just keep it more personal." Keeping it "more personal" is not being in the closet. Marcia's decision about her career has not been shaped by a need to avoid suspicion; she does not lie or deliberately pretend she is straight at work; and her coworkers know she is gay. Caution is dictated by a workplace that tolerates gays but does not treat them as equals. "It would be nice if everybody was accepted . . . but it doesn't happen. . . . You just learn to accept things. You know you can't right now be legally married. It sucks. Tough shit. You have to accept it. It's difficult in a work environment to be completely open with your significant other, holding hands, rah, rah, rah. Tough shit. It's life, accept it." And, while tolerance makes being out possible, it does not, at least in the public world of work, translate into equality.

Marcia made it clear to me that she is not looking for approval from her coworkers. "I don't give a crap about my coworkers. If they don't like me I don't care." What she wants is simple: to be judged by her work and to be respected. "It's my life, you know. I work for them, but they're not my parents. . . . They are not the Lord God. . . . As long as I do my job . . . and they respect me I will respect them."

Marcia's work life is probably typical of a small minority of wage earners. As a house counselor for the disabled, she works in a fairly intimate home setting. Maintaining friendly social ties with coworkers is especially important in her work situation. For many American wage earners, the work setting is impersonal or bureaucratic. We are employees of government agencies, corporations, or some profession.

Consider the case of Mike (b. 1950). Mike grew up and still lives in a suburb of what is called the Capital District—an area that includes the cities of Albany, Schenectady, Troy, and Rensseaer, New York. His coming-out story is similar to Bill's. There was a long period of being closeted, including a marriage and children, followed by a difficult coming-out period in his early forties. Mike's coming-out drama eventually settled into a life that looks more like his straight friend's lives than his earlier closeted phase.

Mike works for a social service department of the State of New York. He has a managerial position that gives him authority over a dozen or so workers. His daily work life also puts him into contact with many clients and agencies. He is answerable to his supervisor. Mike has worked in this government agency for some twenty years.

For most of those years, Mike was closeted. He lied and "acted like I was straight," laughed at jokes at the expense of gays, and pretended to date women. Eventually he married in order to reduce his anxiety that his prolonged status as a single man made others suspicious.

Today, Mike is out to all his coworkers. He prominently displays a picture of his partner, Andy, on his desk that his coworkers and clients cannot fail to notice. He talks as openly about his life with Andy as his coworkers do about their heterosexual partners. For instance, "we went to a union ceremony two weeks ago and I brought in all the pictures and showed them to my secretary and the people I'm closest to."

Because most of his coworkers likely presume that everyone or most everyone is straight, Mike must still make decisions about disclosure. For example, with new clients and coworkers, coming out "depends on the way the conversation runs. If someone asks me if I'm married . . . I say that I'm with a man." Mike won't lie or pretend to be straight.

Mike has not disclosed to all his coworkers and deliberately regulates how much of his gay life will be revealed. However, fear and shame do not guide his coming-out decisions. Instead, decisions about whom to come out to and how much to disclose are guided by his view of sexual identity as something that is "personal," like one's finances or health status. And one is not, Mike thinks, obliged to reveal such personal information to coworkers. Disclosure depends on whether he has or wants a more intimate relationship. With most coworkers he does not disclose, because "I probably would never have an opportunity to share anything personal with them." Moreover, Mike might reveal his gay identity in order to avoid misidentification, but decide that it's inappropriate to divulge personal details of his gay life. "You know in a work relationship somebody will talk about their kids, [or that] they went with their wife somewhere. I'll just say I went out with my boyfriend, but I won't go into details, because nobody does." Mike is forthcoming about the gay aspects of his life with coworkers that he's intimate with or with whom he wishes to build a close bond. For example, he has developed a very close relationship with one of his coworkers, a straight married woman with several children. "We share everything. It's just a really open relationship."

Being out at work is a moral decision for Mike. It's a matter of personal integrity and wanting coworkers to acknowledge and respect him as a gay man. "I don't want anybody to assume that I'm not gay." Coming out at work was made somewhat less difficult because "there is a fellow worker who works with me, who's extremely out. . . . And I think my boss is a lesbian. She has had an extremely close relationship with another woman in the office who has been known . . . to have lesbian relationships."

Mike's decision to be publicly gay at work has not been free of anxiety. While he doesn't worry about job security, he does fret about social acceptance. Mike's coming out to himself and others was very painful. He drank and used drugs to excess, entered into a passionless marriage for the sole purpose of passing, deceived friends for years, and was rejected by his parents. Mike didn't come out at work until about six years prior to our interview. Despite a self-assured way of talking about being out at work, he acknowledged being anxious about the recent hiring of a supervisor—a very "forceful, dynamic, aggressive woman." It turns out that she moved into an apartment opposite the one occupied by Mike and Andy. "This is somebody that I probably would never have had an opportunity to share anything personal with . . . but she's going to know that I'm gay. And I have had . . . not concerns, but it certainly sits in my mind wondering what she's going to think about it. I know my job's not in jeopardy, but if I were heterosexual there wouldn't be a thought about it." I heard some anger and decided to ask about this. Mike did not shy away from confronting his own demons. "A slight bend of self-homophobia . . . there's still a little bit in there that I still deal with."

Like Marcia's sobering sense that coworkers can only be counted on for a limited tolerance, Mike's homophobia is real and no doubt disconcerting to him, especially in light of his hard struggle to win a grounded sense of self-respect. Still, the world of Marcia and Mike is a far cry from that of the closet. Toning down public presentations of gayness or suffering anxiety about what a boss might think is a world apart from passing at work or making job decisions based on avoiding suspicion or being distant from coworkers to avoid exposure or suffering harassment and isolation for being gay. And while fear enters into their decisions about coming out, it is not an overriding factor. Like their straight coworkers, Marcia and Mike make decisions about revealing the personal aspects of their lives by considering whether it's socially appropriate or whether they wish to establish an intimate relationship with a coworker. For Marcia and Mike, and for many gays today, being out at work is driven by a sense of personal integrity and social entitlement, a right to be who they are because of their belief in the essential moral goodness of being gay. Marcia and Mike speak to an era when the closet is disappearing, at least for many gay Americans, but heterosexual domination remains in place.

IDENTITY CHOICES

In the heyday of the era of the closet, the choices confronting individuals were often stark: to stay in or step out of the closet. And even if individuals chose to come out, there were considerable limits to fashioning a gay life. Coming out often meant migrating from hometown to cities in search of a friendlier environment; it frequently involved living a double life, fashioning a private gay life but passing in the public world. The choice to be in or out could potentially shape the very course of an individuals' life.

Identity choices in the era of the closet were also stark: to deny or champion being gay as a core identity.

Many individuals chose to repress their homosexual feelings or, like Lenny, minimized and managed such feelings by narrowing them into sexual impulses. Read virtually any memoir of the post-Stonewall period, from Merle Miller's *On Being Different* to Martin Duberman's *Cures* or *The Original Coming Out* stories by lesbian feminists in the 1970s, and a typical narrative pattern surfaces.[8] The starting point and often a dramatic focus of these coming-out stories is the denial that accompanies the individual's initial awareness of homosexual feelings. Or, recall two of the earliest commercial films—and frankly two of the best that appeared between the 1960s and the 1980s—which presented vivid portraits of the human drama around the initial awareness of being homosexual: *The Children's Hour* (1961) and *Advise and Consent* (1962). The two main gay characters, Shirley MacLaine (Martha) in the former and Don Murray (Senator Anderson) in the latter, struggle with denial; when forced by social events to acknowledge their homosexuality, and when this knowledge threatens to be made public, their deep sense of shame drives them to suicide. When the closet becomes the paramount social reality, denial becomes a chief motif in coming-of-age narratives.

If denial is one typical response to the closet, coming out is the other. And, because the forces lined up against being gay have been considerable in postwar America, coming out is often narrated as a life-and-death struggle to recover one's true self and a life worth living. It is hardly surprising, then, that homosexuality has often been championed as a core identity. The drama of the coming-out stories of the 1960s through the 1980s was the anguished but ultimately triumphant way individuals responded to prolonged denial. These coming-out stories were often about more than discovering and accepting homosexuality; they were about reclaiming a hidden, authentic self.[9] Martin Duberman's early denial was followed by a tortorous double life filled with self-contempt that culminated in a virtual life mission to come out and build a life around being gay. And Paul Monette recounts a youth lost through denial and repression to be recovered by coming out. In the course of reclaiming his true gay self, Monette also finds a voice as a writer.[10] This motif is repeated time and again—a set piece of coming-of-age stories in the era of the closet.

It was not uncommon for coming-out stories to also include a migration from hometown to the urban gay enclaves that were taking shape in New York, San Francisco, Atlanta, Chicago, Denver, and in virtually every big city. Individuals sought the support of others in order to fashion an affirmative gay identity and to recover something of the community lost in leaving the hometown. These subcultures exerted considerable social pressure on its new denizens to create a life around being gay. As a marginal, fragile community, weakly institutionalized through the 1980s, these subcultures celebrated being gay as a primary identity in order to create a solidaristic community in a hostile environment. Political organizations reinforced a culture that made being gay a core identity as a way to sustain a movement that involved considerable personal risk.

Today, the choices are not as stark. Post-Stonewall coming-out motifs are still compelling, but they are only one strand among many.[11] As individuals live outside the closet, they have more latitude in defining themselves and the place of homosexuality in their lives.

Some individuals who live outside the closet continue to make being gay a primary identity. They do so, however, not so much as a way to overcome a socially defined stigmatized identity. Rather, some choose to forge a sense of self around a gay identity for similar reasons as Koreans or Jews center their identity around being Korean American or Jewish—to claim a positive identity, to make a lifetsyle choice, and to feel a sense of social belonging in a multicultural society.

Some gays today still choose to migrate to cities, look to integrate into subcultures, and organize lives around being gay. In particular, individuals living in small towns or places where there is little or no public gay culture will look to urban subcultures, as earlier generations did, to provide a refuge in a hostile world. However, as exiting the closet becomes a more widely available option, individuals may still choose to participate in gay subcultures but less for reasons of protection than as lifestyle choices. These individuals choose to make being gay a core identity and to organize a life—friends, work, residence, leisure—around this identity because they enjoy the company of other gays or because they share its specific cultural or lifestyle pattern.[12] In urban centers such as New York or Los Angeles, but also in small to midsized cities like Syracuse or Tucson, it is possible to organize a thick social life around being gay.

These "subcultural gays" participate in a social world that is somewhat bounded, if not territorially, then symbolically. They signal their exclusive group identification by somewhat distinctive self-presentational and communicative styles; for example, through dress, language, or hypermasculine styles for men or butch gender styles for women. For example, Rhonda, who is part of a lesbian queer network, describes a separate identity culture that is organized around thick symbolic practices. Membership in the lesbian world is densely coded through these practices. A lesbian is recognized, Rhonda says, by "the way a person presents themselves, the way they walk, the way they wear their clothes, what style clothes, the hairstyle, type of glasses, who they hang out with, type of interests, shoes, how they tie their shoes, how many rings they wear."[13]

Many gays today have options beyond denying their homosexuality or integrating into a gay subculture. Individuals may value being gay without building lives around this identity. Being gay might be approached as an identity thread, like, say, gender, class, race, occupation, or religion.[14]

Interestingly, some individals who reached adulthood between 1960 and the 1980s may continue to speak of being gay as a core identity even as their lives suggest otherwise. They have internalized the powerful narrative of coming out of the closet that became pervasive in post-Stonewall culture. This narrative resonated with their lives when they were coming out and may still express something of their lives. However, this narrative is at odds with lives that are often conducted beyond the closet.

For example, you may recall that Mike came of age in the 1970s and 1980s, at the height of the post-Stonewall culture. Mike's coming out followed an almost classic gay male pattern of denial, suppression, passing, despair, alienation, recovery, self-affirmation, and public pride. Mike triumphantly and proudly declares, "Being gay is who I am. . . . It's the most important thing about me." Yet Mike hardly participates in gay life. His life revolves around his partner, mostly heterosexual friends, parenting, Alcoholics Anonymous, his career, and sports. While Mike speaks of a core gay identity, his life suggests otherwise. In fact, at one point in the interview he offered a characterization of his identity that seemed more consistent with his practice. "Being out. . . doesn't change who I am as a person or as a boss or as a father. Being gay is just another part of me."

I pressed Mike to explain how being gay actually shapes his daily life. Does he deliberately present himself as gay in the course of his daily life? "In the ordinary course of the day I don't try to do anything that signals to people I'm gay. . . . I just don't see any purpose to it. I don't think about it." Mike acknowledges that his life is not "very different from my straight friends." However, his present life is very different from his past closeted life.

To the extent that individuals want to integrate being gay into their lives in a deliberate and respectful way, they will often want to be publicly recognized as gay. If being gay is viewed as a good part of who they are, and one that is not signaled by conventional behavior—and a part of oneself that is embraced in relation to a history of shame and secrecy—it's not surprising that many individuals will be forceful about publicly flagging a gay identity. However, while individuals like Mike may at times confuse their desire to be recognized as gay with a primary gay identity, it is more appropriate to describe their approach to being gay as a "thread."

Marcia both echoes this "decentering" theme and takes it one step further. "I wouldn't say that when I think of myself the first thing I think of is a lesbian. Or, I wouldn't say that I think that when people first meet me that's what they need to know. . . . Being a lesbian [is] just like being a woman, or being a redhead. These are things that are part of me." Unlike Mike, in her personal life Marcia tries to minimize sexual identity as a way to define people. "When I see people I don't immediately think, 'Hum, are they gay, bi, or straight?' It just doesn't bother me, its not really a big concern of mine. If someone thinks I'm straight, then . . . yee-haw, that's fine. . . . And, I don't feel the need to, you know, declare myself every day. It's just like you don't need to have people label themselves straight. I dress the way I want to dress. I don't go out of my way to straighten up my appearance . . . but I don't go out of my way to dress gay either, whatever that means." In a theme that we'll return to in the next chapter, Marcia is speaking of the diminishing importance of sexual identity in her personal life, if not in our social institutions. In this wish to minimize the importance of categories of sexual identity we perhaps see something of the experiential underpinnings of a queer sensibility, which likewise both recognizes the social power of sex identity labels and aims to challenge their force in people's personal and social lives.

PRIVATE CHOICES, PUBLIC CONSTRAINTS

Between Lenny's coming of age and Clara's there was a sea change in gay life in America. I've suggested one way to describe this change: the diminishing social significance of the closet. Simply put, more gay people organize lives beyond the closet.

For Lenny and Bill, their homosexuality posed a life choice: to live in or out of the closet. Both men spent a considerable part of their adult lives in the closet. Their homosexuality was denied, minimized, or carefully managed to avoid unwanted exposure that, they were convinced, would bring social disgrace and perhaps material harm. To avoid this fate, they each made life-shaping decisons such as getting married or joining the military.

It would belittle them to characterize their choice to live public heterosexual lives as simply living a lie or a false life. For Lenny, as much as he was attracted to men, he had deep needs and longings to have a wife, to be part of a heterosexual family, and to be respected in his community. Forfeiting the passion and pleasures of being with men was compensated for by the coherent and rich life he has lived. While Bill had many of the same hopes and wants as Lenny, his straight life was deeply unsatisfying and filled him with shame and despair.

The closet experience was perhaps easier for Lenny. Heterosexuality was taken for granted; he had few choices and never seriously considered fashioning a gay life. By the time his children had grown up and the social environment became more hospitable for gays, his life had taken a shape that felt unalterable. The risks of coming out were simply too great. Coming of age in the late 1970s and early 1980s, Bill knew there were alternatives; gays were part of the public world. Still, being exposed to an almost seamless chorus of homophobic voices, from family to peers and ministers, and living in a small working-class town, made passing a compelling choice. As the 1970s passed into the 1980s and 1990s, Bill chose another life. Today, the closet is part of his past.

Baby boomers like Bill were hardly the first generation to step into the closet. They were, though, the first to experience it in a deeply conflicted way—both because of the forces lined up to enforce compulsory heterosexuality and because a national gay movement declared a war against the closet. Many baby boomers like Bill have known both the closet and a life outside, something that cannot be said of Lenny's generation.

For the generations that came after the boomers, those born after 1960, both the closet and the life outside changed considerably. Cracks appeared in the edifice of heterosexual domination. Many straight elites, those who wield cultural, social, and political power, and many organizations from the ACLU to labor unions, the Democratic Party, and the American Bar Association, are on record as supporting gay rights as a matter of civic justice. The wall separating straight and gay worlds is crumbling, as gays become a visible and vocal part of public life. Although coming out for many Americans is still filled with anguish and dread, many of us have stepped into adulthood, or into midlife, convinced of the moral goodness of being gay, feeling sure of our personal worth, and possessing an unflappable sense of social entitlement. This sensibility drives us into the world, refashioning what it means to be gay and making America a little different as well.

After she realized her attraction to women, Karen knew she had choices. Living in the closet was not one of them. Karen felt an inner pressure to be who she is—with herself and others. It was a feeling as much as a thought that, simply put, being gay is something good and is a solid basis for forging a life of integrity, love, and social value. In stark contrast to Lenny and Bill, Karen enthusiastically embraced her identity as a lesbian. It became the basis for forging a coherent and satisfying sense of self and community. Karen stepped into the public world with a sense of self-assuredness and social entitlement. She came out and stayed out. However, Karen understands that prejudice, discrimination, harassment, violence, disrespect, and devaluation will continue to challenge the life she wants to live. But they will not force her to retreat into the closet.

Like Karen, Gordon's coming to terms with his homosexuality is a world apart from that of Lenny and Bill. In one sense there is continuity: all of them experienced an awareness of their homosexuality as youths and each denied or suppressed these feelings. Degrading comments by kin and peers led Gordon to hide his homosexuality, but only until he was twenty. Gordon knew—though in a way that was never the case for Lenny, and only true for Bill as he approached his mid-thirties—that it was okay to be gay. His coming-out story is not really about denial and the struggle for self-acceptance; his anguish was around coming out to his family and to an unfriendly black commuity. Gordon had absorbed something of the cultural shift that valued being gay as natural, as a good part of himself, and as a secure basis for making a life that included love, a satisfying job, and family. In fact, Gordon proceeded to make such a life, even though it cost him the ambivalence of some kin and estrangement from the black community.

Clara was born in 1980, a full ten years after Gordon. But this relatively small generational separation meant that she came of age in 2000, not 1990. In other words, Clara grew up in an America in which gays were becoming a permanent fixture of public life and aspired not merely to be tolerated but to be fully equal citizens.

Like Lenny, Bill, and Gordon, she was aware of her homosexual feelings as a young person. However, Clara had not only accepted who she was but demanded respect from others. Clara came out to her family at age fourteen and, whatever her real feelings were, she used a public language of self-acceptance that was so self-assured that it propelled her into the world as a lesbian.

In Clara's coming-out story, which is better described as a story of living outside, the kernal of a new gay sensibility is clearly visible: a conviction of the equal moral worth of gays and straights, the right to be gay and out, and the demand to have equal opportunities in love and work and to be treated with respect. Yet Clara is not naive about living outside the closet. She may feel like the equal of straights but she knows that others will not always treat her that way. Clara, like others living outside the closet, must manage the contradiction between inner feelings of equal moral worth and a world in which many individuals and institutions at best offer tolerance.

As gays exit from the closet, we have choices that were unavailable to previous generations. This is especially true in the private sphere.

Many of us can choose to be out; we can date and have lovers or intimate partners with whom we share a life. We also have more choices as we step into the public world. For example, we can increasingly choose occupations and career paths that have less to do with avoiding unwanted exposure than with our individual ambitions. Many gays can be out at work without fear of harassment, isolation, or discrimination. Still, being out in the family is not necessarily the same as being accepted; and having more latitude in work life is not the same as having the same opportunities as straights. We don't, because the culture of work life is still normatively heterosexual and many workplaces lack basic protections for gay employees.

If part of the story of gays today is that many of us feel a grounded sense of moral worth and social entitlement, the other part of the story is our reception in a heterosexual-dominated society. A life beyond the closet is unthinkable without personal and social accomodation on the part of straight America. This story is the theme of the next three chapters.

CHAPTER THREE

Straight Encounters

"Terror of being rejected by almost everybody in the world. I felt like I would lose not only my wife and my kids but my parents and my friends. I couldn't imagine what it would be like to be honest about who I was. I was terrified about it." This is how Mike described his feelings about coming out. He was sure that being open would bring public disgrace and an estrangement from the people that mattered most in his life—his parents, wife, son, friends, and coworkers.

Mike (b. 1950) came out in the early 1990s. His fears were not entirely unfounded. Despite living close by, Mike rarely sees his parents and the relationship has strained to a breaking point. Their refusal to acknowledge his relationship with Andy fills Mike with both rage and shame. In the end, he felt compelled to choose between two family loyalties. He sided with his new family, but remains deeply saddened by this turn of events.

To his great surprise, though, his ex-wife, son, coworkers, and friends accommodated, and did so remarkably quickly. In many ways these social ties were deepened and made more solid, as he's been able to share more of his personal life.

Mike would not have been able to fashion a fulfilling life beyond the closet if all or most of these people had disapproved and severed their ties with him. Coming out would have been too costly.

If gay Americans are coming out and staying out, it's in part because family, friends, and coworkers are accommodating. As we'll see, however, accommodation does not always mean acceptance.

The family holds a central place in the drama of coming out. It is among kin that many of us feel our deepest emotional connection; we look to kin for love, validation, and often economic support. In contrast to romantic bonds or friendships, family ties are supposed to last the better part of a lifetime. The family is the one area of life where we want and expect to belong and to be cared about simply because we are family.

For much of the post-Stonewall period, it was not unusual for individuals to exit the closet and, at the same time, their families. For many of us, coming out to kin has been unthinkable. The risk of severing the emotional bonds to parents and siblings has just been too great. Some of us migrated to mid or large cities, to Albany for many upstate New Yorkers or to Los Angeles for southern Californians or to San Francisco or New York for many people across the country. We fashioned gay lives and also sustained our connection to our families, but often kept these two sides of our lives separate. We assembled new types of families composed of lovers, friends, and often ex-lovers. However, our family ties suffered. Irregular visits, carefully managed communication, and withholding from kin some of the most important personal events in our lives created a distance, even estrangement, from family members. Kin ties often became cordial and somewhat formal, lacking the openness, trust, and emotional closeness that we look for in families. For many gays, "families of choice" gradually replaced families of origin as the primary kin unit.[1]

Today, many of us are not willing to surrender strong family ties as the price for living a satisfying and open gay life. We wish to exit the closet and remain integral members of our families. Many of us are coming out and not migrating to urban centers. We're staying in the places where we've established our lives, and this sometimes means in the towns and cities of our kin.

Many gays want and increasingly expect to be recognized as members of families—our own and the families we grew up in. The stereotype of gays as anti-family is being challenged. We wish to be seen and treated as members of families. And we want our lives to be respected and shared with those we care about, including and especially our kin.

The struggle to reclaim a place in our families is a battle less for rights than for respect and emotional caring. It is less a struggle led by a movement than a deeply personal battle waged by each of us in our own families.

Gays want to be recognized as belonging to families. We want to be loved by our families like our straight brothers and sisters are. We seek, and feel entitled to, not just tolerance but a full sense of belonging; we want to share in the family rituals and ties that bond. This has created a new challenge: our families now have to struggle with accommodating to their gay sons and daughters, fathers and mothers, or cousins and grandparents.[2]

For straight America, homosexuality is no longer just an abstract issue of morality or rights but a matter of dealing with real people, indeed the people who matter most. Straight kin are compelled to confront their own beliefs, fears, and hopes. Parents have to struggle with their expectations and wishes that their children marry, have families, and be respected as good citizens. Children of gay parents have to deal with their expectations about their parents. They didn't bargain for mothers and fathers who want to be recognized and accepted as gay.

The family has become a chief battleground in the conflict over the meaning and place of gays in America. It is a deeply personal and emotional issue as real families must wrestle with gay kin who are refusing to migrate or be exiled from their families. It is also an intensely social issue. A cultural battle is being waged over the meaning of family. For a very long time, American culture has assumed that gays are not supposed to be in or have families, and that families are not supposed to include gay kin. As gays demand recognition of their own families, the war over the family becomes an institutional struggle—a battle over laws, social policies, and institutional practices.[3] This deeply intimate personal sphere has become a highly charged political battleground.

DIVIDED LOYALTIES: FAITH OR FAMILY

We met Marcia in the last chapter. She was twenty at the time of the interview and was working as a residential counselor for the developmentally disabled.

Marcia's coming out was relatively abbreviated; she embraced her lesbian identity quickly and confidently. Marcia had never been aware of any attraction to women until she was seventeen. Since early adolescence she had had boyfriends. In her senior year in high school, she was taken aback by a desire she felt for a girlfriend. This triggered a new self-awareness. "It just hit me. Oh my God I think I'm gay. . . . What do I do . . . 'cause I had no idea." Marcia was still unsure. She decided to go to a gay club. To her surprise, she felt comfortable and met a woman she began dating. "I realized I was gay. . . . This is good. . . . I felt like I had the whole realization type thing. I had the sun come up and birds were singing. I was gay and it was nice. It was good." Marcia's self-assured sense that being gay is good gave her a feeling of entitlement that made the closet an unlikely accommodation. Still, she was careful about coming out in school because of her peer's homophobia. But she wanted to come out to the people that mattered most to her, family and friends.

She worried about her family's reaction. She was very close with her mother and feared her response. Marcia was raised a born-again Christian. "I had been raised my whole life [to believe] that homosexuals were wrong. They were perverted; they were going to Hell. They're sick perverts who want to touch children and have sex with animals. . . . They . . . deserved to be killed. I actually believed this when I was little. . . . They are a whole other race. They do not belong with us."

Marcia's fears proved real. "My mother had a nervous breakdown after she found out. She drove home and went into the house and locked herself in the bedroom and didn't eat or shower or anything for three days. It really just shocked me." At first, her mother denied that Marcia was gay. Gradually, she faced the reality; unfortunately, condemnation was her response. "She's like, 'I'm disgusted with you. You are nothing, you are a pervert. This is disgusting.'" Marcia didn't panic or internalize her mother's shaming behavior. "I was just like, 'Okay,

Mom, if that's what you need to tell me because you think that makes it better, it doesn't. And I do understand that you think you're doing your best for me, but you're not, so you need to stop it.' But it didn't stop and it hasn't stopped." Their relationship became strained and shallow.

As Marcia was integrating her sexuality into her life in a positive way, she tried to do the same with her family. For example, she brought a girlfriend to a family Thanksgiving dinner. She was initially surprised at her mother's friendly, even warm, response. Later in the evening, she thanked her mother for being so generous. It turned out, though, that her mother hadn't realized that Marcia's friend was actually her girlfriend. "She's like, 'I didn't know that. Oh my God, she was in our house. Yuck. Did you touch her leg while we were eating.'"

From her mother's Evangelical Christian worldview, a lesbian was a sinful, immoral person that she could not respect. "You're an abomination to God, and we've gotta pray for you." Although her mother has remained disapproving, she has adjusted somewhat by separating Marcia's lesbianism from the rest of her life. Marcia recalls a conversation that marked something of an accommodation for her mother. "Marcia, this is really hard for me to say but you know my feelings towards homosexuality. But you're my daughter and if you're hurting, you can talk to me." Today, something of the closeness between Marcia and her mother has been recovered, but "we still don't talk about it."

Marcia expected a similar reaction from her grandparents, who were also religious and with whom she lived at times while growing up. She fretted about her grandfather's reaction because they were very close. He was a truck driver and sort of rough-edged. She had low expectations. "One day he was like, 'listen, I love you and I'm not gonna treat you any differently.'" Marcia was hopeful. "He was really cool and accepting when I first came out." However, his behavior did not live up to the promise of acceptance. "He doesn't like to hear about it." With cousins and other kin, Marcia's lesbian identity has been treated as a variation of the "Don't ask, don't tell" strategy.

Marcia did not experience a protracted struggle around coming out. She rather quickly accepted her new sexual identity, or at least she embraced a public rhetoric of the goodness and integrity of being a lesbian. Not surprisingly, Marcia wished to be both open about her sexual identity and remain an integral part of the family. Unfortunately, her family accepts her only if she keeps the lesbian aspects of her life outside the family. She has remained in the family but not quite a part of it. "With family it's changed a lot because I like to think of family, you know, you get the warm fire, and it's warmth. That's what I like to think of as a family, it's warmth. And I don't feel like I'm part of the family. I don't feel very warm. My own mother won't give me a hug."

It's not only parents or grandparents who struggle with gay kin. As more of us exit from the closet, our children sometimes struggle with fathers or mothers, aunts and uncles, or grandparents who are openly gay. Although these kin are adults and are likely to be emotionally and economically independent, their ties to family are as powerful as those of their children. Indeed, for many adults, their lives and identities are heavily invested in parenting roles; not only will they be dependent on their children for approval and love, but perhaps for economic support as they grow older.

Frank was sixty-four at the time of my interview with him. His own parents had died many years earlier but he had formed his own family. Frank was married for some thirty-five years and fathered three kids. He had been separated from his wife for about seven years.

I met Frank in a small apartment, which he shared with a housemate. His friendly manner was endearing. The interview proved hard, though. It was clear that it was also difficult for him. Feelings were stirred up, exposing considerable pain, and Frank was often unable to stay with his thoughts.

Still, Frank seemed comfortable with himself and his life. Today he identifies as gay and proudly tells me that he is integrated into a supportive circle of gay friends. Frank is a regular at a local gay bar and participates in various gay groups. He says that he has found a comfortable place in the world, and his sense of self-satisfaction was palpable. "I like the gay life, I mean I love it."

Until he was in his mid-fifties, Frank had lived a straight life. I wondered if he had married in order to conceal and manage his homosexuality. "No, no, no. If I knew then I would not have been married.

She's a great woman and still is." Frank insists that when he married he wasn't aware of being gay. "Well, I don't know how to say this but I didn't think I was gay. I didn't know that I was. I liked women, though I had feelings for men." He fathered three children, and his life felt good. "I was happy with my kids and I was happy with family and with work."

Frank was raised a Roman Catholic. He went to Catholic schools and attended church regularly as an adult. He no longer thinks of himself as religious, though I detected an ongoing struggle regarding his relation to the church. Two of his sisters are practicing Catholics, as are his wife and kids. They attend church weekly, pray regularly, and follow church teachings on many moral questions, especially issues of personal morality.

Sometime around 1990, Frank's homosexual feelings started to surface with an intensity that he couldn't easily deny. Frank thinks he could have managed these feelings to sustain a public heterosexual identity and life. However, his marriage had become passionless, and his homosexual feelings created a sense of fresh possibilities for a satisfying intimate life that he now longed for. Also, times had changed. Gays were public and assertive about their normality and rights. A citywide struggle over gay rights in Albany resulted in an unprecedented level of gay visibility and public support that likely emboldened Frank. This new gay assertiveness made it easier for Frank to reconsider what would be a major life shift. Remarkably, for a man with his history, Frank rather quickly accepted his homosexuality and enthusiastically championed a gay identity. He started going to the bars, meeting men, and before too long realized that this was the life he wanted.

Frank decided to tell his wife. This was, after all, the person with whom he had shared most of his adult life and he still loved and admired her. Unfortunately, she didn't take it well. She threw him out of the house and to this day "she won't let me in the house." Soon his entire family knew and they too didn't react well. His older daughter "won't have anything to do with me." Frank has not seen his grandchildren since she learned of his being gay. "She just doesn't like that I'm a homosexual." His younger daughter will see him but on the condition that he doesn't talk about his gay life. With his son, "I don't talk to him at all about that. He can't believe that I'm gay." Although Frank lives in the same town as his children, he has little contact with them and is unable to share much of what is meaningful and good in his life. They cannot reconcile his being gay with their faith.

Frank has three younger sisters. He was enormously relieved that his older sister accepted him. However, his other two sisters have severed relations with him. "They won't let me in their house. . . . They won't let me go near them." Frank knows why. "They just don't like gay people. They're very prejudiced. They say it's sinful."

Frank seemed bewildered by his family's rejection. How can they be so disapproving and rejecting? He was, after all, a good husband and father for thirty-five years; he grew up with his sisters, played with them, often took care of them, and provided emotional support for them as an adult. Yet, except for one sister, none of them wants anything to do with him. Contact is possible only on the condition that his gay life is not talked about at all. Amazingly, Frank doesn't seem bitter, just hurt. Frank no longer attends church, as he blames Roman Catholicism for the loss of his family. He's thankful for a gay life that makes him feel whole and happy.

Religious people have no monopoly on intolerance. The church itself is a key battlefield in the struggle over gays. Many of the steadiest advocates of gay justice are ministers or rabbis or ordinary churchgoing folk. Division and conflict over the moral and social status of gays is pervasive in American churches.[4]

Still, I don't think it's merely coincidental that, among the people I interviewed, intolerance had staying power primarily among kin for whom religious convictions were fundamental to their identity and moral outlook. For family members who were not deeply religious, discovering a gay kin was often hard and frequently involved a period of tension, and sometimes (as in the case of Mike's parents) the breach was irreparable. In most instances, though, there was some kind of reconciliation. Gay kin were reintegrated, even if not fully accepted. Religious-based intolerance is, I believe, often at the heart of individual intolerance today.

Twenty years ago hostility and intolerance toward gays was deeply felt and widespread among Americans regardless of their religious conviction.[5] The culture that polluted homosexuality was almost seamless. Today, a fundamentalist religious commitment is perhaps the best indicator of the likelihood and force of individual intolerance. To be sure, homosexual hatred can be fierce and aggressive among secular men and women, as we'll see in the case of Malcolm. However, if Malcolm ultimately abandoned homophobia as resolutely as he once embraced it, this was in part because this belief was not rooted in a deeply held religious conviction. My sense is that, in the absence of core religious convictions and community support, homosexual intolerance is harder to sustain today. If individuals such as Malcolm now come out on the side of tolerance, it's in part because there has occurred a weakening of a secular culture of homosexual pollution, a point I make in chapter 4.

HATING AND LOVING A GAY SON: COMING OUT AS HOMOPHOBIC

Malcolm is a straight white man in his mid-forties. He lives in a small town in Wyoming; its population has never reached one thousand. Malcolm was born in this town and vows to never move. Although he's not far from cities like Laramie and Denver, he rarely visits them. He is, in his own words, a small-town guy. This is where he feels at home.

Malcolm is a high school teacher. His wife of some twenty-five years holds a managerial position in the state bureaucracy.

Malcolm was born a Mormon but he doesn't consider himself religious. Many of his kin are practicing Mormons. His son, Alan, spent many years in religious study and at one point imagined a life organized around the church. Malcolm's life revolves around his work, marriage, two children, home, and golf—the concerns of many Americans.

Malcolm is a man's man—athletic, rough-edged, decisive, and someone who likes to take control. I found him to be likeable and engaging, but as his eyes dart about I sensed a restless energy, an aggressivness just below the calm surface. As his story unfolded, I was shocked by his candor—and rage. Ultimately, I was moved by his inner struggle to come to terms with what for him was unimaginable: his son being gay.

Growing up in the 1970s, Malcolm knew that there were homosexuals. Even though he lived in a small town, he was exposed to negative stereotypes of homosexuals in newspapers, television, and in his family and peer culture.

Until a few years ago, his views of homosexuals were very definite. "I figured that people who were queer or homosexual or whatever, was something that they chose. . . . I figured that somewhere in their life, they'd been hurt by a person of the opposite sex and therefore it had turned them completely off." He recalled a young woman who was raped as a young girl and later became a lesbian. His explantion was simple: "She had this built-in hatred for men because she had been raped . . . so she had chosen to be gay." Malcolm had adopted what many of us would consider a homophobic outlook: gays are psychologically damaged individuals who choose being gay to protect themselves from hurt. Homosexuality was not a positive feeling and identity but a defensive, rageful, and abnormal accommodation to psychological pain.

Malcolm was actively homophobic. He recalled an incident as a teenager.

> I couldn't have been more than thirteen. I came in contact with a gentleman who was a homosexual. He invited me and a couple of friends to his house to drink beer. He was in his mid-twenties. I can still remember the three of us drinking beer. We called the guy "Romo the homo." He started getting a little friendly in a different sort of way than what we were used to seeing. We all got to wrestling about in his apartment and . . . he grabbed a friend from behind and started humping him. We realized that this guy was a fucking queer, a faggot. The three of us jumped on him and proceeded to kick the shit out of him.

Malcolm's rage toward homosexuals was relentless.

> For a lot of years after that I made every attempt I could to whip his ass." As I grew older, this experience instilled in me the fact

> that queers . . . were something different, not the same. I didn't think they were the same flesh and blood that I was. I looked down on them. . . . I basically kind of went out of my way to be rude, to occassionally try to pick a fight with them. I was a bully toward most queer men. I think that lasted for a lot of years. . . through the point when I found my own son was gay.

Malcolm has two sons. Alan was the older; Glenn was the favorite. Glenn was husky, solidly built, outgoing, and sports-minded; he played football, and there was, says Malcolm, an easy and special bond between them. Alan was slight but not effeminate. He was quiet and academically oriented. Malcolm attributed Alan's lack of a girlfriend or any serious dating to his strong academic interests. "I never suspected, because that was just not acceptable. I could never accept the fact that my son was gay and I wouldn't even contemplate the fact that he might be gay."

Malcolm discovered Alan's homosexuality by accident. He found a letter in which Alan spoke of being gay. Alan was about sixteen. Malcom was thirty-seven. He responded with "anger and disbelief. How could this be my son? We never had anyone in our family who was gay." Malcolm initially thought that Alan was simply confused or acting out of anger toward him. "I felt like he was probably striking out at me due to the fact that he and I had not had a good relationship. It was his way of getting back at me. It was his way of hurting me like he felt I had hurt him." Malcolm thought of homosexuality as so far beyond the pale of anything acceptable that he could not imagine his son being gay.

Malcolm felt rage toward Alan. "It was very difficult for me to be very civil to him. I wanted to strike out at him. . . . I wanted him to hurt as bad as I hurt. I wanted everybody in the family to hate him because I hated him." Malcolm immersed himself in work to deal with his rage. "Work gave me an opportunity to be out of the house, so I didn't have to be around this kid who was gay. I think at this point that he and I probably hated each others' guts. I know that I did. I was very angry. It was all that I could do when I was around him to contain myself and not just beat the hell out of him. I thought that if I beat the hell of out him, he'd realize that I wasn't going to tolerate him being gay, that he'd better straighten up, because he was going to date girls, get married, and have a family." Malcolm recalls that during this time, Alan "stayed in his room most of the time." Malcolm felt "relief" when Alan moved out of the house to go to college.

His rage did not end after Alan left. "I accidently found his diary. . . and he had put in it that he wished I was dead." Malcolm could no longer contain himself. "Something inside of me snapped at this point. I think the years of anger came to the surface and I thought to myself, 'I don't need this son of a bitch anymore. As far as I'm concerned he's not my son. I don't want anything to do with him. I don't want him in my home. I don't want him around me.'" Malcolm decided to write to Alan telling him in no uncertain terms, "you're no longer my son. I want nothing more to do with you and stay out of my life."

As the relationsip was spiraling downward, Alan surprised Malcolm. He reached out to him wanting some kind of reconciliation. During this time, Malcolm was becoming isolated in his own family. Glenn had accepted Alan and was angry that Malcolm was treating Alan badly. And Glenn was beginning to stake out his own identity and life, which left Malcolm feeling disconnected from both of his sons. Adding to Malcolm's growing sense of estrangement within his family, his wife had sustained a close bond with Alan. Malcolm's homophobic behavior was threatening to tear his family apart.

He resolved to make things better. "I made a hard conviction that I was going to learn to accept and love this son, regardless of who he was or what he was." It's hard to know what triggered Malcolm's resolve—the threat of a family torn apart by his rage, the edge of violence in his anger, or perhaps his guilt and shame for shabbily treating a son that he had raised and loved. As remarkable as his turnaround may seem, it didn't entirely surprise me. I had heard similar stories repeatedly, though not as shockingly frank. Parents do not easily surrender their bond to their children; and they do not lightly threaten to tear apart the emotional denseness of family ties. For a parent to risk losing a son or daughter and to endanger family ties, their belief in the evil of homosexuality has to express a core part of who they are. The obligation of religious purity may be the kind of core conviction that will risk such behavior, but even in this case individuals often find ways to accommodate faith and love.

What I didn't expect was Malcolm's evolution from hatred to acceptance and even advocacy.

Malcolm says that today he has a good relationship with Alan. "I still find myself at times struggling with the fact that he is a homosexual, but I have learned to accept the fact that he is." How did Malcolm manage this change? No doubt, he was moved by his wife's and his younger son's embracing Alan and insisting that he be treated as a respected member of the family. Also Malcolm's own struggle with alchohol and his involvement with AA seemed important. AA culture not only values forgiveness and acceptance but encourages the kind of self-inspection that allowed Malcolm to reconsider his beliefs and actions. Furthermore, the times were changing. The closet door had opened, even in the small-towns of Wyoming. In this regard, Malcolm learned of a gay colleague who was close to Alan. He decided to confide in him. "I made a point of talking to this teacher because I knew that he was gay." They talked frequently, and gradually Malcolm began to redefine his intolerance as expressing his own insecurity. "It finally came to dawn on me that my son was not a threat to me. I didn't realize at the time that what I feared from this kid was the fact that he liked men. I was almost afraid that maybe he'd like me in a sexual way." Malcolm's personal connection to this teacher further shook up his views about homosexuality. "It dawned on me one day when I was in conversation with this teacher that, wait a minute, I sit and talk to this teacher. I know what his sexual preference is, but I don't feel threatened by him. I considered this person to be a very good friend." Malcolm resolved to accept Alan for who he is. "I kind of started putting things in a true perspective for me. My son is my son. He will always be my son. Just accept it! All of a sudden, it doesn't matter why he's gay, just accept it and move on. I think from that point I was able to accept him as being gay."

Accepting Alan was more than just a matter of altering his beliefs and feelings; it meant changing his behavior. Malcolm wanted a level of trust that would allow Alan to be open with him. Malcolm believes that he's succeeded. "I don't think he hides anything from me. . . . I think my son and I are very close now. He's very open to me. We don't seem to have any barriers any longer." Alan hasn't yet established an ongoing romantic relationship, and Malcolm isn't sure how he'd feel about that. However, he is clear about what he believes is right and how he would act. "I would be happy for him if he found someone he was compatible with or if he could spend the rest of his life with someone. In fact I would have as much happiness for him as for my younger son."

Whatever his private feelings, Malcolm's public rhetoric is a major reversal of his earlier homophobia. "I've come to accept homosexuality as something you don't choose, no more than I choose to be heterosexual. You're born with it. It's too bad society can't look at it from the point of view that these are not evil people. These are normal people with normal thoughts, normal attitudes." As Malcolm came to define gays as ordinary or "normal," his tolerance passed into advocacy. "I'm in favor of gay marriage. I'm in favor of gays being able to adopt. . . . I think that society has to accept that. We don't think anything nowadays of a single parent adopting a child. Why would we think anything of a gay couple adopting a child? I think about my son . . . he's got a great way with kids. They love him. And I think he'd be a great father. Why should society step in and say, 'Okay, because you like the same sex you can't have kids?' That's bullshit. So, no, I think society needs to accept this, and the sooner the better."

Malcolm thinks of himself as sort of coming out of a closet, but his closet was a parochial world of prejudice, ignorance, and fear. He continues to struggle with coming out as a father of a gay son. "I'm not entirely out of the closet. There are some people who I may not ever admit to them that my son is gay. I don't think it's fear on my part. I just don't want to get into the big argument with these people, primarily people who are family. . . . I don't feel like it's their business." Also, some of his kin are practicing Mormons who condemn homosexuality. He struggles, as many gays do today, with figuring out when he's withholding information about his son's sexual identity for reasons of shame or for other reasons that may be warranted. "I believe that when the time is right and they find out, they'll accept it to some degree. And eventually they will accept it."

STRAIGHT-IDENTITY CHOICES

For most of the twentieth century, many straight Americans, if they thought about it at all, considered homosexuality something far removed from daily life—and usually it was. Today, homosexuality has become a real, personal issue. As gays exit the closet, straight Americans have to deal with gay kin, friends, coworkers, clients, celebrities, artists, politicians, and service providers. Gays are truly everywhere, and increasingly visible and vocal. Virtually all Americans are more or less compelled to deal with real gay people.[6] Initially, the challenge for many straights is to figure out the appropriate place for gays in their families, workplace, and schools. But gay visibility and integration poses another and different sort of issue: What does it mean to be straight if gay is good?

It wasn't too long ago that most American simply assumed that their fellow citizens were heterosexual. In the 1950s and 1960s, very few American had anywhere real contact with openly gay or lesbian individuals. And no matter where one looked—television, the movies, the theater, or politics, heterosexuality was the reality and the norm. When that reality was challenged by the Stonewall rebellion, the closet was the response. If their existence could no longer be denied, homosexuals could at least be excluded from the respectable public world.

But what happens when the supports of the closet begin to erode, and gays crowd into public life? Well, at least some heterosexuals become more thoughtful not only about gays but about their own sexual identity. If being straight isn't simply a matter of not being homosexual, then what does it mean to be straight today?[7]

I decided to interview individuals who identified as straight. Moreover, I was mostly interested in individuals who were accepting or at least tolerant of gays. I reasoned that the generation born roughly between 1970 and 1980 is the first to come of age in an environment that routinely exposed them to gays through either their daily interactions or popular culture.

"We're All Just People"

David is a nineteen-year-old college student. He describes his family as upper middle class and liberal. David does not recall any openly gay students, teachers, or administrators in his high school. He attended high school in the mid- to late 1990s. He remembers that no one wanted to even be suspected of being gay. Dating was a way to flag a heterosexual identity. "In my high school people were very closed to gays. If they were seeing somebody they made sure everybody knew. [It was] almost [as if to say], 'Well, look who I'm dating,' as if to say, they weren't gay."

David is straight. During high school, though, he never dated. And, although he was part of an all-male friendship circle, homosexual suspicion was minimal if not absent in his circle because "we all talked about women." Also, David believes that few of his peers would have suspected him because he is gender conventional and did not associate with openly gay individuals. Nevertheless, the absence of regular dating throughout high school may have created suspicion on the part of some students. "A few people might [have suspected]. I really don't know, because I never walked around school with my arm around a girl. If they considered somebody that didn't do that gay, then they might have saw me as gay."

At his college campus, gays are visible. This doesn't upset David; he has always been accepting of gay people. His family taught him to respect individual differences. David believes that gays are ordinary, normal people. He supports gay rights and their full equality, including gay marriage. Moreover, for the first time in his life he socializes with gay people. His girlfriend's coworker is a lesbian, and sometimes they hang out together. Asked how he'd react if his best friend came out, David says that "it wouldn't change anything in our relationship."

David does not think of his heterosexuality as a particularly important part of his identity. He doesn't and wouldn't deliberately act in ways to avoid homosexual suspicion. Nor does he purposefully say or do things to flag that he is straight. He acknowledges that his heterosexuality is likely assumed because he has a girlfriend. Still, David insists that he doesn't think of people in terms of their sexual identity.

"I look at people as people." Sexual preference is low on his list of identity markers. "Heterosexuality is an identity in society. However, I identify myself as an owner of a business. This is the way I identify myself in society. I carry myself as a businessperson—not necessarily as a man, as a heterosexual, as a Jewish man, or whatever. I think of everything in a business sense, and that's the way most people look at me now."

Like David, Joe (b. 1980) accepts gay people. He recalls a time when his parents invited a gay couple to dinner. Asked how he felt, Joe said, "I really had no feelings. I wasn't nervous to be in the room. I just sat down, shook their hands, and socialized. It was a like a normal day with people. I talked with them like normal people."

Joe doesn't think much about his or others' sexual identity. He does not deliberately try to signal his heterosexual identity. "I just go strictly on my personality. The way I act is just me. I don't do certain things to say 'hey look I'm straight.' I don't try and correct people if they think a different way [about me]. *I'm not openly heterosexual.*" In this regard, Joe remembered a time when some friends and acquantainces were hanging out in the campus dining room. One of the students casually mentioned his attraction to men. Joe didn't get anxious or uncomfortable. "It wasn't like, I'm not gay, what do you think I am. It was you know just normal, like a normal conversation."

Not all the people I interviewed were college students. My research assistant interviewed Sam, a thirty-four-year-old divorced martial arts instructor.

I expected that Sam might be more inclined to embrace his heterosexuality as a public identity. I was mistaken. An individuals sexual identity carries little significance for him. "I guess when I'm looking at somebody or talking with somebody I'm not looking to categorize them as heterosexual or homosexual. You know, that's not really one of the considerations." Sam is also indifferent to how others view his sexual identity. "I don't really think about it when I'm talking to somebody else, whether they categorize me one way or another. It was never a part of me to worry about what people thought about my sexual orientation." Sam does not intentionally signal his sexual identity. "You know, it was never one of those things where I gotta make sure everybody knows that I like women. It just never occurred to me to worry about it." For example, Sam mentioned that he's been "in places where the majority of people were gay and I wasn't always thinking, God, I got to let them know [I'm heterosexual]. If it came up in conversation, fine; if it didn't, it didn't."

David, Joe, and Sam wish to avoid labeling people by their sexual identity. In fact, they believe that, at least in their social worlds, it is no longer possible to be sure about people's sexual identity. "I don't think you can just look at someone and say 'oh he's straight,' because it may be someone who might look straight and could be gay," said Joe. I was especially surprised to hear that Joe doesn't necessarily interpret gender difference as signaling homosexuality. "A feminine-gendered man or a masculine woman does not necessarily indicate anything about sexual identity." Similarly, Joe would not assume that a person is gay simply because he or she is seen with openly gay people. "I don't think that would be seen as, oh he's talking to gays, he's gay." Dana, a nineteen-year-old college freshman, also straight, agrees. She doesn't assume that someone is gay just because they are with gay people or even at a gay club. Like many of her friends, Dana goes to gay or sexually mixed clubs. "I've walked through an entire crowd of 200 people dancing, holding my girlfriend's hand. So maybe that indicates to somebody that I'm there with her, that that's my girlfriend, but I've seen other girls walking through like that [holding hands] and I wouldn't assume anything."

David, Joe, Sam, and Dana believe that most Americans classify people by their sexual identity. They are aware, moreover, that their own behavior sometimes unavoidably flags a heterosexual identity. If they are dating or otherwise show interest in persons of the opposite gender, they will likely be assumed straight. And sometimes they want people to know that they are straight, but not for homophobic reasons. For example, Dana will let people know she's straight in order to avoid a misunderstanding or to establish a personal social connection. Also, it's important that Dana's close friends and family know she's heterosexual because "that's who I am or who I've been for a period of time.

I like them to know me for who I am." However, "if I walk down the street and someone mistakes me for being a homosexual, its not going to bother me. It's not going to be like, oh no, I'm heterosexual. I don't have to make that known to them."

These individuals live in a world in which sex identity matters; they imagine a world in which it would continue to have personal significance but would lack social weight. Individuals might still want to know if you're attracted to a man or a woman or both for dating or other personal reasons, but sexual orientation would not be a basis for deciding who has rights or who deserves respect.

"Straight but Not Narrow"

Dan and Joe want to be recognized and respected for who they are, and that includes being straight. Although they do not believe that being straight makes them better than gays, they know that it is still socially preferable. Heterosexuality brings material and cultural advantages; homosexuality carries definite risks. If they are relaxed about flagging their straight identity, it is in part because their heterosexuality is likely assumed by others because they are gender conventional, romantically oriented toward the opposite sex, and because they are part of straight social circles. They can enjoy their socially privileged sexual status without having to deliberately declare it because in their ordinary behavior they flaunt it, even if unintentionally and unconsciously.

But what if, despite an inner heterosexual core, your gender self-presentation is sexually ambiguous? How would you publicly claim a heterosexual status without resorting to homophobic behavior? This was an issue for Natasha. She dealt with it, as we'll see shortly, by being purposeful and emphatic about projecting a straight identity.

Natasha's anxiety about how other's read the sexual meaning of her butch persona was heightened because she was black. Natasha already has to deal with social perceptions and inner feelings of status deflation based on being black, especially because she attends a predominantly white university.

David, Joe, and Dana are white and solidly middle class; these socially privileged statuses compensate for any anticipated status deflation if they were to be seen as gay. Sexual identity is less socially weighty for them because of their privileged racial and class status.

By contrast, people of color in the United States are often less valued than whites. Blacks, Asians, and Latinos understand that fighting racism means waging a battle against cultural devaluation that may create feelings of shame and inferiority. A suspect sexual identity would further deflate their social status not only in a white, heterosexual-dominated culture, but also in their racial communities, which already struggle with issues of respect and pride. For Natasha, and perhaps for many people of color in the United States, the issue of sexual identity carries a social and moral weight lacking for many whites. Deliberately and emphatically asserting a positive public heterosexual identity is one response to status anxiety. Instead of minimizing the role of sexual identity and blurring the boundaries between the straight and gay worlds, some individuals, like Natasha, wish to harden the sexual boundaries and to be seen as clearly straight.

Natasha (b. 1978) grew up and still lives in New York City. She often finds herself in the company of gays. While Natasha acknowledges some residual ambivalence that stems from her religious upbringing, she insists that gay people are no different from straights. Indicative of her acceptance of gays, Natasha told me that in high school a woman classmate pursued her romantically. Natasha was surprised, and admitted to feeling initially uncomfortable. She dealt with it in a respectful way, telling her classmate that she didn't feel the same attraction. But the incident raised concerns for Natasha. Why was this woman attracted to her and why did she think she was a lesbian? Natasha thought that perhaps being a large woman who plays sports and looks "butch" might account for this girl's perception. "I was into a lot of different masculine things, like male sports, and I wasn't really into relationships that much. My grandmother even used to question me. She would ask my mother, 'Do you think Natasha's going to be gay?'"

Natasha was uncomfortable with being viewed as gay. However, she would not act in homophobic ways in order to avoid suspicion. "If someone asked if I was a lesbian, I would say no, but I would be critical of friends who said anti-gay things." Natasha chooses to avoid suspicion by distancing herself from any association with lesbianism. "I didn't want anyone to think I was a lesbian. I hung out in the Village and I had a lot of females try to talk to me. I didn't want to be associated with that, so I tried to stay my distance. I didn't want anybody to think that I was that way."

Natasha tries to establish clear boundaries between being straight and being gay. All of her friends are straight because, as she says, "I don't think I want to be associated with it [lesbianism] or think that I'm like that." But because Natasha sometimes finds herself in mixed social environments, her strategy for avoiding suspicion involves deliberately signaling a heterosexual identity. "I talk about men and I let it be known that I'm into men." She says it's intentional. "Yeah, I think I do a conscious thing. I remember being with a girl and I wasn't too sure of what she was but I talked about guys as a way to prove I was into men." Indeed, Natasha says that when she goes to clubs where the company is mixed, or hangs out in the Village, "I would walk around and I would say I'm strictly dickly and I would wear T-shirts that say I'm strictly dickly."

Natasha came of age in a social milieu (New York City in the 1990s) that allowed her considerable freedom to fashion a gender and sexual identity that expressed her inner feelings. Yet her nonconventional gender presentation evoked homosexual suspicion on the part of some friends and kin. In a society that still grants privileges to heterosexuality, Natasha wished to be viewed as straight. However, because Natasha rejected homophobic ways of signaling heterosexuality, she sought to establish clear identity boundaries between heterosexuality and homosexuality. She embraced an assertive, deliberate public heterosexual identity.

Natasha's story illustrates how some individuals respond to the changed status of gay people by making heterosexuality a core identity. Indeed, because she rejected homophobic means of establishing her heterosexual identity, Natasha sought clear, deliberate ways of flagging her sexual identity. Natasha's behavior is perhaps indicative of something new: *the formation of a self-conscious, deliberate public culture of heterosexual identity.*

"Heterosexual and Proud"

Miguel is an eighteen-year-old college freshman, straight and not bashful about it. He proved to be one of my most interesting interviewees. I heard a voice that was unexpected, at times unsettling.

Miguel was raised in a middle-class household in Brooklyn. He describes himself as heterosexual. Indicative of the development of a self-conscious culture of heterosexuality, Miguel has made his heterosexuality a primary identity. "I think being heterosexual is very important. I think it's one of the big things that makes me what I am. I think if I weren't heterosexual I would be kind of a very different person. It's probably a bigger thing than all the others [gender, religion, being Hispanic]."

Until recently, Miguel described himself as very homophobic. This changed as he found himself working with several gay men in a New York City clothing store. "I was really uncomfortable, since I wasn't familiar with any homosexuals. I was pretty uncomfortable at first and out of ignorance made fun of them. After I got to know the guys I realized there's nothing different about them. I became a really good friend with them and now it doesn't matter to me at all. I don't have any problems with it." Yet, because of his religion, "I feel that homosexuality is wrong. I still see them as normal people. I wouldn't support gay marriage and I really don't think that they should have children. But I don't treat them any different." Gays should be treated respectfully, says Miguel, but not accorded full social equality.

Miguel is part of an all-male friendship group. He describes a network of friends bound by dense intimate ties. For example, "today I went to sit on the bed in my friend's room and he was laying on it. So I pushed his feet off the bed and put his leg on my leg. We touch a lot without doing anything really homosexual." The line separating homosexual physical contact from friendly play is "actually touching genitals." The playful homosocial intimacy of Miguel's friendship circle is made possible by the unambiguous and aggressive assertion of their heterosexuality.

Miguel's social world is thickly coded in sexual-identity terms. And he is deliberate, almost compulsive, in presenting himself as heterosexual. In a world fraught with suspicion and the risk of being ridiculed or excluded by his peer group, his heterosexual credentials must be established in an unambiguous, aggressive, and repetitive way.

Staking out an unimpeachable heterosexual identity involves, in the first instance, establishing clear boundaries between men and women. Women are to be approached as sex objects or romantic partners, not as friends. "I don't have any female friends, because I'm very open with my friends. Girls that are my friends I tell them I want sex." Miguel further explains, "I'm a man, and really all we want is sex. If I were gay that means I would like men also for sex." Homosexual suspicion is avoided, then, if men make their sexual interest in women known. "You don't have to date but talk about it, talk about sex, or look at girls. If you talk a lot about women, you know, you can't be gay." For Miguel, heterosexual guys talk about girls; they don't befriend them. "Guys who hang out with girls will be seen as gay. There's this guy who hangs out a lot with girls. These girls are his friends. He practices dance steps with them. It's like he's one of the girls." Men establish their heterosexual credentials then by sexualizing women—in talk and practice. "I've been in college and I met girls the first day and had sex with them. Like things like that for a guy are good, especially when you can talk about that with other guys."

Sustaining an unambiguous heterosexual identity requires that Miguel distance himself from all stereotypical markers of femininity. "If you're a straight guy also you can't be very sensitive. If someone says an insult at you, you say it right back. Somebody hits you, you hit them right back. Like there's a friend of mine, he has feminine tendencies. He does a lot of things that are very feminine. Like if somebody hits him playing around, he'll say something like, 'Oh, that's it. I'm not your friend anymore.' That's very feminine. That's not something a guy would do." Miguel's identification of heterosexuality with a seamless masculine self extends deep into his self-presentation. Thus, everyday talk is said to be coded with gender- and sexual-identity significance. He purposefully speaks and acts to convey a masculine identity. "I won't say anything nice. It's like, men are very, very hard core. You're not supposed to say nice things and do nice, especially when you're with other guys. You're very rough and tough and things like that."

Miguel acknowledges that he is very self-conscious about his looks. Because men who are overly attentive to grooming and dress may be labeled as gay, this sphere is fraught with risk for him. As a self-defined "pretty boy," Miguel has to find ways to avoid homosexual suspicion. "One of the things about gay men is they can supposedly dress. But I can dress also. A lot of people call me pretty boy. But there's a big difference between being a pretty boy and being gay. A gay guy will come up to me and talk about how good I look. [Straight] guys don't do that." Clearly anxious about his susceptibility to being read as gay, Miguel has chosen a dress style that he thinks is coded as nonfeminine and nongay. "I wear a lot of baggy clothes. I think since girls wear tight clothes, then for men they don't wear that; they wear baggy." There are, moreover, certain types of clothing he won't wear because they are supposedly understood as gay. "If there's a certain suit that just looks a little too fruity, I wouldn't buy it. I wouldn't wear a pink shirt. I would never wear anything feminine. I wouldn't wear colored socks. A lot of the guys that I know that are gay wear funny kinds of socks with figures on them and different colors. I wouldn't wear that 'cause I think it's kind of gay."

Miguel does not avoid gay people, which would be homophobic. Instead, he tries to manage these interactions to avoid suspicion. He seeks to create clear boundaries between a straight and gay world and to situate himself clearly in the former. Maintaining these boundaries became a major problem when he worked, as sometimes he and his gay coworkers would socialize after work. "I think you can be the straightest guy, but if you hang out with a lot of gays, people would think you're gay." Miguel tried to avoid both a homophobic rejection of his coworkers and homosexual suspicion by limiting his association with his gay coworkers. For example, he would "never go with them to a gay bar. If a girl goes to a gay bar, if it's both male and female, then it's not that big a deal. If a guy goes, then people start to think, because girls go to clubs just to hang out, to dance, but guys don't. Guys go out looking for women." However, Miguel would join his gay coworkers if they went to a restaurant, but only under certain conditions. "We've gone to restaurants, but it wasn't just me, it was like a lot of people. Some were gay, some weren't, and there were girls. It wasn't like we went out just me and my three gay friends to a bar." Living outside of New York City at the time of the interview, Miguel feels that he must limit his association with gay people. "In New York people are more mature. . . . Here there's a lot of immaturity and there's a lot of homophobia. I think maybe if I met them [gays] and talked to them I would say hi but I wouldn't be real friends with them. No, not here. Not at school. And I don't think I would hang out with them." His friends would disapprove. "I don't think they'd stop being my friend but they would make fun of me, and I wouldn't want to be made fun of."

As public expressions of homophobia are less tolerated today, some individuals wish to project an unambiguous straight identity as a way to flag their heterosexual status. Both Natasha and Miguel disapprove of homophobic behavior but are still anxious to be recognized as heterosexual. The reason seems obvious: a public heterosexual identity validates their subjective sense of self and confers status and privilege. Natasha and Miguel rely on a deliberate, highly monitored public performance to establish an unimpeachable heterosexual identity. If Natasha and Miguel are not exceptional in this regard, their behavior suggests something new: *heterosexuality has become a primary identity.* Ironically, this involves an intensification of a culture of heterosexual signification and identity management that recalls a (closeted) homosexual pattern. As almost every gesture and behavior assumes sex-identity significance, Miguel's daily life has taken on a self-consciousness or performative deliberateness that resembles that of the closeted homosexual.

QUEER KIN

Growing up, Lenny (b. 1930) never, ever considered coming out a possibility. As you may recall, Lenny's attraction to men was ambiguous both in its intensity and its meaning. It wasn't until the 1960s and 1970s that he began to think of this attraction in identity terms. Moreover, in Lenny's social world of first-generation Italian immigrant kin and peers, he would surely have been ridiculed, ostracized, and likely harassed. Coming out was simply unimaginable; the very thought was foreign to him until well into his adulthood. His life had, by then, a coherence and richness that he would not jeopardize.

It was both similar and different for Bill (b. 1960). Bill was certain that he was a homosexual by early adolescence. But coming out in his working-class family in a small upstate New York town would have risked public disgrace and perhaps the loss of his family. Unlike Lenny though, Bill did what many in the post-Stonewall generation did. He moved away from his hometown and family and fashioned an open gay life.

There are still many Americans for whom the risk of public disgrace and losing the family make Lenny's or Bill's strategies of accommodation compelling. This is beginning to change. For Clara, Karen, Gordon, and Marcia, coming out didn't require relocating a gay life apart from kin. Many gays are today exiting the closet but not exiting their families or hometowns.

As gays step outside and stay inside their families, straight America must react. Parents, grandparents, aunts and uncles, and children confront gay kin who wish to be recognized as family. This is new, at least in its current scope. As a result, the family has become a major battleground for gays in their struggle for personal integrity, social inclusion, and equality.

If my interviews speak to broader social trends, gays' reception in their families is mixed. Tolerance is a prominent pattern. Roughly speaking, a period of strain and estrangement is often followed by some type of reconciliation. There are innumerable variations to this pattern. Reconciliation often amounts to a grudging acknowledgment of a gay family member, whose reintegration into the family is contingent on the condition that his or her gay life remains outside or marginal to family life. The lengths that some families go to sustain some version of the 'Don't ask, don't tell" military policy is mind-boggling. I've heard stories, over and over again, of long-term gay couples who gather with kin to share holidays, exchange gifts, celebrate weddings, and grieve together. But there is no explicit coming out; it's as if there's a tacit agreement that while the fact that a member of the family is gay is generally known to kin it will not be explicitly acknowledged. Still, gay kin are often treated respectfully and as kin. These are tough adjustments, on both sides. And while they don't signal acceptance or equality, neither are they rejection. Some sort of tolerance seems to best describe the dominant pattern of families accommodating gay kin.

Individuals do not sever ties of kinship lightly. They may bend but will adjust, sometimes in seemingly ludicrous ways, to keep the family intact. Moreover, as homosexuality is losing its polluted status and as openly homophobic behavior is less tolerated, families feel social pressure to manage their unease in ways that preserve family unity. Where homophobia runs deep among kin, the resiliency of kin will be seriously challenged. I think that today this is mostly, but not only, true of kin who have fundamentalist convictions. Antigay religious convictions strike me as the most hardened and intransigent. But rejection even in these cases is not inevitable; too much is at stake.

Marcia's mother is a case in point. Her born-again Christian faith condemns homosexuality in severe terms. She could hardly countenance her daughter's homosexuality, let alone accept it. She showered Marcia with damning, hateful comments. Fortunately, Marcia was strong and confident; she knew that being gay was good. She read her mother's hatred as prejudice, religious dogma, fear, and dashed expectations. Eventually, Marcia's mother found a way to accommodate her faith and her kin love: she embraces Marcia without embracing her sexual identity. Marcia will be loved as kin so long as her lesbianism is not in evidence. Still, Marcia expects to bring dates and girlfriends to her home; she expects to be loved by her mother and kin. She doesn't expect that the close bond with her mother will ever be recovered, unless her mother changes. But Marcia can be who she is and retain her family-member status, something that would have been rare just a few decades ago. My guess is that her mother will further accommodate, as social and personal pressures weigh on her.

Alan was both less and more fortunate than Marcia. His father was more aggressively rejecting. He threatened physical violence and family ostracism. Alan suffered greatly. But, in the end, Malcolm accommodated. He accepted Alan, embraced who he is, and reestablished a level of openness, trust, and emotional connection that was previously absent.

The realities of Marcia's mother's grudging and limited tolerance and Malcolm's arrival, no matter how tortured, at acceptance express something of the ambivalent, conflicted position of gays in America. In the post-Stonewall period, gays expected little from straight Americans; bare tolerance, often at the cost of family estrangement, was often the most one could realistically expect. Hostile rejection, including being pushed out of the family, was not exceptional. In a world in which many gays live outside the closet, the expectations have changed. Tolerance is the likely response, but gays can realistically hope for acceptance. The struggle in our families over gay kin tells a larger story of the uneasy place of gays in America.

Uneasy not only because straights are unsure and unsettled about gays, but also because gays are restless too. Many of us feel good about who we are; we feel that we are the psychological and moral equals of our straight brothers and sisters. We feel entitled to the same rights, opportunities, respect, and social support. We will surely not tolerate intolerance and will not settle for tolerance for very long. Acceptance—or in political terms, social equality—not only expresses how we feel about ourselves and what we expect, but also speaks to personal lives in which we in fact have more choice about our intimate relationships, friendships, family, and where we live and what we do for a living.

There are reasons for the current social uneasiness and restlessness surrounding gays in America. The social supports of the closet are under attack. A culture of homosexual pollution, state-driven homosexual repression, and a psychology of victimization rooted in feelings of shame and subjective corruption have weakened considerably. In the next two chapters I turn to the social forces that have made possible a life beyond the closet, making the struggle for equality the focus of gay politics today.

CHAPTER FOUR

From the Polluted Homosexual to the Normal Gay

Many individuals who grew up gay in the early-postwar years suffered an oppressive sense of isolation. At the root of their isolation were feelings of shame and a fear that exposure would bring public disgrace, or worse.

Individuals learned to feel shame and fear as they grew up realizing that homosexuality is considered to be something awful, like a horribly contagious disease or some unimaginable perversion. In their families, schools, and churches, they were taught that there is only one normal, right, and good sexuality: heterosexuality. And, by the 1970s, there was a world of television, movies, and news media that had a very clear message: homosexuals are child molesters, predators, and gender and sexual deviants.

It was inevitable that many individuals would come to feel shame and fear. Isolation is one way to accommodate a spoiled inner sense of self. To be isolated is to live with a keen sense of being both inside and outside of the social world; it is to be a member of a family yet separate; to have friends but to feel walled off from them because they don't really know you. Robert says, "I never gave myself a chance to get to know my coworkers. . . . It's really very few people [that] I open up to. Not my parents or friends. I always feel on the outside looking in."

To be isolated or "contained," as Lenny described the feeling, is at the core of the closet experience. The closet is less about denying than about acknowledging one's homosexuality and "choosing" to conceal and manage it. The closet allows one to be in the world as a respected, good person, despite possessing a stained identity. Shame, fear, terror, and disgust not only are the emotional stuff of the closet, but sustain it.

Struggling against the closet is in the first instance an inner, emotional battle. It is a war waged to recover a feeling that one's core self is worthy of being loved and respected. Closet rebellions are inevitably cultural rebellions as this inner struggle for integrity compels individuals to engage a culture that pollutes homosexuality. To escape the grip of isolation, feelings of shame and disgust that have collected around the inner self must be defended against so they no longer have the power to control behavior. In struggling against the closet, individuals have to resist the weight of a homophobic culture.

For some, shame and fear is so deeply lodged in the psyche, and the culture of homophobia so firmly entrenched among kin, peers, and coworkers, that there is no escape. For Lenny, the weight of a homophobic past, now absorbed as part of his inner life, was just too heavy to throw off. But Frank, a man of Lenny's generation, managed to escape. As he related his story, it seemed almost heroic. Despite being rejected and effectively abandoned by his family, and despite being condemned by his church, Frank fashioned a rich life beyond the closet.

For individuals born well after Lenny and Frank, the past has been less weighty. Perhaps fewer years of exposure to a culture that hates homosexuals meant that it was less deeply internalized. More important, individuals who came of age in the 1970s and after lived in a world far removed from that of Lenny and Frank. A homophobic culture was challenged by a national gay movement. By the 1980s, gay subcultures were established in many towns and cities across the country. These institutionalized gay worlds provided the social support for individuals to step out into the straight world. The stories I heard of individuals coming of age in the 1980s and 1990s were often organized around the theme of closet rebellion. For the generation coming of age in the 1980s and after, a feeling of cultural change was in the air—the degraded moral status of homosexuals and the rightness of homophobia could no longer be taken for granted.

If an institutionalized gay world made it possible for individuals to resist a homophobic culture in the 1970s and 1980s, two developments in the 1990s made it much easier for gays to step outside and live beyond the closet.

First, there was a sea of change in the social texture of gay life. Throughout the 1970s and 1980s, organized gay life was centered in major cities such as New York, San Francisco, Los Angeles, and Chicago. Many lesbians and gay men left their hometowns for urban gay enclaves in hopes of finding a place where they could fit in and fashion a life of integrity and purpose. By the end of the 1990s, an institutionalized gay world of social and political organizations, community centers, and gay-owned or gay-friendly bars, restaurants, bookstores, and businesses of all kinds were part of many small towns and cities across the nation. Gays could now look to organizations in their own communities to find support to forge lives somewhere between the closet and beyond.

Second, the wall separating the straight and gay worlds began to crumble. In the early 1990s, gays became a visible, seemingly permanent part of the American mainstream. They were on television, they held public office or were political candidates, and were regularly and respectfully reported on in the news media. And public gay Americans often looked, sounded, and acted like their straight counterparts. This explosion of gay visibility contributed to the breaking up of a seamless homophobic culture.[1] For lesbians and gay men who were not directly exposed to organized gay life, this unprecedented social visibility allowed them to imagine alternatives to the closet.

Also, while the fight for gay justice found allies in the straight world in past decades, in the 1990s there was a glacial shift: many public figures openly criticized homophobic statements and actions as bigoted. Many writers, editorialists, celebrities, and politicians embraced the cause of gay rights. By the late 1990s, "the homosexual question" was as much about homophobia as about homosexuality.

These changes signal a change in the status of gay Americans. *The cultural underpinning of the closet is under assault by a new discourse that asserts the "normality" of being gay.*

In this chapter, I chart a cultural shift from images of the polluted homosexual to the "normal gay." I focus exclusively on portrayals of gays in Hollywood movies between 1960 and 2000.[2] The evidence suggests that the weakening of homophobic representations is also occurring in other cultural sectors, such as science, the law, television, the news media, and advertising.[3]

The social and political significance of the "normal gay" is ambiguous. The image of the normal gay accounts for a narrow slice of the gay world. It does not, for example, typically include lesbians or gays of color. At least in commercial films, it is primarily white men that represent the "normal gay." Many lesbians and gay men will continue to feel that their very existence is invisible or denied; these individuals will find it harder to emerge from the shadows of the closet. Furthermore, gay normalization is *not* necessarily, or inevitably, occurring across the varied cultural communities, populations, and regions that make up America. Anecdotal evidence suggests that a firmly rooted homophobic culture remains in place in our secondary schools and in the military; and surveys consistently report high levels of moral disapproval of homosexuality among men, older Americans, fundamentalists, nonwhites, and the less educated.[4] In point of fact, we know very little about the respective power of polluting versus normalizing beliefs across different cultural communities and populations.

In any event, I only wish to claim that gay normalization is one prominent trend, not that it's uniformly remaking the cultural landscape of America. My chief concern is to understand the political logic of normalization. How do constructions of the normal gay make possible a life beyond the closet while leaving heterosexual dominance in place?

THE POLLUTED HOMOSEXUAL

The Children's Hour (1961) and *Advise and Consent* (1962) were among the very few star-studded Hollywood films of the early 1960s that featured an explicitly homosexual character. These films tell a story of homosexual calamity as a social tragedy. For example, in *The Children's Hour*, Shirley MacLaine plays a lesbian, Martha. The audience learns of her sexual identity after she is exposed by others. Despite her status as a good citizen (she's a devoted teacher, competent administrator, compassionate friend, and law-abiding citizen), she and everyone associated with her are stigmatized and shunned after she is outed. Ruin and misery are depicted as the product of social intolerance: Martha commits suicide; Joe (James Garner), an aquaintance of Martha's, loses his job, then his fiancée (Audrey Hepburn); and the school for young girls that Martha owns and manages is shut down. The message of the film seems clear: the problem of homosexuality today is not that there are homosexuals but that social prejudice exists.

The meaning and place of homosexuality in the heartland of America was still somewhat unsettled in the 1950s. While a film such as *The Children's Hour* criticized intolerance toward homosexuals, as did Alfred Kinsey's famous studies, the government was aggressively engaged in the harassment and persecution of homosexuals. For the most part, the politics of homosexuality was not a major focus of public attention. The figure of the homosexual scarcely registered a presence in popular culture.[5]

By the early 1970s, however, lesbians and gay men had established a national public presence. In contrast to the quiet, barely noticeable political activities of the homosexual movement in the 1950s and early 1960s, lesbian feminism and gay liberationism championed gay pride and visibility; these movements challenged a homophobic culture and the network of state-enforced laws and practices sustaining the closet. Gays began to come out—in their families, at work, and in the political arena. Popular culture discovered the homosexual.[6] The idea of an exclusively heterosexual public sphere was challenged.

Hollywood, like the rest of America, had no choice but to respond to the new public visibility of the homosexual. Mainstream films of the 1970s and 1980s were almost uniformly condemning. These films reveal something of American's anxiety toward "the new homosexual"—proud and assertive. There were some exceptions. For example, *Ode to Billy Joe* (1976) tells the story of the romantic and tragic Billy Joe (Robby Benson). Despite being madly in love with a woman, Billy Joe takes his life because he could not shake feelings of shame and defilement for having had a single homosexual experience. Billy Joe's suicide is a statement about the power of homophobia rather than about the self-destructive impulse of homosexuals. This film speaks to the ruinous effects of a culture of homosexual pollution.

But Hollywood overwhelmingly framed "the homosexual problem" as a personal tragedy, as a tale of individual sickness and deviance. The social drama in these films revolves around the danger that the homosexual presents to the children, families, moral values, and the very integrity of America as a nation.[7]

As the homosexual stepped into public life in the 1970s, Hollywood fashioned images of this figure as an outsider and social threat. If the homosexual's public presence could not be denied or effectively suppressed, this figure could at least be portrayed in ways that clearly reinforced the norm and ideal status of heterosexuality. *The homosexual became the impure other to the pure heterosexual.*

Consider some of the films in the 1970s and 1980s that featured gay characters. A comedy about black working men, *Car Wash* (1976) introduced an openly homosexual character—Lindy (Antonio Fargas). Excepting Lindy, all of the other characters were not just assumed to be heterosexual but were often emphatically presented as heterosexual. For example, the men were either married, had girlfriends, dated women, hired prostitutes, or flirted with women customers. Lindy's polluted status is dramatized by stereotyping him as a "queen"—swishy, limp-wristed, and exhibiting an exaggerated, affected feminine style. This film presents the male homosexual as a gender invert—a feminized male preoccupied with his looks and obsessed with sex. Lindy is tolerated as part of the public world but only because he reinforces the purity of heterosexuality by presenting homosexuals as defiled and deviant. Lindy clearly belongs outside the circle of the respectable heterosexual citizen.

Viewing the homosexual as a freakish, cartoonlike figure was a way to minimize his or her threat to a social order that made heterosexuality the only acceptable way to be a good citizen. However, many Americans viewed the new homosexual, who demanded respect and challenged heterosexual privilege, as dangerous. This menacing figure was translated on celluloid into posing a real physical and moral threat to the heterosexual citizen. In films of the 1970s and 1980s the homosexual was often portrayed as a sociopath—an aggressive, violent, evil figure.

In *Sudden Impact* (1983), the fourth of the Dirty Harry films, Harry (Clint Eastwood) is a police detective who wages a war against a corrupt world. Harry believes that crime, incivility, and immorality are ruining America. He dedicates himself to purifying America—by any means necessary.

Harry is investigating a series of murders. The perpetrator is Jennifer (Sandra Locke), whose killing spree is revenge for her and her sister's rape. One of the rapists is Ray—a white lesbian in her twenties. Reflecting the new social reality of gay visibility, Ray is portrayed as part of the public world, but the film proceeds to characterize her as the very antithesis of the respectable citizen.

We first meet Ray in a bar. Flagging the lesbian's suspect moral character, the bar is crowded with deviant social types. Ray is the only woman in the bar. She has short hair and wears blue jeans and a jean jacket with the sleeves cut off. She smokes, curses, and talks in an aggressively masculine style. Ray is the stereotypical butch, a mannish woman who is also violent and dangerous. Ray is a moral and physical threat. She participated in the rape and plans to kill Jennifer. However, Jennifer kills Ray first. The presentation of the lesbian as a psychopathic killer who is murdered perhaps expressed American's unconscious fear of the homosexual's new public assertiveness and a desire to expel her from civic life.

Films such as *Car Wash* and *Sudden Impact* construct a sharp opposition between the pure heterosexual and the polluted homosexual. The latter figure appears as a gender freak, moral degenerate, sociopath, or psychopathic killer. There are films of the 1970s and 1980s that are more complex, though they don't challenge the inferior status of the homosexual.

Looking for Mr. Goodbar (1977) depicts a world shaped by the sexual and gender liberationist ideas of the 1960s. Teresa (Diane Keaton) grew up in a repressed Irish Catholic family in Brooklyn. She moves to Manhattan to find herself. Teresa's journey of self-exploration involves a certain blurring of the line between good and bad or polluted sexual desires and acts. For example, the film exposes the dark side of a heterosexual marital norm by showing the repressive and violent aspects of her parents' marriage. And through Teresa the film explores, in a morally ambiguous way, a world of sexual experimentation—from one-night stands and group sex to commercial and rough sex.

In the course of her sexual coming-of-age story, we encounter homosexuals. In one scene, Teresa finds herself in a gay bar. Men are dancing and laughing. At first, the viewer might think that this is a positive portrayal of gay men; the intermingling of heterosexuals and homosexuals might even suggest the film's advocacy of social tolerance. This generous impulse, however, is quickly contradicted.

The bar scene focuses on two men. Gary (Tom Berenger), a muscular, handsome man in his twenties, dressed in clone-style jeans, a T-shirt, and jean jacket, approaches a much older, wealthy-looking man. They kiss in a way suggesting that they have an intimate bond.

The two men reappear in a New Year's Eve scene some time later in the film. They are celebrating in Times Square. The older man is dressed as a clown and Gary is in drag, complete with wig, high heels, and makeup. Abruptly, the scene turns dangerous; chaos descends as crowds of drunken men are fighting and destroying property. Gary and his friend run to escape the violence.

> OLDER MAN: Did they hurt you?
>
> GARY: No, don't ever ask me to wear this crap again. I'm no nellie. You ought to know that. Christ, look at us. We're a couple of freaks.

OLDER MAN: [crying hysterically] I'm sorry.

GARY: I've had it with you . . . and your fancy shirts, shoes . . .

OLDER MAN: [desperately holding Gary] Please don't go. [Gary hits him]. Please don't go . . . I'll wait for you at the apartment. You need some money.

GARY: You're the nellie, not me. I'm a pitcher not a catcher and don't you ever forget that.

Gary expresses one of the pillar fears about gay men: they are not real men, but sissies or nellies. They are men who can be fucked, just like women. The film also offers a portrait of homosexual relationships that is damning. In contrast to the heterosexual ideal of a love-based companionate intimacy, a homosexual relationship is presented as an exploitative and corrupting exchange of youthful beauty for material comfort. The older man is wealthy, closeted, and effeminate; Gary is an ex-con who trades on his masculine good looks for material comfort. Gary's true sexual identity is unclear. If he is in fact a homosexual, perhaps breaking with his benefactor will lead him to an affirmative gay identity.

Gary's status is clarified in the final scene, when he meets Teresa for the first time in a bar. Enjoying each other, they decide to go to her apartment. Gary is unable to fuck. He is upset. "In my neighborhood if you didn't fight you were a fruit. In prison if you didn't fight you spread ass." Gary again tries to fuck but cannot. Teresa asks, "What are you trying to prove?" Gary says, "You think I'm some kind of flaming faggot." Gary will prove his manhood at any cost: he violently rapes her. However, he can only enter her from behind, as if he were having sex with a man. Humiliated by this implicit acknowledgment of his homosexuality, and his failed manhood, Gary stabs Teresa repeatedly and kills her.

The older man may be a pathetic and pathological figure who confuses desire with love and purchases the affections of young, handsome men, but Gary is a psychopath. Filled with rage and self-hatred, he murders to cleanse himself of his homosexual feelings. Both figures are presented as social threats. The older man represents the power of the homosexual to seduce and corrupt innocent vulnerable youth. Gary presents a mortal danger to Americans. Like *Sudden Impact*, this film reveals Americans' wish to purge homosexuals from public life. In its portrayal of gays, the film enacts the social death of the homosexual by rendering this figure into a virtual subhuman species (psychopath) who should not be part of civic life.[8]

Hollywood films of the 1970s and 1980s acknowledge the reality of homosexuals but represent them either as harmless but freakish and pathetic figures (*Car Wash*, *Next Stop Greenwich Village*, *St. Elmo's Fire*), or as serious physical, moral, and social threats (*Sudden Impact*, *Looking for Mr. Goodbar*, *Cruising*, *Deliverance*). These films view heterosexuality and homosexuality as mutually exclusive social identities. America is imagined as divided into a heterosexual majority and a homosexual minority. This is a moral division: the heterosexual represents a pure and good human status in contrast to the impure and dangerous homosexual. The link between homosexual pollution and social repression is established through the notion of moral contagion. Heterosexual exposure to homosexuals threatens their seduction and corruption. Accordingly, homosexuals must be excluded from the public world of visible, open communication by means of repressive strategies such as censorship, civic disenfranchisement, and sequestration. In short, these films construct a social world in which heterosexual privilege is reinforced by purifying the heterosexual while vilifying the homosexual and positioning him or her outside of normal, respectable American civic life.

THE NORMAL GAY

Stereotypes that scandalize homosexuals are hardly a thing of the past—not by a long shot. But images of the polluted homosexual are now often publicly criticized as a form of prejudice and bigotry; tolerance of public homophobic expressions can no longer be taken for granted.[9] A shift in the cultural status of the homosexual is clear in films of the 1990s. Polluting stereotypes are giving way to another representation: the normal gay.

The normal gay is presented as fully human, as the psychological and moral equal of the heterosexual, and accordingly gays should be integrated into America as respected citizens. However, the normal gay also serves as a narrow social norm. This figure is associated with specific personal and social behaviors. For example, the normal gay is expected to be gender conventional, link sex to love and a marriage-like relationship, defend family values, personify economic individualism, and display national pride. Although normalization makes it possible for individuals to conduct lives of integrity, it also establishes a moral and social division among gays. Only normal gays who conform to dominant social norms deserve respect and integration. Lesbians and gay men who are gender benders or choose alternative intimate lives will likely remain outsiders. And, as we'll see, the normal gay implies a political logic of tolerance and minority rights that does not challenge heterosexual dominance.

Philadelphia (1993) was in many ways a breakthrough movie. In a big studio production starring Tom Hanks and Denzel Washington, Hollywood brought AIDS and homosexuality to middle America. This was one of the first big-budget, star-studded Hollywood productions to present the gay individual as a normal, good citizen.

The movie tells the story of Andy (Tom Hanks), a rising star in a prestigious law firm, who is fired for having AIDS. Represented by Joe (Denzel Washington), Andy files an AIDS discrimination suit and wins. The film simultaneously tells a larger story of the changing moral status of gay Americans.

Andy's experience in his law firm pointedly depicts a society that fears and discriminates against gays. The culture of the firm is aggressively masculine and heterosexual. Andy's good standing at the law firm is maintained by concealing his homosexuality. This decision is a response to homophobic comments (fag jokes) made by the senior law partners. Andy's dismissal from the firm is related less to his having

AIDS than to his being homosexual, though AIDS is shown to be the ultimate fear of homosexual pollution and contagion come to literal life. In a telling scene, the law firm's senior partner (Jason Robards) advises against settling the lawsuit by invoking the image of the homosexual defiling the firm. "Andy brought AIDS into our office, into our men's room, brought AIDS to our annual family gatherings." Andy's boss is saying that just as AIDS can literally spread by contact, so might Andy's homosexuality. In short, the film's portrayal of the law firm depicts a social order in which gay people are forced to either pass or suffer considerable personal harm.

If the focus of the film was Andy's decision to pass and his firing for homophobic reasons, it would describe the world of the closet. Rather, the main drama of *Philadelphia* centers on Andy's decision to fight anti-gay prejudice and his triumph in the American criminal justice system. Instead of surrendering to the power of prejudice and intolerance, Andy fights back by suing the law firm. His legal victory suggests that America is changing and that gays will not and should not accept the closet as a condition of social integration. *Philadelphia* advocates a view of gays as normal human beings who deserve equal rights and respect.

While the film depicts the fight against homosexual pollution as an institutional drama, it powerfully dramatizes this struggle through the character of Joe.

Joe, as in your average Joe, represents the typical American. Newly married, hard working, he is a "guy's guy." Predictably, then, his homophobia is established early in the film. After being turned down by many lawyers, Andy approaches Joe, a gritty streetwise lawyer. As they are shaking hands, Andy tells Joe that he is seeking counsel for an AIDS discrimination suit. Joe abruptly withdraws his hand, takes several backward steps away from Andy, looks at Andy with apparent fear and loathing, watches everything that Andy touches in his office, and refuses to take the case for personal reasons, which he subsequently discloses as a hatred of homosexuals. This scene reveals the logic of homosexual pollution: Joe's behavior establishes a division between the pure heterosexual and the impure homosexual. Andy's polluted status is illustrated by Joe's fear of contamination, his refusal to represent Andy, and his frank expression of disgust toward homosexuals.

Philadelphia is not a coming-out film, at least not in the classic sense. Andy doesn't struggle with self-acceptance. From the very first scene, Andy is out and reveals no moral anguish over being gay. He lives with Miguel (Antonio Banderas) and is integrated into a dense network of kin and friends. Instead, it's Joe's personal struggle with his own homophobia, and ultimately with America's intolerance toward gays, that is the moral focus of the film.

Anticipating the end of his trial, and his death, Andy and Miguel have a party. At one point, Andy and Miguel are intimately embraced as they dance. Similarly intimate with his wife, Joe glances, then fixes, on Andy and Miguel. Andy notices and smiles, as if he is signaling that his love for Miguel is equivalent to Joe's love for his wife. Joe is beginning to recognize Andy as fully human. His realization comes later that evening. After the guests leave, Joe and Andy are supposed to review Andy's testimony. Instead, in a poignant scene, Andy relates to Joe the story of a Maria Callas opera that is playing in the background. It's a sad tale of love, injustice, and tragic death. As Andy is absorbed in the operatic narrative, Joe is fixed intently on Andy. Tears begin to well up. No words are spoken, but the meaning seems clear. For the first time, Joe is seeing Andy as someone who, like him, feels joy and sadness, love and loss, justice and oppression. By the end of the film, Andy has ceased to be polluted for Joe. As Andy is dying in the hospital, he signals for Joe to sit next to him. This is a dramatic moment as their physical and emotional closeness marks the end of Andy's polluted status. Joe sits on the bed and touches Andy's face as he adjusts his breathing apparatus. This act symbolizes Joe's acknowledgment of the moral equivalence of the heterosexual and the homosexual.

The film's moral standpoint is clear: it asserts the normality of homosexuality and the bigoted status of homophobia. As a typical Hollywood story of good versus evil, *Philadelphia* depicts the anti-gay behavior of the law firm and the "early" Joe as evil, while Andy and the "latter" Joe become symbols of goodness.

Philadelphia abandons polluting stereotypes and condemns social intolerance. Still, the normal gay remains a distinct social minority to be tolerated but not considered the equal to the straight majority. Heterosexual domination is not threatened.

First, homosexuality is not presented as an emotional and sexual orientation that is diffusely distributed across a population but rather as an identity of a small minority. The majority of citizens are either assumed or act as heterosexual; they are married or display a sexual interest in the opposite gender. Indeed, the heterosexuality of all of the main characters, except Andy and Miguel, is unambiguously conveyed. For example, in the opening scene of the movie, Joe is in a hospital celebrating the birth of his first child. Andy's parents and their adult children are all married. Andy's law partners are married or otherwise signal their heterosexuality by their homophobic comments or their interest in the opposite sex. The film does not challenge the dominant and privileged status of heterosexuality.

Second, gays, or some gays, may be normal and good citizens, but heterosexuality is still the ideal. The figure of Andy as the normal gay is surrounded by idealized images of the straight American. For example, Andy's parents live in a white picket–fenced colonial home in a small town where, we are led to believe, they've lived happily—as they celebrate their fiftieth wedding anniversary—for their entire adult lives. Andy's family is an extended heterosexual kin unit, presented as lovingly bonded and intact. The film projects an almost 1950s family ideal—the white colonial home in small-town America, the extended loving family, the parents who live and love together for life, and the conventional gender division between men and women. So, while the film assigns a normal status to being gay, it continues to endorse the norm and ideal of heterosexuality.

Third, Andy exhibits personal traits and behaviors that many Americans would consider "normal" or ideal in every way other than his sexual identity. He is conventionally masculine; he is in a quasi-marital relationship; he is part of an extended close-knit family; he is hardworking and economically independent; and he is a champion of the rule of law—a core part of the American creed. This characterization of Andy doesn't challenge a social order that assumes that the division and complementarity of men and women is natural and right; and it doesn't question the ideal of heterosexual marriage and family; it only creates a space of social tolerance for gays, or, more correctly, for normal gays.

Finally, in the ideal society imagined in *Philadelphia*, discrimination toward gays would be uncivil—that's the message of Andy's legal victory. However, the culture and institutions of America would remain organized around heterosexual privilege. Thus, the law firm that fired Andy may no longer be able to discriminate but it remains organized around a binary gender order that sustains men's domination; the men in the firm are still the senior partners; the women are still the receptionists, secretaries, or junior partners; and all of the men, including Andy, are conventionally masculine, and the women conventionally feminine. A gender order that divides men and women into different and complementary identities and roles underpins a social order that assumes the naturalness and correctness of heterosexuality. Moreover, the culture of the law firm remains organized around the ideal of heterosexuality in its public rituals of sexual play, dating, romance, weddings, marriages, and family celebrations. The film's sexual politics do not go beyond claiming a minority but continued subordinate status for the homosexual.

If *Philadelphia* represents Hollywood's film debut of the normal gay, *In and Out* (1997) suggests that middle America is ready and willing to accept gays as full citizens. This is a coming-out story, but less the classic closet tale of individual's struggling for self-acceptance in a hostile society. Rather, this film narrates a moral drama of a nation that comes of age through recognition of the gay individual as one of its own.

In and Out tells the story of the coming out of Howard (Kevin Kline). As he is unintentionally "outed" by a former student turned actor, Cameron Drake (Matt Dillon), Howard's family and friends are forced to deal with the issue of homosexuality. The film rehearses a conventional coming-out story. Initially in denial, Howard gradually acknowledges and accepts that he is gay.

Coming out is not, however, the chief story of the film. Howard's coming out is almost painless. For example, after Cameron's outing of Howard, his parents are immediately comforting. "Howard, we want you to know that we love you—gay [or] straight. It's not a bad thing." Another coming-out scene also conveys its routine character. As the outing of Howard becomes national news, a television reporter, Peter Malloy (Tom Sellek) is assigned to cover the story. Peter matter-of-factly tells Howard that he's gay. Howard asks Peter how others have reacted to his revelation.

PETER: I came out to everyone, my folks, my boss, my dog. One day I snapped. I couldn't take lying to the people I love.

HOWARD: What happened?

PETER: My mom cried for exactly ten seconds. My boss said who cares. My dad said "But you're so tall."

By portraying people's response to Howard's and Peter's coming out in a matter-of-fact and accepting way, the film suggests that not only do gay people approach being gay as a normal identity but much of straight America does as well.

In this regard, it is not coincidental that the movie takes place in a small town in the midwest (Greenleaf, Indiana). If the film is announcing America's growing acceptance of the normal status of being gay, where else should it take place than in the national heartland? Greenleaf is pure Americana—white picket–fenced homes, a gemeinschaft-like community, marriages that are permanent, men who work as farmers (Howard's father), and women who are housewives and mothers (Howard's mother). If Greenleaf citizens can accept the gay citizen, the film seems to be saying, all Americans can and should.

Howard comes out on the day of his wedding, but it's anticlimactic because he's already been accepted by his parents. The most dramatic scene is graduation day at the high school. Howard has been fired by the principal and was not expected to attend. Encouraged by his father, Howard shows up just in time to hear Cameron Drake—

who returns to his hometown to set things right—ridiculing the homophobia of the school administration. Drake asks the principal why Howard is no longer a teacher.

> PRINCIPAL: The community felt that it was a question of influence. It's all right to be this way at home, but Mr. Bracket is a teacher.
>
> DRAKE: So you're thinking about the students. What you're saying is that because Mr. Bracket is gay he's going to send out some kind of gay microwaves to make everyone else gay. Well, kids, you've had Mr. Bracket: Is that the way it worked?

Mocking the belief in the contagious polluted status of homosexuality, a student says, "I had Mr. Bracket and I must be gay." After other students similarly ridicule this homophobic logic, the principal declares that the community has made its decision. At that point, Howard's father declares, "I'm his father and I'm gay." Howard's mother chimes in, "I'm his mother and I'm a lesbian." Soon the entire community joins in what I would describe as a public ritual of gay normalization. Greenleaf citizens are announcing the end of the polluted status of the homosexual. By publicly identifying with Howard, they are declaring that the gay individual is a normal human being, one of their own.

The film's defense of the normality of being gay does not, however, mean that it challenges the norm of heterosexuality. As in *Philadelphia*, the homosexual is presented as making up a very small social minority. The social world of Greenleaf is overwhelmingly heterosexual. Aside from Howard and Peter, whose sexual identity is known only by Howard and his fiancée, Greenleaf citizens are assumed to be heterosexual. And the film celebrates the institutions of heterosexual marriage and family. In an uncanny parallel with *Philadelphia*, Howard's parents' marriage is portrayed in ideal and nostalgic terms. They are small-town folks who grew up and still live in Greenleaf, and they are so happily married that they celebrate their fiftieth wedding anniversary with renewed wedding vows. In short, the film champions the normal gay self, but America—as symbolized by Greenleaf—is a nation where almost all citizens are heterosexual and the institutions that sustain heterosexual dominance, such as binary gender roles, weddings, marriage, and the nuclear family, remain unchallenged.

In a further striking parallel to *Philadelphia*, Howard (like Andy) represents what many Americans would consider to be a "normal"—indeed, an ideal—American citizen in every way other than his homosexuality. In fact, Howard betrays a kind of wistful longing for an America that is long gone, if it ever was a reality. With a midwestern, small-town backdrop, Howard could have stepped out of a 1950s television sitcom such as *The Andy Griffith Show* or *Leave It to Beaver*. His character exemplifies small-town respectability. He's a devoted, popular high school teacher who wears a bow tie and seersucker suit and pedals his bike to work. He's been engaged for three years to a hometown girl whose femininity is thoroughly conventional, including her virginal status. Howard personifies middle-American virtues: he's honest, hardworking, trustworthy, devoted to family, and respectful of tradition. So, while the film declares the normality of being gay, it also champions conventional gender roles, sex linked to love and marriage, family values, and a Protestant work ethic. In short, the film's message is one of tolerating the homosexual as a part of America but leaving unchallenged the ideal of a nation anchored by heterosexual marriage and the family.

Philadelphia and *In and Out* substitute an image of the normal gay for the polluted homosexual. However, the norm of heterosexuality remains institutionally secure. Both films evoke idealized images of an America that are strikingly nostalgic and conservative. The gay citizen, it seems, can be tolerated only if a norm and ideal of America is defended that asserts the good, right, and normal status of dichotomous gender roles, heterosexual love, marriage, and the family.

The social and political meaning of the notion of the normal gay is potentially ambiguous and unstable. While it can easily coexist with a norm of heterosexuality, it can also unsettle that norm. For example, except for his sexual identity, the Tom Hanks character (Andy) in *Philadelphia* expresses the traits and behaviors of the ideal American citizen. And part of Andy's normality is his intimate life. By portraying Andy in a loving relationship the film in effect declares the reality and legitimacy of gay families; at least implicitly, *Philadelphia* would seem to endorse such policies as gay adoption, gay marriage, domestic partnership, housing and hospital visitation rights, and so on.

In some films of the 1990s, admittedly exceptional, the normal gay citizen is portrayed in a way that is more directly troubling to an exclusive norm of heterosexuality. *Boys on the Side* (1995) is one such film. It's about the lives of Jane (Whoopi Goldberg), Holly (Drew Barrymore), and Robin (Mary Louise Parker). At one level it is a story of a generation of women who have the freedom to define their own lives. Each woman has her own personality and story. Jane is a freewheeling black lesbian. Holly is a somewhat naive, sexually active straight white woman whose life is defined by her relations with men. Robin is a career-oriented, conventionally feminine straight white woman who, because of a one-time lapse, is HIV positive. The relationship between Jane and Holly is the emotional center of the film.

This is not a coming-out film. Jane doesn't anguish over her homosexuality. She does not exhibit any shame or ambivalence. Moreover, others don't fret over Jane's sexual identity. When Holly matter-of-factly tells Robin about Jane's sexual identity, Robin is surprised but accepting. And when Robin tells her mother about Jane's sexual identity, her mother is initially upset but soon comes to care deeply about Jane. The fact that Holly and Robin live with Jane underscores the film's moral conviction of the normal status of gays.

Interestingly, *Boys on the Side* projects an image of the "good gay" without her thoroughgoing normalization. Whereas Andy and Howard reinforce dominant social norms in every way but their homosexuality, Jane is nonconventional in many respects. For example, her economic values are less middle American than countercultural and working class. She is a struggling musician who survives by driving a taxi in New York. Moreover, Jane is not conventionally feminine. Her self-presentation (for example, her grooming, dress, and talk) is much more masculine than Holly's or Robin's. However, she is not a stereotypical "mannish lesbian," and her gender nonconformity is not associated with individual pathology or social deviance. Jane retains conventional markers of black femininity (for example, braids), and psychologically she exhibits stereotypical feminine traits, such as being empathetic and nurturing. Finally, Jane is neither settled in a quasi-marital relationship (like Andy) nor desexualized (like Howard); she is depicted as a sexually assertive woman who eventually finds another woman.

The way Jane is portrayed challenges an exclusive norm of heterosexuality. For example, her androgynous gender identity contradicts the norm of a binary hetero-gender order. Similarly, against norms of feminine sexuality that link sexual desire to nurturing and love, Jane is erotically adventurous but not predatory. More to the point, Jane presents a credible lesbian alternative to heterosexuality. Her lesbian sexual desire lacks any trace of shame or guilt. And the film cautiously legitimates lesbian relationships as an alternative to marriage by suggesting in a final scene that Jane and Anna will live together as lovers. Indeed, the film legitimates the idea of multiple types of families—not just gay families (Jane and Anna) but the chosen family of Jane, Holly, and Robin. As Robin is dying she decides to live with Jane and Holly, not with her family of origin.

Boys on the Side is also one of the few commercially successful films of the 1990s that feature lesbians. Of the twenty-odd films produced in the 1990s that I looked at, only *Boys on the Side* featured a normalized lesbian character—though less mainstream films such as *Chasing Amy* (1997) and *Set It Off (*1996) also present affirmative lesbian characters.

The politics of gender is crucial to explaining the relative absence of respectable lesbians compared to gay men in recent popular culture. While both gay men and lesbians threaten the norm of heterosexuality, the lesbian also challenges men's dominance. Lesbians are women who live independently of men or without being economically, socially, and sexually or emotionally dependent on them. Lesbians claim masculine privilege—in the choice of socioeconomic independence, in the pursuit of women as sex and love partners, and at least for some lesbians in the integration of masculine styles of self-presentation as a way to flag their sexual identity and to claim social respect and power. The lesbian, moreover, may be understood as a threat to the heterosexual family as she signals to all women the possibility of roles outside of wife and mother. As a perceived threat to men's dominance, to a conventional dichotomous gender order, and to a norm of the heterosexual family that has relied on the domestic labor of women, it's hardly surprising that American culture remains reluctant to legitimate the figure of the normal lesbian.[10]

As movies such as *Basic Instinct* (1992) illustrate, the perceived lesbian threat has been responded to by projecting a stereotypical, polluting image of her as a menacing predator and seducer. However, as polluting representations are less tolerated, another strategy is prominent: the homosexuality of women is, if not denied, then depicted as not stable or fundamental. The lesbian is imagined as a transitional status—an immature phase or a case of gender maladjustment.

The idea that homosexuality is somehow transitory or less stable for women is in evidence in two movies. In *Silkwood* (1983), Cher plays a "lesbian," Dolly. She lives with a heterosexual couple (Meryl Streep and Kurt Russell) who accept her. Yet her self-presentation as a plain, depressed, and isolated individual conveys a rather dreary, if not polluted, sense of self. Moreover, Dolly never publicly comes out as a lesbian, leaving her identity somewhat ambiguous. Dolly's sexual identity is suggested when Angela (Diana Scarwid) enters her life. Dolly and Angela are shown as an ordinary, loving couple. They decide to live together and share a house with Karen and Drew. However, Angela soon leaves Dolly to return to her husband. It turns out that Angela's lesbian experience was a response to being badly treated by her husband. After Angela leaves, Dolly returns to her former lifeless and ambiguously identified self. The movie trades on a sense of the unstable, ambiguous status of lesbianism.

A similar ambiguity surrounds the presentation of lesbianism in John Singleton's *Higher Learning* (1995). Kristen, a naive, attractive, and initially straight-acting college student, becomes romantically involved with a somewhat older woman student. Tellingly, Kristen's lesbianism is introduced only after a man rapes her. As her emotional scars heal, Kristen rediscovers her true heterosexual nature. Her psychological healing parallels her involvement with a man. Her lesbianism, it seems, was a temporary response to a traumatic event. Interestingly, the older woman is presented as a politically active feminist, leaving the audience to wonder whether her lesbianism is more about gender politics than her actual sexual desires.

If the lesbian is not polluted in these films, her literal reality is denied or doubted. She is viewed as a straight woman who is confused, manipulated, or acting out. Sometimes, lesbianism is denied by interpreting it as a type of intense bonding between women. This has been a prominent pattern in recent films such as *The Color Purple (*1985), *Thelma and Louise* (1991), and *Fried Green Tomatoes* (1991). *Boys on the Side* trades on the ambiguous meaning surrounding the intimate bonding between women. For example, in a courtroom scene in which Robin is explaining the kinship status of the three friends, she says, "I don't know what it is but there's something that goes on between women. . . . I'm just saying like speaks to like. Love or whatever doesn't always keep, [but] you find out what does, if you're lucky." Robin's statement blurs the line between women bonding and lesbianism and allows Jane's "lesbianism" to be read as an instance of the former.

Jane's ambiguous sexual status is suggested by her overriding identity as an eccentric person. Jane is a black woman with no apparent ties to a black community; her dearest friends are white women. She is a musician with little or no integration into a network of musicians. And, to really mark her as an outsider, Jane has apparently no kin ties. Jane is presented as a free-floating, marginal individual whose identity, sexual and otherwise, seems fluid and ambiguous.

While the film doesn't explicitly deny Jane's lesbianism, its political significance is considerably diminished by her isolation from any sense of a lesbian or gay community. Her closest social bonds are with straight women. Her journey of self-discovery takes place entirely in the straight world. And Jane's self-presentation and behavior are free of any lesbian subcultural markings. Accordingly, whatever challenge Jane might present to men's dominance or to heterosexual domination might easily be read as a merely personal, idiosyncratic statement rather than an expression of a community or social movement.

Films that fashion images of gays as normal typically present homosexuality as an individual sexual identity. In contrast to a gay movement that understands being gay as a social and political identity, these films avoid or minimize any affiliation of being gay with a community, subculture, or movement. The life drama of the normal gay takes place in a thoroughly heterosexual setting. If there is any acknowledgment that many gays are part of a community, the latter is reduced to superficial lifestyle or consumer choices (for example, fashion, skin piercings, decorating styles). The minimizing of the subcultural or group status of being gay has the effect of reducing politics to a personal struggle for respect and acceptance.

In contrast to the presentation of the normal gay as an individual identity, consider what we might call "gay-standpoint films." Movies such as *Love! Valour! Compassion!* (1997), *Longtime Companion* (1990), *Jeffrey* (1995), and *Kiss Me, Guido (1998)* are different from the gay-friendly films of the 1980s such as *Making Love* (1982), *Personal Best* (1982), or *Desert Hearts* (1985). In the latter films, the chief drama is coming out in a hostile heterosexual society. Gay-standpoint films feature individuals who are self-accepting and are part of an institutionalized gay community. Gay life is understood from the perspective of this subculture. These films offer a critical view of the straight world—for example, exposing anti-gay violence, social discrimination, and a culture that stereotypes gays.

One of the few Hollywood films that situates a gay character in both straight and gay contexts is *The Object of My Affection* (1998). The story takes place in New York City in the 1990s. George (Paul Rudd) has just broken up with Robert (Tim Daley) and moves into an apartment with Nina (Jennifer Aniston). Nina gets pregnant and wants George, rather than the biological father, Vince, to help raise the child. The film focuses on the intimate ties between George and Nina, Nina and Vince, and George and his boyfriends.

George's gay identity is established early in the film. There is no coming-out scene. George lacks any trace of shame or anguish about being gay. Moreover, Nina, her family, and their heterosexual friends are accepting.

As is typical of films that normalize being gay, George exemplifies ideal personal and civic traits. He's good-looking but not a dandy or narcissistic; he's sincere, reasonable, and considerate. George is a devoted friend and dedicated schoolteacher, conventionally masculine, links sex to intimacy and love, and is committed to family values, which explains his decision to help raise Nina's child.

Departing from most Hollywood films of the 1990s, George is presented as part of a gay friendship circle. There is his ex-boyfriend Robert, his new boyfriend Paul, and Paul's admirer and benefactor (Nigel Hawthorne). However, these gay individuals show no interest in sexual politics. Indeed, the movie naively suggests the absence of any tension between being gay and being an American, as if heterosexuality were no longer an institutional norm and cultural ideal.

The gay characters in this film are exclusively associated with a nonpolitical world of consumerism and high culture. For example, Robert is a handsome, stylish (he drives a red convertible sports car) English professor. Paul is an aspiring actor, and his benefactor is a literary-theater critic who lives in an elegantly decorated apartment and dresses impeccably. Gay men take on feminine roles. They serve a (male) dominant heterosexual world by making the social world beautiful and by sustaining the machinery of production (the heterosexual world) through their voracious cultural consumption. By positioning gay men squarely in the cultural realm of lifestyle and consumption, this film disassociates being gay from a political movement seeking social justice.

Moreover, as the film introduces several gay characters, a politics that divides gays into "good" and "bad" is evident. Representations of the normal gay cannot avoid a politics of moral classification. For example, *Philadelphia* doesn't champion the normal good status of the gay individual in general but fashions a specific norm of being gay. The "good gay" (Andy) is gender conventional and committed to marital-family-work ethics and values. Lesbians or gay men who deviate from the norm of the normal or good gay fall outside the charmed circle of social respectability. In *The Object of My Affection* this division between the good and the bad gay is made explicit. Whereas George occupies the moral space of the good gay, Robert is the bad gay. George is honest, trustworthy, empathetic, altruistic, and committed to marital and family values. Robert is egocentric, insincere, consumer- and status-oriented, and sexually promiscuous. This film normalizes not the gay citizen in general, but only the good gay.

While many lesbians and gay men will not find their lives reflected in the image of the normal gay, the status of "normality" will make it possible for many individuals to conduct lives beyond the closet. And many of these postcloseted gays will feel entitled to full citizenship rights and integration into a national culture that is respectful of them and their relationships.

THE RETREAT FROM GAY NORMALIZATION

The political implications of recognizing gays as "virtually normal" are ambiguous. As we've seen, Hollywood has generally aligned normality with a politics of minority rights and tolerance. But a normal status can just as easily justify a politics aimed at full social equality. Perhaps sensing this political ambiguity, some films have retreated somewhat from gay normalization.

This retreat is obvious in films such as *Basic Instinct*, *Father of the Bride*, and *Ace Ventura*, which populate the screen with the polluted figure of the pansy, the mannish lesbian, or the sociopathic homosexual. These movies illustrate an almost backlash response to gay mainstreaming and a wish to reinstate the conditions of the closet. In other films of the 1990s, these polluted figures are absent, but an ambivalence surfaces in a subtle gender stereotyping and the desexualizing of gays.

In the 1997 commercial hit *My Best Friend's Wedding*, Julianne (Julia Roberts) is a free-spirited, independent woman. She is single by choice, a writer, politically opinionated, and socially assertive. Julianne realizes that she's in love with Michael (Dermot Mulroney), her best friend, after he announces his engagement to be married. Julianne enlists her close friend George (Rupert Everett), who is gay, in a scheme to derail the wedding.

The film's view of gays as normal is conveyed in the close friendship between Julianne and George. Moreover, George's gay identity is presented in a respectful and routine way. There is no personal or social drama around his homosexuality—neither on his part nor on Julianne's. In fact, like Andy (*Philadelphia*), Howard (*In and Out*), and George (*The Object of My Desire*), George is in many respects an idealized figure: handsome, cultured, empathetic, funny, successful, and an exceptionally loyal friend. When Julianne tries to make Michael jealous, she recruits George to pass as her boyfriend, which he does with great humor and charm.

Although George lacks polluted traits, he is subtly stereotyped as a feminine man. The contrast between George and (the heterosexual) Michael is instructive. Whereas George is impeccable in his grooming and dress, elegant in his manners, and presented as something of a cultural dilettante, Michael is careless about his dress, he associates culture with sports (he's a sportswriter), and his rugged good looks project the image of a thoroughly masculine man. George's feminization is further dramatized by his desexualization. While Michael is coupled to Kimmie, and Julianne desires Michael, George seemingly lacks sexual desire, except his pretended heterosexual desire for Julianne. And, to further mark his femininity, George is always available to listen, advise, and support Julianne. He is, in short, Julianne's "sisterly" best friend.

The film's ambivalence is also suggested by the privatization of George's gay identity. George lives, we are led to believe, an open life, but in the course of the film Julianne is the only one who actually knows about his sexual identity. George is always pretending to be Julianne's heterosexual lover, and his "passing" is never exposed. There is a parallel here with Peter, the television reporter in *In and Out*. Peter discloses to Howard and his fiancée, but his true sexual identity remains unknown to anyone else in Greenleaf. The message of *My Best Friend's Wedding* seems clear: while gays should not be forced into a condition of invisibility and silence, they should be out only in the private, intimate confidence of friends and family.

The Oscar-winning film *As Good as It Gets* (1997) reveals a similar ambivalence toward the figure of the normal gay. In this film, Melvin (Jack Nicholson), an obsessive-compulsive misanthrope, falls in love with Carol (Helen Hunt), a waitress whose life is extremely stressful because of a sick son and financial hardships. Melvin's neighbor is Simon (Greg Kinnear), a gay artist. The lives of these three characters get intertwined, though the drama centers on the relationship between Melvin and Carol.

The film presents Simon's gay identity in a matter-of-fact way. Only Melvin exhibits any discomfort, but he dislikes everyone, especially people who are different from him because of their race, ethnicity, or sexual identity. By making Melvin's homophobia, not homosexuality, into a disease, the film is making a statement about the normality of being gay. Furthermore, Melvin's steady progress in the course of the film toward psychological normality is narrated as paralleling his acceptance of Simon. In the early scenes, Melvin fears and despises Simon because he is gay. In the course of the film, Melvin grows attached to Simon. In a poignant scene toward the end of the movie, Melvin offers to share his apartment with Simon after he suffers a series of financial and emotional setbacks.

SIMON: I love you.

MELVIN: Simon, I tell ya, I'd be the luckiest man alive if that did it for me.

The film's ambivalence toward accepting gays as normal citizens is suggested by the presentation of Simon as asexual. He does not have a boyfriend, lover, or sex partner—nor, apparently, is he looking for one. Simon's sexual passion is sublimated into an obsessive attachment to his petite, adorable dog and a passion for art. And, while the film avoids homophobic effeminate stereotypes, almost everything about Simon suggests a feminine man. His good looks evoke a feminine beauty. He's almost adolescent or androgynous in figure and demeanor. Simon is presented as passive, hypersensitive, prone to whining and hysteria, and intimidated by "real men" like Melvin and his father. Thus, while Melvin struggles to manage an obsessive-compulsive disorder, and Carol is burdened with a sickly child whose medical care demands all of her free time and money, it is Simon who is presented as a victim. He is robbed and assaulted, abused by his parents, rejected by a public that doesn't buy his art, and homeless by the end of the movie. Simon is not the (polluted) effeminate queen or pansy, but as a hysterical, childlike, desexualized victim he occupies a feminine role. He shares with women a subordinate social status in relation to straight, masculine men.

Hollywood films of the 1990s document a cultural shift: the polluted homosexual gives way to the normal gay. The status of being normal makes possible a life outside the closet, but only gays who display the traits or behaviors associated with normality are accepted. Only gays who are gender conventional, and who connect sex to romantic, quasi-marital, and family values are considered "normal." Individuals who do not conform to these social norms may be considered deviant or inferior and will not necessarily merit respect and integration. And, to the extent that the normal gay is typically imagined as male, white, or middle class, individuals who do not possess these statuses will not be recognized in the public image of the normal gay. Finally, the very behaviors that have the status of "normal" (for example, gender binary) reinforce a heterosexual norm and ideal.

THE GOOD/BAD SEXUAL CITIZEN

Many scholars hold that the beliefs people have about being gay are not simply a reflection of what they know or don't know about homosexuality. Rather, the meaning of being gay is in part fixed by its being the opposite of what it means to be straight.[11] For example, if heterosexuality is associated, ideally, with behaviors such as being loving and being monogamous, homosexuality is often associated in the public's mind with being hedonistic and promiscuous. From this perspective, stigmatizing representations of homosexuality affect both homosexuals and heterosexuals. Behavior associated with homosexuality, such as promiscuity, are defined as bad for both homosexuals and heterosexuals. If public meanings surrounding being gay change, we would expect changes in norms of heterosexual behavior.

In one respect, though, the meaning of homosexuality has apparently had no influence on general sexual norms. Whether films pollute or normalize homosexuality, all the films I viewed hold to an ideal that values sex as a medium of love, relationship building, and family making. Accordingly, these films operate with a global division between the good and bad sexual citizen. The bad sexual citizen weakens or uncouples body- and pleasure-centered sex from intimate bonding. In the shift from polluting to normalizing representations there is, however, a change in the role of homosexuality in shaping the image of the bad sexual citizen. In films of the 1960s through the 1980s that pollute homosexuality, the homosexual is the exemplar of the bad sexual citizen. In films that promote gay normalization, the homosexual, at least the normal gay, is no longer associated with the bad sexual citizen. Indeed, the division between the good and the bad sexual citizen is less closely tied to the division between the heterosexual and the homosexual.

A public culture that pollutes homosexuality took shape in the 1960s and 1970s. No doubt this was a response to the rise of a national gay movement. However, it is not coincidental that the figure of the homosexual gained social prominence during a period of turmoil in America. Rebellions of youths, women, gays, and sexual liberationists challenged dominant social norms that linked sex to intimacy, love, marriage, and the family. Many of these sex rebels championed a culture of sexual variation.[12] They defended the idea that sex has multiple meanings. Sex was valued not only as a way to establish intimacy or a family but as a type of pleasure, self-expression, and communication apart from love or relationship building. Some rebels championed a minimalist ethic: as long as sex was between consenting adults it should be considered legitimate and free of state control.

Stigmatizing the homosexual was in part a reaction to these efforts to renegotiate sexual norms to permit more choice. The polluted homosexual restricted the field of legitimate sexuality to heterosexuality. Moreover, to the extent that American culture has associated homosexuality with a cluster of sexual meanings such as multiple sex partners, public sex, and recreational sex, polluting homosexuality also discredited these practices. Heterosexuals who engaged in these behaviors experienced something of the defiled status of homosexuals.

Polluting the homosexual, then, functioned to defend both heterosexual privilege and a specific heterosexual and gender order.

Midnight Cowboy (1969) expressed something of the rebellious spirit of the time. For example, the figure of Joe Buck (Jon Voight) gave expression to a culture that valued individuals who fashioned lives independently of social roles and standard conventions.

Joe is a handsome, small-town, working-class Texan who sets out to make his fortune in New York by hustling women. Through the character of Joe, the film explores and cautiously endorses a culture of sexual variation. For example, scenes of commercial sex are depicted in a morally neutral way. Indeed, the women he has sex with are presented as sexually autonomous; they make sexual choices based on need and desire. Joe seems to flourish in the giving and receiving of sexual pleasure, as do the women.

Although the film is tolerant toward sexual variation, homosexuality is off limits. Both Ratso (Dustin Hoffman) and Joe view the homosexual as a despicable human type. Ratso, the lowest of street hustlers, is aggressively hostile toward homosexuals. He refers to them as "faggots," a term signaling their defiled moral status. And Joe, who turns to men after he proves inept in hustling women, is repulsed by homosexuals. In one scene, an older, closeted man purchases Joe's sexual favors. However, this man is unable to go through with the sexual exchange for reasons that apparently have to do with his religious convictions. Despite being paid, Joe assaults the man because, we are led to believe, the mere anticipation of homosexual sex is so disgusting and repulsive to him. Joe avoids any taint of being homosexual by both his homophobic actions and repeated flashbacks to a past girlfriend.

As this film explores an underground world of street people, hustlers, and sexual rebels, it is not merely coincidental that the figure of the polluted homosexual appears time and again. Gay "queens" and closet types, along with countercultural figures whose gender presentation and erotic fluidity might suggest homosexuality, are a striking presence. At one level, the polluted homosexual serves to establish a clear, absolute moral boundary for legitimate sexual variation. Heterosexuality is the exclusive field of legitimate sexuality. But the haunting presence of the polluted homosexual suggests that this figure performs a further boundary-defining role. The continuous juxtaposition of homosexuality and "deviant" sexualities (for example, commercial sex, public sex, casual sex) suggests the dangers of an eroticism loosened from its solid mooring in love, intimacy, marriage, and the family. In other words, the figure of the polluted homosexual is perhaps a cultural response to the sense of danger and disorder that surrounded the relaxation of sexual controls.

In *Five Easy Pieces* (1970), Bobby (Jack Nicholson) steps forward as a sexual rebel. Although he lives with his girlfriend, Bobby has sex with many women, sometimes at the same time and sometimes with prostitutes. The movie portrays Bobby's sexual behavior as meaningful, and valuable, not only as a medium of intimate love but also as a form of pleasure and self-expression. In the spirit of the 1960s, the film seems open toward Bobby's ethic of self- and sexual experimentation. His freewheeling, guiltless eroticism is presented as an almost pure realm of self-expression and freedom.

Bobby's pursuit of sexual variation, however, does not extend to homosexuality. Despite exploring a wide range of nonconventional sexual behaviors, Bobby has no homosexual encounters. Indeed, his masculine swagger and (hetero) sexual bravado establishes Bobby's unequivocal heterosexual identity.

Bobby's sexual experimentation is tolerated because it is confined to the field of heterosexuality. If his sexual adventures included homosexuality, he would have likely forfeited a normal and respectable status. However, to the extent that he prefers erotic play over marriage and family values, Bobby's character looks more and more like the cultural stereotype of the irresponsible, sex driven, dangerous homosexual.

In the course of the film, Bobby's self-control weakens. Desire threatens to take over his life. His passion ceases to be playful; it becomes menacing. Thus, Bobby not only cheats on his girlfriend, but he has an affair with his brother's fiancée. And in a final scene in which Bobby must decide between marriage and sexual freedom, Bobby chooses the latter even though it means abandoning his pregnant girlfriend. As the quest for erotic pleasure and expressiveness becomes his chief sexual value, the film presents him as a social danger. Bobby's "liberated" sexuality threatens the institutions of marriage and the family—and ultimately endangers society by projecting a world of fatherless children. The fear of an eroticism that in its boundless quest for pleasure and excitement tears apart the fabric of moral order is a threat that has been closely associated with the homosexual.

Looking for Mr. Goodbar is, as we've seen, a coming-of-age story narrated as a journey of sexual self-exploration. Teresa grew up in a sexually repressed family. Having polio as a child reinforced feelings of shame around her body. Sexual liberation is her chosen path to adulthood. Teresa tries it all—one-night stands, paid sex, group sex, affairs with married men, and rough sex. Her sexual adventurousness is part of a struggle to be free of shame and guilt; it is her chosen path to freedom.

Teresa's sexual experimentation is exclusively heterosexual. In a scene depicting group sex, a woman invites Teresa to participate. She declines.

In the course of the film, a sense of danger surrounds Teresa's erotic openness. As her experimentation takes her further away from norms of sexual romanticism, marriage, and family making, it comes to signify a world of risk—to herself and society. For example, in one scene Teresa gets involved with a man (Richard Gere) whose free-spirited sexuality passes into sexual violence. And, in the end, Teresa's sexual adventurousness results in her brutal murder by, tellingly, a homosexual—the very symbol of a desire free from social convention.

In *All That Jazz* (1979) the "liberated" heterosexual is symbolically associated with the homosexual. This movie offers a portrait of an artist, Joe Gideon (Roy Schneider). His creativity in the theater, dance, and movie worlds is depicted as inseparable from his sexual adventurousness. Joe has a regular lover but also has sex with friends and especially with younger aspiring artists. The film presents his sexuality as an expression of a creative artist who is responsive to subconscious desires. His artistic and sexual creativity seems to have no boundaries, except when it comes to homosexuality. Joe may violate many sexual norms, but he is unambiguously, aggressively straight.

And yet, Joe exhibits an almost stereotypical gay male pattern that associates sex exclusively with its sensual and expressive qualities. The association of Joe's eroticism with homosexuality is further suggested by his gender nonconventionality and, most pointedly, by his social location in the world of dance and the theater.

In the course of the 1960s and 1970s, sexual norms were being renegotiated to permit more individual choice. Reflecting the times, these films explore the moral meaning of a culture of sexual variation. Homosexuality is used to establish moral boundaries. The exclusive legitimacy of heterosexuality is established by polluting homosexuality. Moreover, to the extent that homosexuality was associated with specific behaviors such as multiple-partner sex, recreational sex, a body- and pleasure-centered sexuality, or public sex, its defiled status also meant the pollution of these behaviors. To the extent that characters such as Bobby, Teresa, and Joe champion an eroticism that uncouples the pleasurable and expressive qualities of sex from love, marriage, and the family, they evoke the very same fears of social disorder associated with the homosexual. Introducing the figure of the polluted homosexual regulates sexuality by restricting legitimate sexual variation to heterosexuality and to a narrow heterosexual pattern. The homosexual circulates, so to speak, as a free-floating signifier of a dangerous desire.

Turning our attention to films that portray gays as normal, I found, unexpectedly, a tightening of heterosexual regulation. These films retreat from a culture that values expanded sexual choice and variation. Heterosexual practices that deviate from a narrow romantic-companionate norm are devalued and disrespected. Indeed, gay normalization, at least in the films of the 1990s, is accompanied by a sexual ethic that legitimates sex—for both heterosexuals and homosexuals—exclusively in intimate, preferably love-based, monogamous, preferably marital-type relationships. *In other words, these films establish a division between the good and bad sexual citizen that is uncoupled from the hetero/homosexual binary.* The narrowing of the range of legitimate sexual variation is a response to fears of moral and social disorder raised by gay normalization. The social integration of gays creates an anxiety that other "deviant" sexualities (sex workers, sadomasochists, pedophiles, polygamists) will make similar claims to normality and also demand respectability. Bringing homosexuality into the American heartland evokes fears of unleashing an unbridled eroticism that will bring chaos and decline.

In and Out uses humor and parody to mock homosexual pollution. Gays are viewed as normal Americans. But, as we've seen, the ideal of heterosexuality is not threatened. Heterosexual marriage and the family are celebrated. After Howard's coming-out scene, the movie ends, tellingly, with a renewal of his parent's wedding vows after fifty years of marriage. The idealization of marriage not only serves to reinforce the norm of heterosexuality but to enforce a particular heterosexual norm—lifetime marriage based on love and family obligations.

The narrowing of legitimate heterosexual behavior to a romantic intimate norm is dramatized in the character of Cameron Drake (Matt Dillon). Cameron, the Oscar-winning movie star, lives a "Hollywood lifestyle." He is surrounded by beautiful women and lives lavishly. Cameron returns to Greenleaf, where he grew up, to help Howard. Unexpectedly, he falls in love with Howard's ex-fiancée, who, in contrast to his beautiful bimbo girlfriend, is a plain-looking, overweight, clumsy, small-town high school teacher. The film creates a good/bad moral division between the hedonistic, narcissistic sexual values associated with Hollywood and the romantic, marital, and family values of Greenleaf.

In and Out was a huge commercial success in part because it trades on a nostalgic image of America. It champions an America in which individuals marry as virgins for love, in which marriage inevitably leads to family, and in which men and women occupy different and complementary social and sexual roles. The real threat to America is not the normal gay, who is a variation of the ideal national citizen, but hedonistic, narcissistic, and consumerist sexual and social values that are dramatically symbolized by Hollywood culture.

The tightening of heterosexual regulation that accompanies gay normalization is also evident in *As Good as It Gets* and *The Object of My Affection*. In the former film, the central drama is a romantic love story oriented toward marriage. Neither Melvin nor Carol has sex with anyone before they declare their love for each other. This romantic comedy depicts a virginal courtship that is based on love and that will end, we are led to believe, in marriage and a family. The audience sits comfortably with a normalized gay character in part because this movie recalls an almost 1950s ideal of a love-based, virginal marriage with a breadwinner husband and, if not a domestic wife, then a motherly one.

The harkening back to an idealized, illusory past is to some degree absent from *The Object of My Affection*. This film in certain respects stretches the normative boundaries of American sexual culture.

Nina is an attractive Manhattan woman who is independent and nonconventional in many ways. For example, she rejects her sister's consumer- and status-oriented lifestyle for a low-rent walk-up apartment and a low-paying job working with underprivileged adolescent women of color. Her nonconventionality is conveyed in her decision to live with George, despite his being gay and to her boyfriend's dismay. Yet the chief drama of the film revolves around Nina's desire to be a mother—and George's wish to be a father. Moreover, throughout the film, Nina is either in a monogamous intimate relationship or falling in love with George. And George is either breaking up with his ex-boyfriend or establishing a new romantic relationship. The film establishes a binary: sex coupled to love and monogamous intimacy is valued, while sex for pleasure apart from love and marriage is devalued.

Ironically, then, as films of the 1990s champion a notion of the normal gay they also narrow the range of legitimate sexual-intimate choices, for gays and for straights. As the normal gay assumes the status of a respectable citizen, it is the "bad" sexual citizen, defined by his or her violation of a romantic, monogamous intimate norm, that is polluted. The division between the good and the bad sexual citizen may make it possible for the normal lesbian and the gay man to become full American citizens, but one effect is a tightening of sexual controls for all citizens.

One of the few Hollywood films of the 1990s that positively explores a fluid, expansive erotic culture is *Threesome* (1994). The film narrates a coming-of-age story of three college students who share a dorm suite.

Eddy (Josh Charles) is gay but only acknowledges this in the course of the film. His coming out is quick and relatively painless. In fact, Stuart (Stephen Baldwin) "outs" Eddy.

> STUART: I think you were checking out my butt yesterday. Are you a homo?
>
> EDDY: Fuck off.
>
> STUART: It doesn't bother me. I'm secure enough about my own sexuality to not be threatened by it. I don't have anything against homosexuals. I mean you are what you are.

Later that day Stuart casually remarks to Alex (Lara Boyle), "Guess what, Eddy is a proud homo." Eddy doesn't dispute Stuart's statement. In fact, Eddy argues that sex between men or between women is superior because each gender knows its own sexual needs and how to satisfy them.

Eddy exemplifies the idea of the normal gay. He is gender conventional, an excellent student, a loyal friend, and exhibits valued civic qualities such as self-control, rationality, modesty, empathy, and respect for social rules and the law.

If Eddy is respectable and sexually repressed, Stuart is nonconventional and sexually expressive. Stuart is body and pleasure oriented and freewheeling in his sexuality. In other words, Stuart is a heterosexual who exhibits many of the sexual values and practices that are stereotypically associated with gay men. Until the final scene, the film celebrates Stuart's eroticism and sensual exuberance in contrast to Eddy's repressed sexuality and unhealthy asceticism. In this regard, Eddy's coming of age revolves less around coming out as gay than around accepting an expressive, exuberant eroticism. In other words, the film's critical edge is less about contesting homosexual pollution than about challenging a good/bad sexual citizen binary that would associate Eddy with the former and Stuart with the latter. Thus, in a triumphant scene virtually announcing the subversion of the good/bad sexual citizen division, the three friends are in bed together. Spontaneously, they start kissing and soon they're naked. We see Stuart and Eddy passionately kissing Alex; Stuart reaches across Alex to bring Eddy's hand to his much-coveted butt, signaling the film's ideal of a sexual-intimate order that is not regulated by the hetero/homosexual binary nor by a narrow notion of the good sexual citizen.

In the end, the film retreats from this sexual ethic of erotic play and variation. Stuart becomes hysterical when he learns that Alex may be pregnant. Astonishingly, he tries to kill himself. We see him lying on the bathroom floor crying and rambling incoherently about finding Jesus. He wants to be castrated, as his exuberant sensuality is now understood as self-destructive. The movie ends with the narrator explaining that Stuart subsequently married. A final scene shows him groomed for corporate life, symbolizing his coming of age as a respectable, "normal" adult. Stuart's "queer" eroticism turns out to be an adolescent phase on his way to the maturity of being a good sexual citizen.

THE TROUBLE WITH NORMAL

Between 1960 and 2000, Hollywood films have gradually, if unevenly, exchanged polluting for normalizing images of lesbians and gay men. The significance of this development should not be discounted. Extending the status of normal to homosexuality weakens a culture of shame and self-deprecation; it furnishes a forceful rationale for making claims for individual rights, cultural respect, and social inclusion; it permits individuals to live an ordinary existence in which decisions about love, friendship, work, or place of residence can be made without considering the need to hide or deceive. In short, it makes possible a life beyond the closet.

There are reasons to pause in the face of this cultural change. While blatant homophobic representations have less credibility and perhaps less social force, subtle stereotyping persists. If the effeminate queen or mannish lesbian is as likely to be viewed as a bigoted stereotype as laughed at, the subtle feminization of gay men and the sometimes buffoonish and almost always sexless presentation of lesbians and gay men indicate a resistance to gays' equal social status. *Until gay men and lesbians routinely play lead roles, until they are presented as fully sexual and in loving relationships, until gay women and people of color are a reg-*

ular presence in films, and until gays are presented from the standpoint of a subculture that is critical of heterosexual privilege, media representations at best promote a fairly narrow type of social tolerance, not equality.

Moreover, films that champion the normal gay establish a division between the good and the bad gay citizen. The good gay functions as a narrow social norm; she must be gender conventional, committed to romantic-companionate and family values, uncritically patriotic, and detached from a subculture. The normal gay just wants to blend in, to be an ordinary American. The normal gay does not challenge or threaten the norm of heterosexuality. Moreover, individuals who deviate from this norm—for example, gays who are gender benders, who like sex apart from love or intimacy, or gays who want to change society—may not gain entry into the magical circle of normality and respectability.

I've also suggested that gay normalization doesn't necessarily lead to expanded choice for straight Americans. In films that normalize gays, there is a tightening of heterosexual regulation. Films such as *Philadelphia* and *In and Out* appeal to strikingly nostalgic images of an America of small towns, of men who work and women who mother, of virgin courtship and marriages that last a lifetime, and of Gemeinschaft-like communities. This is an America that is intolerant of sexual variation—of sexually active youths, of children born outside of marriage, of cohabitation, of multiple sex partners, of an eroticism loosened from the grip of romantic love and intimacy. Only individuals whose behavior conforms to norms of the good sexual citizen can claim the full privileges of heterosexuality.

Gay normalization does not cause a retreat from a culture that values sexual variation. There are many social factors, from gender politics to sex panics around youth sexuality, teen pregnancy, single mothers, and sexual disease, that might account for the social pressures to narrow the range of legitimate sexual choice. Still, I think that the link between gay normalization and the tightening of social control is more than coincidental. Assigning a fully human, normal status to gay individuals fuels a fear of disorder because of the association of homosexuality with a freewheeling, promiscuous desire. It also creates a fear that other sexual outsiders will demand inclusion, further fueling anxieties of impending disorder. It is to be expected that every step toward gay integration will likely prompt some opposition that will appeal to fears of children being confused and abused, of families and marriages being weakened, and of a nation tumbling down the path toward moral chaos.

As gays are viewed as normal, they are no longer necessarily associated with the bad sexual citizen. Of course, the homosexual was never the only bad sexual citizen; there was the prostitute, the sex offender, pornographer, and the sexual libertine. Still, in the early postwar years the homosexual emerged as the personification of the menacing sexual citizen. The homosexual became a kind of symbol of a perverse, dangerous eroticism that was detached from romantic, marital, and family values. Accordingly, the hetero/homosexual division came to serve as an important regulatory force. This has changed somewhat as gays are viewed as normal; designation as the good or the bad sexual citizen is less dependent on sexual identity. The bad citizen today is someone who violates romantic, intimate, familial norms, regardless of his or her sexual identity. The bad sexual citizen, not the homosexual, at least not the normal gay, is becoming a chief focus of social control.

CHAPTER FIVE

From Outsider to Citizen

The 1950s and 1960s were not easy times to be different. The Cold War, the red scare, and a culture of patriotism promoted a narrow ideal of the American citizen. He loved his country, worked hard, married the girl next door, and fathered happy children. (Or, loved her country, stayed at home, and was a dutiful wife and mother.) This good citizen was, of course, heterosexual, preferably white, middle class, and churchgoing, and took front and center stage with a vengeance. Think of Ward and June Cleaver. As this nation aggressively made heterosexuality into a condition of citizenship, gays became "aliens," outsiders in a nation that many had just recently risked their lives for.

Many gays in the 1950s and 1960s perhaps suffered more because they were damned to silence and invisibility than because of an open, aggressive homophobic culture (something that truly crystallized after Stonewall). We need to be mindful that gays barely registered on the screen of popular culture in the immediate postwar years.[1] Outside major urban centers it is likely that few people were either very aware of, or particularly exercised over, the issue of homosexuality. Career, marriage, family making, home, the Soviet threat—these were the preoccupations of most Americans.

Ironically, the barely noticed presence of gays allowed some of them to carve out inconspicuous social lives. These often courageous individuals cautiously sought out those few public spaces where others like themselves could be found. Despite considerable risk, gay men searched out cruising spaces (parks, tearooms, highway stops, YMCAs), while lesbians discovered each other in such spaces as bars and softball leagues.[2]

But these tentative steps into public life were marked by a sense of fear. The places where gays gathered were often under surveillance and lacked a solid institutional footing. Bars would be raided and closed down; parks and tearooms were subject to police patrols; and softball leagues were seasonal. There was risk, often great, for anyone who ventured into these public places. Gays were vulnerable to arrest, harassment, violence, and public exposure, which threatened social disgrace and worse.

In the day-to-day struggle to eke out some sense of a gay life, individuals encountered a government intent on preventing this. Gays not only lacked basic legal rights (for example, to freely associate), but they encountered governmental authorities (federal, state, and local) that were aggressively turning against them. Moral reformers, politicians, and public officials wishing to brandish their moral purity enlisted the state to persecute homosexuals. Perhaps the most infamous of the time, and now known to have been a closeted homosexual himself, was the director of the FBI, J. Edgar Hoover. In this atmosphere of heightened risk and fear, many individuals understandably chose to pass as straight. The closet was a product of both cultural defilement and the repressive, coercive power of the state.

If the social status of gays has changed between the 1950s and today, it is not only because of a change in American culture. Stepping outside the closet would not have been possible without at least some individuals and some elites (e.g., newspaper editors, writers, or politicians) redefining homosexuality as something natural and good. Yet tens of thousands of Americans can today choose to live outside the closet only because the state has retreated from its campaigns of homosexual persecution.

Gays are becoming citizens. But what kind of citizens are they becoming? And what kind of citizens should they be?

GAYS AS "ALIENS"

From the founding years of America through the nineteenth century, sex laws were passed with the primary aim of strengthening marriage. Nonmarital and nonprocreative sexual behaviors were proscribed. Accordingly, a wide range of sexual practices, from fornication and adultery to "lewd and lascivious" behavior, were criminalized. A culture of sexual respectability took shape that valued sex only between married adults in the privacy of their home and for the purpose of procreation.[3]

Through most of the nineteenth century, the American government was not especially involved in regulating homosexuality, at least not enough to direct the criminal justice system to aggressively suppress homosexual behavior. The very term *homosexual*, or terms like *invert* and *Urning* that circulated in Europe in the nineteenth century, were absent from the American vernacular.[4] In fact, there were no laws that focused exclusively on homosexuality.[5] Homosexual behavior was classified and punished under the category of "sodomy." Initially understood as a sinful immoral act, in the course of the nineteenth century sodomy was reinterpreted as a criminal offense that included a wide spectrum of nonprocreative, nonmarital sexual acts such as oral or anal sex or sex with an animal.[6] The fact that few individuals were convicted of homosexual sodomy until the last decades of the nineteenth century speaks to its marginal status in Victorian sexual culture.[7] At the same time, the adoption of sodomy laws by most states and the severity of the punishment for those convicted (whipping, banishment, and imprisonment) speaks to the status of homosexual behavior as outside of respectable society.

Restricting sex to a private, marital, and procreative act was the ideal. Victorians believed that sex should have a high moral purpose. Sex should be a way to display moral self-control and could acquire meaning as a selfless act under the guise of the need to create a family. The realities of the time no doubt greatly disappointed the keepers of moral virtue. A world of illicit sex flourished, especially in seaports, mining towns, and large cities.[8] Regulating sexual behavior was by and large the responsibility of the family, churches, and various moral reform and purity groups. The state mostly stayed out of the business of regulating its citizens' intimate affairs. For example, although contraception and abortion was illegal, these practices were widespread and barely regulated by the state.

In the course of the nineteenth century, this laissez-faire state practice was criticized for being unable to address what some people viewed as threats to the Victorian ideal of sexual respectability. Pornography and prostitution were somewhat tolerated, so long as these vices were far removed from respectable society. This sexual underworld, however, began to find its way into the lives of ordinary Americans through romance novels and magazines. The very heart of Victorian culture, its ideal of marriage, seemed threatened by another, unprecedented development: the rise of divorce. By the 1920s, scholars estimate, one in six marriages was ending in divorce.[9] In short, the Victorian cultural ideal of sexual respectability was threatened by a new set of realities that were becoming undeniable: a world of sex outside marriage.

Sensing a crisis in American sexual culture, social reformers turned to the state to enforce a Victorian sexual morality. Against the grain of a long-standing American tradition that championed privacy, the state took greater responsibility for regulating individuals' sexual lives.

Between 1860 and 1890, forty states enacted anti-abortion statutes.[10] This legislation was initially spearheaded by a variety of so-called purity groups and moral crusaders. Medical doctors soon joined the battle to end abortion. A fledging American Medical Association sought to enhance its power in relation to other medical practitioners by backing the criminalization of abortion. The historians John D'Emilio and Estelle Freedman write that "by the end of the century, the physicians campaign to criminalize abortion had succeeded. . . . Congress had outlawed the dissemination of birth control information through the mails; many states restricted the sale or advertising of contraceptive devices. . . . Comstock was waging a ceaseless battle to enforce these laws. . . . Large sectors of the medical profession were declaring against artificial methods to limit fertilization. Birth control information had virtually been driven underground."[11]

Paralleling this campaign against abortion, an alliance of suffragists, purity crusaders, and the AMA backed sweeping anti-prostitution legislation. For example, the American Social Hygiene Association proposed legislation that would give states wide latitude in regulating commercial sex. Provisions such as the "Red Light Abatement Acts" would authorize states to regulate saloons, dance halls, and bars, as well as the people that owned and managed them. Another statute permitted ordinary citizens to petition to close places suspected of harboring prostitutes. Such aggressive, far-reaching anti-prostitution laws were promoted in state after state. As the sociologist Kristin Luker notes, "By 1920, ten states had passed laws that enacted these provisions . . . and thirty-two states had laws that enacted at least some of these provisions."[12]

Social groups enlisting the state to defend the purity of women, marriage, and the family also launched an attack on public sexual images. The courts and state legislatures expanded the legal meaning of obscenity in order to suppress sexual representations in public life. "The American courts heard very few obscenity cases between 1821 and 1870. . . . Only four state legislatures enacted obscenity laws prior to the civil war." However, in 1873 the Congress passed "an act for the suppression of trade in, and circulation of obscene literature and articles of immoral use."[13] By the early twentieth century, virtually every state monitored books, art, or magazines for their sexual content; this extended beyond pulp novels and pornography to literary publications and sex-education and birth-control documents.

Finally, a powerful eugenics movement successfully enlisted the state to promote an aggressive policy of sterilization. Invoking fears of the spread of sexual immorality and mental feebleness stemming from interracial intimacy, this movement targeted people of color, the poor, rebellious youths, immigrants, and other unruly, outsider groups for sterilization. Legal scholars Linda Hirshman and Jane Larson observe,

"By 1930 half of the states had enacted compulsory sterilization laws. These laws covered convicted criminals, but also persons considered 'feebleminded' or suspected of 'sexual immorality.' In the first third of the century, approximately 20,000 involuntary sterilizations were performed by order of state law."[14]

By the early twentieth century, birth control, abortion, interracial marriage, prostitution, commercial sex, forced sterilization, and public sexual representations had become the business of the state. The state now exercised unprecedented control of the sexual-intimate lives of Americans. "Sex law, once limited to prohibiting adultery, rape and whoredom or lewd behavior, by the end of the nineteenth century ran to pages of elaborate and detailed prohibitions."[15]

While the web of governmental control of heterosexual behavior expanded by leaps and bounds between the 1860s and World War I, homosexuality was only marginally targeted. For example, in his highly regarded book *Gay New York*, the historian George Chauncey argues that while laws prohibiting cross-dressing, loitering, solicitation, and public lewdness were sometimes used to control homosexuality, New York municipal authorities were erratic in their persecution of homosexuals.[16] There was an informal understanding that gays were to be tolerated so long as they moderated their public visibility. In fact, Chauncey documents a fairly robust public gay life that in many respects was integrated into the mainstream of New York. Contrary to standard accounts of the pre-Stonewall past as blanketed by silence and invisibility, Chauncey holds that, at least in New York, an open gay life flourished in bars, cafés, speakeasies, certain streets, cafeterias, and grand balls.[17]

In the years between the two world wars, the tide slowly, if unevenly, began to turn. State control of consensual heterosexual adult behavior was relaxed. For example, a flourishing birth-control movement challenged its criminalization. Restrictive birth-control legislation such as laws prohibiting the advertising of birth-control devices were repealed. One result was the takeoff of the condom industry and the easy availability of condoms. Another result was the establishment in 1942 of the Planned Parenthood Federation of America.

Championing contraception as a legitimate strategy of family planning, birth-control clinics cropped up in cities and towns across the country. And while abortions were still illegal, they were widespread and rarely prosecuted. Similarly, by the 1940s sexually provocative images began to regularly appear in the public realm. Big business had discovered that sex sells, and artists and writers found in sex a powerful avenue to explore the character of personal and social life in America. This new sexual openness was met with opposition by organizations such as the National Organization of Decent Literature, but the tide had already turned.

The retreat of the state from controlling consensual adult heterosexual conduct and expression continued in the decades following World War II. State liberalization is evident in sex-law reforms and court decisions.

In 1962, the Model Penal Code became the most important guide to legal reform through the 1970s and 1980s.[18] A product of the American Law Institute, sex law was recast in a way to expand personal choice. The code aimed to decriminalize adult consensual behavior. Its guiding idea was that sex is an individual right. Sex was thought to be so integral to individual well-being that sexual choice needed to be protected from the arbitrary interference of other citizens and the government.

The code became the model for criminal legal reform; it shaped a series of key court decisions that expanded sexual rights. For example, in *Skinner v. Oklahoma* (1942) the courts struck down the practice of sterilizing individuals convicted of a wide range of nonsexual crimes. Subsequent court decisions decriminalized fornication and declared unconstitutional laws that banned or limited birth-control practices such as the use of contraceptives. In *Griswold v. Connecticuit* (1965) the Supreme Court declared state laws that criminalized the use of contraceptives by married couples unconstitutional. The Court appealed to a zone of privacy in marriage that was said to be established by the Constitution. This court decision in effect recognized the legitimacy of nonprocreative sex. In *Eisenstadt v. Baird* (1972), the courts extended this protection to unmarried couples. Nowhere has the retreat of the state from intimate life been more apparent than in the sphere of the heterosexual family. One scholar has argued that "over the past twenty-five years, family law has become increasingly privatized. In virtually all doctrinal areas, private norm creation and private decision making have supplanted state-imposed rules and structures for governing family-related behavior."[19] In short, a clear trend in court rulings defined sex as an important sphere of personal expression or individual choice that, like religious or occupational choice, merits state protection.

The legal safeguarding of consensual adult heterosexual behavior in private was paralleled by the liberalization of laws regulating public sex speech. In *Roth v. U.S.* (1957), the Supreme Court ruled that "obscenity" covers only sex speech that appeals to clear prurient interests. Subsequent cases further weakened obscenity laws. In *Memoirs of a Woman of Pleasure v. Mass.* (1966), the court narrowed what was to be considered obscene to material "utterly without redeeming social importance." In *Miller v. Ca.* (1973) the Court further liberalized public sex speech by appealing to "community standards" as the criteria to determine obscenity. Commenting on the consequences of the retreat of the state from regulating public sexual materials, D'Emilio and Freedman write, "From the 1930s onward . . . the courts in the United States steadily narrowed the definition of obscenity until . . . they had virtually removed barriers . . . against the presentation of sexual matter in literature and other media."[20]

By strengthening a zone of privacy that included sex, and by expanding protections for public sex speech, the postwar state enlarged the sphere of sexual autonomy for heterosexual adults. These reforms in sex laws were a return to long-standing American traditions championing minimal state regulation of consensual adult intimate behavior.[21]

As the state was relaxing controls over heterosexual behavior, homosexuality became the focus of considerable social regulation between the 1930s and 1960s. For the first time in American history, the state mobilized its growing authority and resources to control same-sex behavior.

Gay individuals initially stepped into the public eye in the later decades of the nineteenth century. If ordinary citizens weren't directly exposed to such individuals, newspapers began to report gatherings of so-called sexual and gender deviants. Already geared up to combat vice of all kinds, the guardians of a Victorian morality expanded the scope of their crusade to include people who engaged in sodomy. The state was enlisted to suppress these acts of sexual and gender deviance. Existing laws were now being enforced, and new legislation was enacted to address this perceived social danger.[22] In particular, cross-dressing laws figured prominently because of the association of homosexuality with gender inversion. Despite agitation by moral crusaders, governmental agencies acted spottily rather than launching a full-scale methodical campaign of homosexual persecution.

This changed in the 1930s and dramatically so in the postwar period: the state stepped forward as the chief guardian of a respectable heterosexual order. Homosexuals were to be pursued, persecuted, and prosecuted. Chauncey writes,

> The very growth and visibility of the gay subculture during the Prohibition years of the 1920s and 1930s precipitated a powerful cultural reaction in the 1930s [and] . . . a new anxiety about homosexuals and hostility toward them. . . . A host of laws and regulations were enacted or newly enforced in the 1930s that suppressed the largest of the drag balls, censored lesbian and gay images in plays and films, and prohibited restaurants, bars, and clubs from employing homosexuals or even serving them.[23]

By the 1950s and 1960s, as homosexuals were being publicly demonized as an invisible, menacing threat, government agencies were issuing executive orders and enacting new laws aimed at persecuting them. Homosexuals, real or suspected, were routinely arrested and their names and places of employment often printed in newspapers; they were discharged from the military and civil service; denied immigration; harassed in bars and the streets; their businesses or businesses they frequented were closed; and their publications were censored and destroyed.

The legal scholar William Eskridge summarizes the status of the homosexual in 1960:

> The homosexual in 1961 was smothered by law. She or he risked arrest . . . for dancing with someone of the same sex, cross dressing, propositioning another adult homosexual, possessing a homophile publication, writing about homosexuality without disapproval, displaying pictures of two people of the same sex in intimate positions, operating a lesbian or gay bar, or actually having oral or anal sex with another adult homosexual. . . . Misdemeanor arrests for sex related vagrancy or disorderly conduct offences meant that the homosexual might have her or his name published in the local newspaper, would probably lose her or his job. . . . If the homosexual were not a citizen, she or he would likely be deported. If the homosexual were a professional . . . she or he would lose the certification needed to practice that profession. If the charged homosexual were a member of the armed forces, she or he might be court-martialed and would likely be dishonorably discharged and lose all veterans benefits.[24]

Eskridge concludes, "This new legal regime represented society's coercive effort to normalize human relationships around 'heterosexuality.'"[25] The effort by the state to "normalize" heterosexuality between the 1930s and 1960s helped create what we've come to call the closet.

BECOMING CITIZENS

Sex laws and policies are guided by a norm of the good sexual citizen. By criminalizing and disenfranchising certain sexual acts, identities, or intimate arrangements, the state helps to create a sexual hierarchy. Some acts or identities are tolerated but barely; others are not tolerated at all; still other sexual expressions are deemed so intolerable that those who engage in them are scandalized as "bad sexual citizens"—immoral and dangerous to society. Bad sexual citizens become the targets of social control, which may include public stereotyping, harassment, violence, criminalization, and disenfranchisement. In the early decades of the twentieth century, women who had children out of wedlock, sexually active youths, adults who sexually desired youths, and individuals who engaged in interracial sex were often labeled bad sexual citizens.

The good sexual citizen was most definitely heterosexual. However, it was only after World War II that homosexuals became perhaps the personification of the bad sexual citizen. As they took on the role of a social and moral menace, a network of controls evolved that had the effect of creating the closet. And the closet clearly marked gays as outsiders, as moral, social, and political aliens.

As the closet became the defining reality for many gay Americans, a political movement took shape that challenged this condition. This movement was and still is divided between, roughly speaking, a "liberationist" and an "assimilationist" ideology and agenda.

If assimilationists aim to broaden the notion of the good sexual citizen to include homosexuals, liberationists challenge this ideal. If the norm of the good sexual citizen defines sex exclusively as a private act, liberationists defend public forms of sexuality (for example, sex in parks, tearooms, or bath houses); if the ideal sexual citizen is gender conventional, liberationists aim to scramble gender norms such that being active or passive, aggressive or submissive, is not coded as masculine or feminine; if the good sexual citizen tightly binds sex to love or intimacy, liberationists relax the bond, allowing for legitimate sex within and outside intimacy; and if the ideal sexual citizen is married, liberationists advocate either the end of state regulation of adult intimate relationships or state recognition of a diversity of families. In short, assimilationists want homosexuals to be recognized and accepted as good sexual citizens; liberationists challenge the sexual norms associated with this ideal.

A liberationist politics emerged after the Stonewall rebellions in 1969.[26] Liberationists opposed the system of compulsory heterosexuality that produced the closet. They were also critical of the assimilationist politics of the Mattachine Society and the Daughters of Bilitis, which, they argued, left heterosexual domination in place.

Gay liberationism arose during a time of extraordinary social turmoil. The protests against the Vietnam War and the rise of militant, in-your-face movements for racial and gender justice stirred hopes of revolutionary change. Liberationists absorbed the spirit of radical feminism, lesbian feminism, and black liberation. Gays were not just the targets of prejudice and discrimination but were oppressed by a heterosexual dictatorship. Writes one liberationist, "One is oppressed as a homosexual every minute of every day, inasmuch as one is restrained from acting in ways that would seem normal to a heterosexual. Every time one refrains from an act of public affection with a lover—in the park, on the movie line—one dies a little. And gay people, of course, die a little every day. . . . Everything in society—every movie, every billboard, everything . . . reminds the gay person that what he or she is is unnatural, abnormal."[27] Liberation required dismantling the "system." The fight for gay justice was viewed as inseparable from struggles to transform gender roles, the institution of marriage and the family, and the political economy of capitalism and imperialism.[28] Challenging gay oppression meant changing America, from top to bottom.

The early 1970s were the heroic years for gay liberationism. Groups such as the Gay Liberation Front, the Fairies, the Furies, and Radicalesbians created their own political organizations, published newspapers, newsletters, and books, and forged distinctive cultures with their own ideologies. They marched, organized sit-ins, met with newspaper editors, appeared on television, published manifestos, and formed alliances with other movements. Their militancy and almost swaggering sense of pride and confidence was for many individuals a welcome departure from the subdued, cautious politics of assimilationism that had dominated the 1950s and 1960s. For a moment it looked as if liberationism would become the chief political and cultural force in gay life.

This did not happen. By the mid-1970s, gay liberationism virtually disappeared as an organized political movement. Many liberationist groups dissolved or were greatly weakened by the incessant battles over ideology and strategy. Their Marxist or radical feminist rhetoric, which portrayed America as fundamentally corrupt and in need of a revolution, alienated many gays who gravitated toward reform-minded groups such as the Gay Activist Alliance. In the end, liberationism proved more effective in shifting gay politics away from the cautious assimilationism of the previous decades than at mobilizing mass support for its own radical vision and agenda.

Liberationists never managed more than a marginal presence in organized gay politics after the mid-1970s. Yet artists, writers, activists, and academics have sustained its critical spirit. And, in response to AIDS and an organized anti-gay politics from the late 1970s onward, a broadly liberationist political agenda surfaced in the organized politics of ACT UP, Queer Nation, Lesbian Avengers, and Sex Panic![29] Except perhaps for ACT UP, none of these groups managed more than a short-lived organizational life. Liberationism lives on primarily as a cultural sensibility.

An assimilationist agenda has been and still is the driving force of the gay movement.[30] Although there are differences among assimilationists, they share an agenda aimed at bringing the homosexual into the circle of sexual citizenship. These reformers do not wish to change America beyond altering the status of gays from outsider to citizen. An assimilationist agenda does not necessarily protest the dominant status of heterosexuality; it's about minority rights, not toppling the majority. Nor do these reformers wish to challenge the broader spectrum of sexual-intimate norms that govern behavior, such as the norm of marriage, monogamy, or gender norms of sexuality. Assimilationists press America to live up to its promise of equal treatment of all of its citizens; they wish to be a part of what is considered a basically good nation; this requires reform, not revolution.[31]

In the initial wave of political organizing in the 1950s, the focus of an assimilationist politics was to end the harassment and persecution of homosexuals that was sanctioned and often initiated by the state. The key political organizations of the time were the male-oriented Mattachine Society and female-organized Daughters of Bilitis.[32] Without much public fanfare, these organizations cautiously but courageously, given the times, challenged state-driven discrimination. They protested the firing of homosexuals by government agencies and their persecution by the random enforcement of laws such as those prohibiting loitering, solicitation, lewdness, or cross-dressing. However, because they believed that the source of prejudice is ignorance or a misinformed view of homosexuals as different and dangerous, their chief political strategy was public education. Through sponsoring public talks, promoting research, and encouraging positive public role models to step forward, these organizations sought to persuade the public that homosexuals are no different from heterosexuals. The Mattachine Society declared that its chief task was to "dispel the idea that the sex variant is unique, 'queer' or unusual, but is instead a human being with the same capacities of feelings, thinking and accomplishment as any other human being."[33] The ultimate purpose was to end legal discrimination and public stereotyping; social integration would mean the end of the homosexual as a separate identity and subculture.

As the 1950s gave way to the 1960s a gay movement pursuing an assimilationist agenda grew more confident. Appealing to constitutional principles of privacy, due process, and basic rights of free speech and association, municipalities were taken to court to end street harassment and police entrapment, to halt bar raids and unnecessary search and seizure, and to stop government actions that shut down businesses catering to gays. For example, the California State Supreme Court and legislature took giant steps in deregulating consensual same-sex adult behavior by narrowing the meaning of public decency, lewdness, and vagrancy statutes so that they could no longer be used to persecute homosexuals. Most impressively, invoking recent judicial rulings gay organizations successfully challenged obscenity laws that were used to censor gay public speech (for example, in gay magazines, newsletters, books, art, and pornography).

By the mid-1970s, provoked and inspired by the defiant spirit of liberationism, a more assertive rights-oriented gay movement challenged laws that criminalized homosexuality. In the aftermath of the Griswold, Eisenstadt, and Stanley Supreme Court decisions, gay rights advocates argued that acknowledging the fundamental role of sexuality in personal liberty, which was at the heart of cases that extended privacy rights to adult private consensual sex, should apply to homosexuals as well. Appealing to a constitutional right to privacy and equal treatment, state laws that criminalized sodomy were challenged. By 1983, twenty-five states had decriminalized consensual sodomy, while eleven states reduced sodomy to a misdemeanor. In the 1990s, many states and cities banned anti-gay discrimination in state employment. And, while Congress has continued to block federal civil rights legislation that would include sexual orientation, the Civil Service Commission and ultimately a executive order by President Clinton, ended legal job discrimination in all federal agencies.

Strategies aimed at decriminalizing homosexuality were supplemented by deliberate efforts at gaining equal civil rights. From the mid-1970s on, the gay movement turned its attention and resources to gaining positive rights. In small towns and large cities across the country, organizations dedicated to enacting gay rights ordinances were formed. And well-financed, professional national organizations such as the Lambda Legal Defense, the National Lesbian and Gay Task Force, and the Human Rights Campaign made gaining equal civil rights the chief aim of a national gay movement. The intent of so-called gay rights laws is to get the state to recognize lesbians and gay men as citizens deserving the same positive liberties and protections as any other citizen. In the course of the 1970s, there were few victories—only forty communities passed gay rights. However, by 2000 the number had swelled to well over three hundred. Moreover, gay rights laws are no longer confined to urban centers but have been passed in small towns and suburban communities, and not just in the northeast and west, but in the south, midwest, and northwest. The wave of domestic partnership law beginning in the mid-1990s is indicative of moderate but real success at legal integration. By the late 1990s, 421 cities and states, and over 3,500 businesses or institutions of higher education offered some form of domestic partner benefit.[34]

William Eskridge summarizes the considerable gains toward legal and social integration during this period:

> The gay rights movement had won many successes by 1981—judicial nullification or legislative repeal of laws criminalizing consensual sodomy in most jurisdictions, of almost all state criminal laws targeting same-sex intimacy, and municipal cross-dressing ordinances, of the immigration and citizenship exclusions, of all censorship laws targeting same-sex eroticism, of almost all laws or regulations prohibiting bars from becoming congregating

> places for gay people, and of exclusions of gay people from public employment in most jurisdictions. . . . Since 1981 an increasing number of states and cities have adopted laws affirmatively protecting gay people against private discrimination and violence, recognizing gay families as domestic partnerships, and allowing second-parent adoptions by a party of a same-sex partner.[35]

This wave of legal reform made possible a "post-closeted regime where openly gay people could participate in the public culture."[36]

Legal reform has brought gays into the national community, but not as equal citizens. The battle over the meaning of legal and social equality has become the chief focus of the gay movement today.

TOLERATED BUT NOT EQUAL

The legal and social integration of gay Americans has not been an unqualified story of success, to say the least. A majority of cities and states lack laws that protect gay people from housing and job discrimination. The Federal Gay and Lesbian Civil Rights Bill, introduced in Congress in 1975, has virtually no hope of passage. The more modest Employment Non-Discrimination Act (ENDA), introduced in 1994, has few realistic prospects of passage at this time. The result: the jobs and homes of the overwhelming majority of gays and lesbians are not legally protected by any local, state, or federal laws. Moreover, anti-gay legislative proposals, at the local and state levels, may very well have exceeded positive legislative efforts in the 1990s. One analyst counts 472 cases of proposed anti-gay legislation.[37] And government policies such as "Don't ask don't tell" and the Defense of Marriage Act and judicial decisions like *Bowers v. Hartwick* (1986) and *The Boy Scouts of America and Monmouth Council, et al. v. James Dale* (2000) underscore gays' second-class citizenship status.

Many Americans stand opposed to the social integration of gays. They would like to reinstate the conditions of the closet or at least to maintain gays' status as outsiders.

Surveys document continued widespread moral disapproval. Polls through the early 1990s indicate that an overwhelming majority of

Americans believed that homosexuality is wrong or immoral.[38] Summarizing data from thirteen surveys between 1973 and 1991, two political scientists conclude, "Between 67 percent and 75 percent of respondents said that 'sexual relations between two adults of the same sex' were 'always wrong.'" However, researchers document a dramatic and unexpected shift in moral attitudes in the mid-1990s. "Surprisingly, given almost twenty years of stability, the percentage saying 'always wrong' dropped 15 percent between 1991 and 1996 [to 56 percent], suggesting the first major decline in disapproval."[39]

Moreover, as survey questions shift from abstract moral beliefs about homosexuality to the morality of discrimination, the trend toward social tolerance is even clearer. A majority of Americans—and in the late 1990s the support has climbed to around 70 to 80 percent—support a wide range of rights for gays. Assessing the available survey data, two researchers conclude, "Americans increasingly support civil liberties for gay people. Between 1973 and 1996, the percentages saying that 'a man who admits he is a homosexual' should 'be allowed to teach in a college' and 'to make a speech in your community' and who would *not* favor taking 'a book he wrote in favor of homosexuality . . . out of your public library' rose steadily by 28, 20, and 15 percent, respectively. By 1996, substantial majorities (75 percent, 81 percent, and 69 percent, respectively) supported each of these rights. Between 1977 and 1996, the percentage saying 'homosexuals should . . . have equal rights in terms of job opportunities' rose 27 percent (to 83 percent)."[40]

The battleground of gay politics is shifting away from whether or not gays should be socially integrated to the meaning of gay citizenship. The politics of the closet is hardly history; still, public anti-gay campaigns are increasingly local rather than national and are spearheaded by ad hoc groups that lack the backing of the state and often major cultural elites (for example, newspaper editors, television commentators, and national political and public figures). Indeed, the absence of anti-gay politics in the last Republican primary and the distancing of the Bush administration from the anti-gay politics of the Christian Right underscore just how marginal such politics have become, even within the conservative wing of the Republican Party. Legal and social integration is the chief trend, no matter how unevenly, across different regions and populations. Today, the question of whether gays' integration means tolerance or equality is at the center of social conflict.

It is telling that gays' greatest successes have been in weakening the twin supports of the closet. Many laws criminalizing homosexuality have been repealed or today go unenforced, and though homophobic representations are still a part of American public life they are now often criticized as a form of bigotry and prejudice. Gays are increasingly being viewed as fully human and as part of the American community. This is a significant change. It makes it possible for many gays and lesbians to exercise greater personal choice and to conduct lives of integrity. However, as the gay political agenda shifts from the struggle for toleration to establishing real social equality, resistance has stiffened.

The push for equal citizenship has exposed the limits of state liberalization. The refusals to grant gays the right to marry and serve in the military stand as telling statements of the government's denial of gays status as first-class citizens. This opposition may at first glance seem puzzling. After all, heterosexual dominance is hardly in jeopardy if equal rights are extended to a small minority, so what's the big deal?

I think that part of the explanation lies in the connection between the issues of gay equality and national identity. First blacks challenged a white-defined America; Latinos and other people of color followed; then women protested a masculine understanding of national identity. Establishing gay equality would challenge another core feature of American national identity. It would effectively mean, as some members of the Supreme Court understood in *Bowers v. Hartwick*, ending or weakening the historical association of nationhood with heterosexuality. It was Chief Justice White who explicitly repudiated any association of homosexuality with American nationality: "Proscriptions against that conduct [homosexual sodomy] have ancient roots. Sodomy was a criminal offense at common law and was forbidden by the laws of the original 13 states when they ratified the Bill of Rights. . . . In fact, until

1961, all 50 states in the Union outlawed sodomy . . . Against this background, to claim that a right to engage in such conduct is 'deeply rooted in this nation's history and tradition' . . . is, at best, facetious."[41]

The sexual politics of national identity are at the heart of the conflict over gays in the military and gay marriage. If gays were to openly serve in the military and to marry, this would be a major challenge to the national ideal of the heterosexual citizen.[42]

From this perspective, the military policy of "Don't ask, don't tell" is a striking sign of gays' unequal status and their ambivalent status as not quite ousiders or citizens. The military is not an institution like, say, a bank or a hospital, but it is symbolically linked to Americans' core sense of nationhood. As many scholars remind us, citizenship is not just a legal reality but is symbolic—something we have an idea and ideals about.[43] Serving in the military or being eligible to serve are key markers of being a good American. The strong tie between the military and the nation is captured in the memorializing of soldiers and national wars in the nation's capital and in a popular culture that celebrates military triumphs and heroes. For a fully abled adult to be excluded from military service because of his or her race, national origin, or sexual identity publicly marks the individual as an outsider.

It was perhaps a mistake on Clinton's part to approach the issue of gays in the military as merely a question of rights. As Congress, the military brass, and the American public weighed in, it was apparent that the battle around gays in the military had become part of a symbolic national drama. Some supporters of ending the ban on gays in the military misread the opposition as old-style closet politics. No doubt some critics longed for a return to the days of state-supported homosexual repression. However, opponents may have also understood in a way that Clinton and some gay activists did not that incorporating gays into the military would signal the beginning of the end of the historical association of national identity and heterosexuality. The "Don't ask, don't tell" policy signaled a rejection of gay equality and of any challenge to the heterosexual meaning of American nationhood. Many Americans, not just in the military and Congress, are not ready to uncouple heterosexuality and being an American.

The institution of marriage is equally invested with national significance in American culture. Whether it's the legal restriction of marriage to heterosexuals, the state privileging of heterosexual marriage over all other intimate unions, or the idealization of marriage in popular culture and commerce (for example, the wedding industry), the ideal national citizen is married.[44] Americans may be more tolerant today toward individuals who choose to be single or cohabitate, but these choices occupy a lesser status than marriage. For this reason, the struggle to extend marital rights to gays is as much about symbolic struggles over national identity as about the politics of equality.[45]

The issue of whether the state should, as a matter of morality or law, recognize gay relationships has bounced around the courts for some time.[46] However, in the last decade or so, as lesbians and gay men have been creating stable, long-term families, and as the question of intimate rights became an urgent health-care issue because of the AIDS crisis, the gay movement has made the legal recognition of gay relationships a priority. While some individuals in the gay community oppose gay marriage because it legitimates the state's regulation of intimate life and devalues all nonmarital intimate arrangements, most gays and lesbians consider the denial of the right to marry as compromising their goal of achieving social equality. Gay marriage became a national issue after the Hawaii State Supreme Court, in *Baehr v. Lewin* (1993), ruled that not allowing gays to marry was a form of gender discrimination. However, even before the courts could resolve the issue, the Hawaii legislature acted in 1994 to restrict marriage to heterosexuality. Other states quickly followed suit, and in 1996 the U.S. Congress passed, with the overwhelming support of the Democrats and President Clinton, the Defense of Marriage Act. This reaffirmed a national ideal that defines marriage as an exclusively heterosexual institution.

To summarize, in the last decade or so the gay movement has shifted its focus from tolerance to social equality. Gays want to be equal citizens; we already have the same obligations and duties; we want the same rights, opportunities, and respect as any other American citizen. And while the state and other institutions have retreated significantly from the repressive practices that produced the closet, they have also refused to grant gays equal citizenship. Gays' continued unequal status reflects a public that is still divided over the moral status of homosexuality; it reflects, as well, a public that worries that gay equality means the end of heterosexual privilege and the ideal of a heterosexual national identity.

The declining social significance of the closet can only have the effect of intensifying demands for equality. Gays will not be satisfied with tolerance. As many of us approach being gay as an ordinary and good status, as we live outside the closet, and as our lives have individual integrity and purpose, we will demand full social inclusion and first-class citizenship. There is no turning back to the days of the closet. Efforts to reinstate the closet are a losing cause. And activists who interpret every anti-gay action as evidence of the still-dominant reality of a homophobic, repressive heterosexual dictatorship are no less stuck in the past than anti-gay crusaders. With the decline of the closet, the battleground shifts: from the politics of coming out, pride, and visibility to equality—before the law and across social institutions.

BEYOND ASSIMILATION AND LIBERATION

As a civil rights agenda has come to dominate the gay movement, some gays have raised doubts about its politics. No one questions that equal rights is a condition of personal freedom and political democracy. However, critics rightly ask, would gaining equal rights establish social equality? Would gaining rights bring about social respect, equal treatment, and full social integration? Can and should the pursuit of social equality be separated from a wider agenda of sexual and social justice?

The current debate over the politics of sexual citizenship expresses a long-standing division between the civil rights or assimilationist and the liberationist ideologies. At the heart of this political division are contrasting images of America.

Generally speaking, rights advocates view America as a fundamentally good society. America is faulted for incompletely realizing its promise of delivering individual freedom, equality, and happiness. Rights advocates expect America to live up to its ideals, to include gays in the circle of full citizenship. By contrast, liberationists tend to see America as deeply flawed; this nation is said to have betrayed its promise of freedom and equality, and not only to gays. For liberationists, a rights-oriented agenda amounts to a wish to be integrated into a flawed, repressive society. Real social progress requires something like a social revolution.

It's time to get past these polarizing positions. Liberationism emerged during the heyday of the making of the closet. This period is passing. Gays have gained considerable personal freedom and are being incorporated into American life. This change undercuts a liberationist view of a seamless world of homosexual hatred and repression.

My own preference is to take a rights-based agenda as the starting point. The view of America as incompletely realizing the promise of a good society is compelling both as a social perspective and as a political strategy. However, I share liberationist criticisms that the rights agenda assumes a thin sociological understanding of heterosexual dominance and a one-sided view of social change.

I intend to sketch a view of the politics of sexual citizenship that blends a rights-oriented and a liberationist approach. This "third way" brings together the forward-looking, reform-minded politics of rights activists and the deep sociology and broad political vision of liberationists.[47]

Consider the strengths and weaknesses of the most serious theoretical defense of a rights-oriented politics. In *Virtually Normal*, the well-known writer and political commentator Andrew Sullivan defends a movement oriented to establishing gay's equal civil and political rights.[48] He offers an elegant, if minimal, liberal defense of gay equality. Sullivan maintains that the cornerstone of liberalism is the idea of a separation between the public and private spheres. The guiding principle of the public or political sphere is the formal or legal equality of its citizens. All individuals who are citizens are bearers of the same rights and duties. By contrast, the guiding principle of the private or civil sphere is personal freedom and social diversity.

From this liberal standpoint, America's gay citizens suffer a glaring injustice. "Gay citizens vote for their own government, pay for it with their own taxes, and have an equal right to participate in it in the same manner as any other citizen. Their unequal treatment by their own state is a fundamental abrogation of fundamental rights."[49] The focus of the gay movement should be, according to Sullivan, establishing gays' legal political equality. "This politics affirms a simple and limited principle: that all public . . . discrimination against homosexuals be ended and that every right and responsibility that heterosexuals enjoy as public citizens be extended to [homosexuals] And that is all. No cures or re-educations, no wrenching private litigation, no political imposition of tolerance; merely a political attempt to enshrine formal public equality."[50]

Sullivan recognizes that there are inequalities in the private or civil sphere as well. Growing up gay, he encountered the shame, isolation, and prejudicial treatment that many gays still experience. However, he maintains that the state should not be used to remedy civil inequalities; for example, through such policies as affirmative action, quotas, hate-crime legislation, and anti-discrimination policies in the workplace. This would violate the core liberal principle of the separation of the public and the private spheres. Enlisting the state to remedy these social injustices might advance the cause of equality but at the potential cost of our individual freedom. Of course, individuals can privately organize to challenge inequalities in the private sphere. "While I would passionately support Microsoft's adoption of antidiscriminatory regulations, I would passionately oppose the government's attempt to impose them."[51]

Sullivan's ideas reveal many of the strengths of a rights agenda. In particular, I would recommend the following: a view of America's core institutions and culture as partially realizing positive types of freedom, social diversity, and a democratic public life; a principled defense of political equality; an uncompromising conviction that rights are the basis of individual freedom, democracy, and justice; and a healthy suspicion of agendas of top-down, state-based social reform.

The underlying weakness of Sullivan's argument, which is indicative of rights-oriented politics in general, is its thin sociology. Sullivan is not naive. He understands that disrespect and discrimination toward gays are pervasive in private and civil life. He believes, however, that a movement focused on establishing legal political equality would go a long way toward bringing about real social equality. If gays were recognized as equal citizens, they would be more likely to be open and visible; And as straight Americans routinely encountered gays as fellow citizens—for example, in the workplace, in the army barracks, and as neighbors—discrimination would diminish as gays were seen as "virtually normal." Sullivan's faith in the positive effects of an agenda of equal citizenship rights is forcefully expressed in the significance he attaches to establishing equal marital rights. "If nothing else were done at all, and gay marriage were legalized, ninety percent of the political work necessary to achieve gay and lesbian equality would have been achieved."[52] Gay marriage, Sullivan believes, would encourage gays to be more open, as they would feel a stronger sense of integrity and social belonging; and it would encourage straight Americans to view gays as like themselves, and therefore worthy of respect and integration.

But Sullivan offers no evidence or reason to believe that formal political equality would gradually translate into social equality. He relies on the hope that gays' increased social visibility and social integration will weaken prejudice and stigma. If the examples of people of color, women, or the disabled are at all telling, however, there is little reason to be sanguine; these groups remain social unequals despite their legal equality and social visibility. Just as most social scientists understand white racial privilege and men's dominance as built into American social structure and culture, heterosexual dominance must also be understood as deeply rooted in social life, not just a product of law or individual prejudice.[53] The strength of the liberationist tradition is precisely its sociological understanding of heterosexual dominance.

From early statements by lesbian feminists and gay liberationists to contemporary queer perspectives, liberationists hold that heterosexual dominance is maintained less by unjust laws and individual prejudice than by the very social structure and organization of American life. For example, many liberationists assert a tight fit between gender norms and heterosexual dominance.[54] America is said to be a society organized around dichotomous norms of gender. From birth, individuals are expected to exhibit a consistency in their self-presentation and behavior between their assigned sex identity as male or female and their gender identity as man or woman. Institutions from the family to schools and the mass media impose expectations that individuals should adopt masculine or feminine gender roles reflecting their status as males or females. These contrasting gender identities and roles are said to reflect the complementary physical and psychological nature of men and women. From this point of view, heterosexuality is understood as expressing the natural fit of gendered bodies, psyches, and social roles. Men and women form a natural unity, each attracted to the other and each finding fulfillment in the other.

Individuals who deviate significantly from gender norms are stigmatized as homosexual. For example, women who are masculine, aggressive, or erotically assertive may be called whores, but also dykes; men who are passive or too emotional or feminine in their self-presentation are labeled sissies, fags, or queers. These disparaging labels aim to enforce a binary gender order that also assumes the normality and rightness of heterosexuality. So long as there are binary gender norms there will be heterosexual dominance. There is little evidence that extending rights to gays weakens dichotomous gender norms. This is so because gender norms are not primarily upheld by laws but by institutions (for example, family, economic institutions, military, schools) and by culture—that is, the media, advertisements, popular music, television, film, scientific and medical knowledge, and the daily customs and practices in families and peer groups.

A rights agenda cannot stand alone. Legal equality easily coexists with social inequality. Gays' equal status will only be achieved when heterosexual dominance is ended, and that requires challenging its deep cultural and institutional supports. Urvashi Vaid has stated this position sharply and forcefully:

> Civil rights strategies do not challenge the moral and antisexual underpinnings of homophobia, because homophobia does not originate in our lack of full civil equality. Rather, homophobia arises from the nature and construction of the political, legal, eco-

> nomic, sexual, racial, and family systems within which we live. As long as the rights-oriented movement refuses to address these social institutions and cultural forces, we cannot eradicate homophobic prejudice.[55]

A rights-oriented political agenda should be broadened in at least three ways. First, equality is about more than political equality or equal rights; it's about social equality across the spectrum of national institutions from the government to the workplace, schools, families, and welfare and health-care institutions. And no matter how important it is to gain equal rights, opportunities, and protections, equality is also about respect and representation. Gays may have the right to vote and hold office, but we remain unequal citizens if our interests and points of view are not respected and are not represented in political agencies. For example, if we don't have spokespeople in political parties or if public officials do not promote our social interests or agendas, equal political rights will not translate into social equality. Rights without respect and representation in the institutions that make up social life is only the shell of social equality.

Second, equality is not only about becoming equal citizens and participants in social life, but also about a right to be heard and to have our interests taken seriously. Equality is not about extending equal rights to gays but only on the condition that we conform to dominant gender, sexual, familial, and social norms. Equality is about institutions encouraging dialogues in which gays participate as equals in shaping the social norms and conventions of our institutions. In other words, equality means encouraging the distinctive voices of gays to be heard and to potentially shape social life.

There is a third problem with a rights agenda: it severs any tie between the pursuit of gay equality and broader issues of sexual and social justice. Consider the politics of citizenship from a sexual justice perspective. Rights activists fight for gays to become first-class citizens. Becoming a citizen is understood as being integrated into a network of rights, duties, and state protections. But citizenship is not only about rights and duties. Citizenship also involves an ideal of the citizen or a notion of the kind of personal traits and behaviors that a nation values and would like to see in its individual members. In other words, citizenship involves a norm of "the good citizen."

In contemporary America, the good sexual citizen, roughly speaking, is an individual whose sexual behavior conforms to traditional gender norms, who links sex to intimacy, love, monogamy, and preferably marriage, and who restricts sex to private acts that exhibit romantic or caring qualities. While rights advocates protest unequal citizenship rights, they have not challenged the sexual norms associated with the good sexual citizen. Accordingly, gays might gain equal rights, but those who deviate from norms of the good citizen would still be considered outsiders. For example, women who are sexually aggressive and dominant, individuals who choose to be single or enjoy commercial sex or are coupled but nonmonogamous, or individuals who like rough but consensual sex might have formal rights but their sexual-intimate choices would be disrespected and perhaps be targets of social control. While it may be the case, as some rights advocates claim, that a majority of gays support all of the sexual norms associated with the good sexual citizen, surely some don't. What's crucial is that the very issue of the legitimacy of these sexual norms is not even part of a civil rights political discussion.

A narrow rights agenda ignores the way ideas of sexual citizenship establish social boundaries between insiders (good citizens) and outsiders (bad citizens). And, while same- or opposite-gender preference is surely one boundary issue, there are many other dimensions of sexuality that are used to separate the good and bad sexual citizen; for example, gender norms, the age of the sex partners, whether sex is private or public, commercial or not, casual or intimate, monogamous or not, gentle or rough. In particular, a rights-oriented movement does not challenge forms of social control that create sexual victims and outsiders of individuals whose sexual preferences are between consenting adults. By narrowing its agenda to gaining equality and integration, a rights-oriented movement leaves the dominant sexual norms, other than gender preference, in place and removed from political debate.

The strength of a liberationist perspective is its understanding of heterosexual dominance as being deeply rooted in social life and as part of a broader pattern of sexual and social inequality. Liberationists argue that the struggle for gay equality should be linked to other battles for sexual-intimate and social justice. There will be, of course, disagreements about which norms beyond compulsory heterosexuality are unjust and which regulations are defensible. The point, though, is that a rights agenda can't avoid being implicated in broader patterns of sexual and social inequality; it should, then, be blended with a liberationist politic.

RIGHTS AND JUSTICE: THE DEBATE OVER GAY MARRIAGE

To illustrate something of what a blend of a rights and liberationist politics might look like, I briefly consider the debate over gay marriage. This debate has been polarized between a rights-based defense of gay marriage and a liberationist critique.[56]

Rights advocates defend gay marriage as a matter of establishing equal rights and a respected social status. There can be no equality without the right to marry. In America, marriage is a marker of first-class citizenship and carries an assortment of economic and social benefits. Furthermore, to the extent that gays are excluded from marriage, their intimate relationships will be viewed as inferior; they will be less stable and solid. And, because of the centrality of intimate love to personal happiness in American society, lacking marital rights translates into diminished prospects for self-fulfillment.

Liberationists offer two key criticisms. First, marriage has been and still is a male-dominated, repressive institution. The gay movement should challenge marriage, not endorse and participate in it. Second, as a state-recognized institution, marriage imposes a narrow and uniform norm of intimacy that has the effect of symbolically and materially devaluing all nonmarital intimacies, which has particularly bad effects on the poor and people of color, who are less likely to marry. Also, supporting a norm of marriage contradicts the values of erotic freedom and variation that have been at the heart of gay culture. The gay movement should focus on either ending the state's regulation of intimate life (long-term goal) or extending state recognition to a multiplicity of intimate arrangements (short-term goal).

At the root of these polarizing positions are two contrasting views of the institution of marriage and its effect on gays. Rights advocates emphasize the benefits of marriage; it will enhance personal happiness, bring stability to gay relationships, and advance their full integration into what is considered a basically good society. By contrast, liberationists criticize marriage as a chief source of male dominance and compulsory heterosexuality; it reinforces a repressive society. Moreover, marriage domesticates sexuality and has been part of an ideology of "familialism" that has been hostile to a playful, erotic culture that values choice, experimentation, and variation. Marriage will benefit a small slice of gay America while leaving in place the privileged status of men and heterosexuality.

Differences in values and social perspectives between rights advocates and liberationists cannot simply be smoothed over. However, it's useful, I think, to try to stake out a less polarizing position.[57]

Defenders of gay marriage make a compelling and to my mind winning point: to the extent that marriage in the United States is associated with first-class citizenship, including social respect, being denied this right is a pointed public statement of the disrespected and socially inferior status of gays. Lacking marital rights positions gays as outsiders, denies us a host of crucial material benefits and rights, devalues our relationships, and reduces our chances for personal well-being and a meaningful sense of social and civic belonging. These are real effects of being denied marital rights. Accordingly, no matter how compelling critics' arguments against marriage, there is no credible evidence and no reason to believe that Americans would even consider ending the state sanctioning of marriage or its material and symbolic support of marriage. Marriage is here to stay for the immediate and near future; this reality must be the starting point of any serious political discussion.

Yet, liberationist criticisms of marriage should not be dismissed. Marriage has been and still is organized by gender roles that reinforce male dominance; this is not an incidental part of this institution; it's not merely a fact of the past; it must still be reckoned with. However, contrary to what some liberationists seem to assume, it is not a fixed part of marriage. There is evidence that the gender ordering of marriage has weakened significantly and, at a minimum, has lost considerable cultural authority.[58] Moreover, there is little reason to believe that gays would adopt gender roles if permitted to marry; in fact, the evidence strongly suggests that gender roles do not have much impact on patterns of gay intimacy.[59]

So, whereas rights advocates miss the broader significance of the politics of marriage by narrowing the issue into one solely of equal rights, liberationists often collapse this politics into one of sexual and gender repression. However, approaching marriage as an institution worth defending but in need of reform suggests an alternative political standpoint: gay marriage should be defended but not only on the basis of equal rights arguments but as part of the defense of an institution that promises intimacy between equals. This approach would connect the struggle for equal marital rights to a struggle over the very social meaning of marriage. In other words, gays should make the case for same-sex marriage but in the context of arguing for a view of marriage as an intimate union of equals. The defense of marriage would then be connected to a critique of the male dominated organization of this institution.

But what about the liberationist point that state-sanctioned marriage devalues nonmarital arrangements, deprives the poor and especially minority populations of much needed benefits and resources, and betrays a gay culture that has valued erotic experimentation? Here, too, I think that marriage can be defended but not in a narrowly individualistic and legalistic language. Rights advocates often rationalize the marginalizing effects of marriage by appealing to a language of individual choice. The right to marry, they say, merely gives gays a choice that they presently lack; it doesn't preclude individuals from choosing to not marry, and it doesn't necessarily devalue other intimate arrangements. Individuals choose intimate arrangements that reflect their specific wants, needs, and values; the point, they say, is to give gays the range of options available to straight citizens.

This argument is sociologically naive. If the poor or people of color marry less than other Americans it is not merely a "lifestyle" choice; it relates to social factors such as job insecurity, low income, transient living conditions, racism, or high rates of unemployment and incarceration among men. And, contrary to what rights advocates seem to think, a nonmarital status is a social, economic, and cultural disadvantage. Marriage establishes a privileged status (rights, resources, benefits, prestige) in relation to being single and to being in nonmarital intimate arrangements. The state enforces this hierarchy.

Liberationists understand well the politics of marriage. As a state-sanctioned institution it creates a social hierarchy among intimate choices. But opposition to marriage doesn't necessarily follow. While marriage is a socially privileged type of intimate arrangement, there does not have to be a huge gap in terms of status, rights, and benefits relative to nonmarital arrangements. The fact that more Americans are choosing cohabitation, are divorcing, or are remaining single for longer periods of time suggests that marriage is losing its "normalizing" status or its role as a marker of respectability. And nonmarital arrangements such as civil unions, common-law relationships, cohabitation, and domestic partnerships are gaining many of the rights once restricted to marriage. So the hierarchy is being weakened from both sides—marriage is less exulted, and nonmarital arrangements are gaining respectability and rights.[60]

Instead of raging against marriage, a more politically effective strategy would be to argue for enhanced state recognition and support of nonmarital arrangements (in the short term) and to make the case for uncoupling basic health-care and social security benefits from marriage (in the long-term).[61] These strategies would have the effect of further diminishing the normative status of marriage while equalizing intimate choices—symbolically and materially. Such strategies would also have the added political benefit of avoiding opposing an institution that remains a fundamental type of value commitment for the vast majority of Americans.

BEYOND THE POLITICS OF TOLERANCE

The closet has been at the center of gay politics in the United States since at least the 1950s. At the root of the closet has been a culture that views gays as not only different in basic ways from heterosexuals but inferior and threatening—to children, families, and to the nation's moral and military security. Accordingly, the dismantling of the closet has meant persuading Americans that gays are just ordinary people, that like heterosexuals, we can be disciplined, productive, loyal, and loving. If homosexuality is understood as a natural or ordinary human trait, the closet would be judged unfair. Gays would be welcomed into the community of Americans.

Gays are winning this cultural battle, even if some of our enemies remain resolute and the social landscape is littered with the victims of a terrorizing hatred of homosexuals. Whether we look at television, the movies, literature, art, book publishing, newspapers and magazines, science, or elite opinion (expressed in editorials and political party platforms, for example), images of gays as just people or as fully human are steadily gaining ground. Public expression of homophobia, though by no means rare, is more and more being challenged as a form of bigotry or as a marker of being unenlightened in a global, multicultural world that values a cosmopolitan respect for social diversity.

As gays are viewed as fully human and as deserving to be citizens, there is pressure for institutions to be accommodating. This has not always gone smoothly. Battles are being waged in virtually every institution. In general, institutions that cultivate a cosmopolitan outlook such as big corporations and unions, colleges and universities, and health and civil service bureaucracies are more welcoming than small businesses, secondary schools, and churches that are highly responsive to local and parochial interests and sentiments. The major exception to this rule is the military, whose resistance, I've suggested, is perhaps explained by its powerful symbolic association with American nationalism.

The public integration of gays has created new sources of tension. In particular, conflicts have surfaced around whether integration involves tolerance or equality. To date, tolerance has been the dominant type of social accommodation. Tolerance entails decriminalization and the delegitimation of blatant homophobic behavior. Gays are to be acknowledged as part of America, but not necessarily accepted or valued as equals. It is hard, however, to draw the line at tolerance. Once homophobic practices are criticized as hateful and hurtful, there is an implicit acknowledgment that gays are ordinary folk deserving of respect and equal treatment. The tension between the cultural legitimation of gays and their continuing institutional inequality is at the core of contemporary lesbian and gay politics.

It is not only that America's public culture is becoming more respectful and welcoming toward gays. More and more gay people accept themselves, define being gay as a good part of themselves, and feel a sense of entitlement—to be treated respectfully by all other Americans. This sense of personal integrity drives the political struggle for equality into every institution. Yes, equality before the law is important, but so is equality in our schools, health-care and welfare agencies, in our churches and political parties, in our local YMCAs and American Legion clubs. The struggle for social equality across the institutional spectrum pushes a rights agenda to the left, to a more expansive understanding of equality and a broadening of its political strategies.

These escalating expectations for inclusion, respect, and equality in a context of continued resistance, indeed sometimes spirited opposition, have spurred the renewal of the spirit of liberationism. In particular, the AIDS epidemic, which simultaneously exposed a reality of intolerance as well as growing mainstream support for gay integration, was especially important in pressuring a rights agenda to edge toward the left. This radical spirit expresses something of the sense of integrity and entitlement that many of us who are living beyond the closet feel; it also exposes the real limitations of a rights agenda by grasping heterosexual dominance as rooted in our institutions and culture, not just in laws, attitudes, and ignorance.

However, as in the past, liberationism has largely failed to find a solid organizational footing in gay political culture. No doubt there are many reasons for this. My own sense is that liberationism alienates many gays to the extent that its social vision is wedded to a romantic rejection of America. Many liberationists seem temperamentally unable to see in the present anything more than repression, exclusion, marginalization, and domination. Rights are discounted as benefiting only middle-class whites; integration and legal equality is said to reinforce a repressive social order; culturally respectful images are "exposed" as assimilationist or exclusionary. In short, a good America can only be imagined as a future possibility. This sort of romanticism, which parades as a left politics, must be abandoned. But the heart and soul of liberationism is its understanding of the social roots of heterosexual dominance and a political vision that connects rights and equality to social justice. This should also be the heart and soul of the gay movement.

EPILOGUE

"We are all multiculturalists," says the sociologist Nathan Glazer.[1] And it is in no small part because we are all becoming multiculturalists that gays are gaining entry into the American mainstream. But what kind of multiculturalists are we becoming? And how will gays fit into a multicultural America? One thing seems sure: the fate of gays is tied to the fate of other outsiders.

Many Americans, past and present, have believed that the genius of this nation is its friendliness to people of varied backgrounds and beliefs. But we've not always agreed on which differences matter and how diversity should shape our national culture. For a very long time, the idea of America as a melting pot was compelling. According to this metaphor, America was seen as welcoming to different kinds of people and cultures. Citizens would be encouraged to pray as they wish, to celebrate their ethnic traditions, and would still be considered good Americans. But, this theory went, individuals should not stand apart from the American community; they should not organize their lives chiefly around their own religious or ethnic community. A good American was expected to participate in national life and to gradually become part of America. As individuals did this, their differences would melt away or become merely personal and symbolic, for example, a matter of culinary or musical taste.

The melting pot was in many ways a wonderful national idea and ideal. The differences among Americans would get stirred together, creating something new; this would happen again and again as new cultures were continuously introduced through immigration or other means. Foreigners were to be looked upon favorably, as contributing to America's vitality. This was the ideal. The reality was often something quite different. Throughout American history, immigrants and other strangers were regularly treated as outcasts or pressured to conform to a dominant national culture that expressed the values and ideas of a small minority.

From the founding years of this nation through at least World War II, American society has been dominated, to speak in shorthand terms, by Anglo-Protestants, men, whites, the rich, and by norms of heterosexuality and ableness. Being respected as an American was often conditional on displaying those behaviors (for example, styles of dress, grooming, and speech) associated with these statuses. Only individuals who were not white, not Protestant, not men, or not abled were labeled as "different"; and to be different was to occupy a lesser social status, and sometimes to be viewed as a threat. For native Americans, Hispanics, blacks, the Chinese and Japanese, for Jews and Catholics at various times, and for the disabled, the melting pot ideal was often experienced as a demand to assimilate or suffer as an outsider or "alien." This history is today well known, as the story of the past has been retold through the lens of multiculturalism.[2]

By the early twentieth century the idea of the melting pot came to be closely linked to a national policy that aggressively enforced social conformity. Reacting to the waves of southern European and Asian immigrants, to the domestic turmoil associated with the suffragist and black rights movements, and to the red scare, America turned against those who did not look, act, and sound like true-blue Americans. Scholars speak of a national agenda of "Americanization." Writes one historian, "The Americanization movement . . . is charged with promoting an Anglocentric conception of the United States. . . . Such a conception was, by definition, not inclusive of all members of the polity, for instance, excluding African Americans, Chinese- and Japanese-

Americans, and some poor whites. The movement also required new Americans to detach themselves from ethnic groups, to sacrifice multiple allegiances in favor of a uniform national identity."[3] Against this assault on pluralism, critics such as Horace Kallen, John Dewey, Jane Addams, and many others fashioned an alternative to the melting pot national image: America as a social "mosaic." Cultural pluralism was said to express the soul of America. Pluralists declared that America has always been a nation of diverse cultural communities and that these social groups will not and should not melt away. Their preservation and respect is what gives this nation its identity and vitality.

Cultural pluralism was a minor current in American society through the first half of the twentieth century. The intense nationalist fervor stirred up by the two world wars, the Great Depression, and the Cold War put a premium on national unity. But, as America emerged from World War II triumphant, confident, and affluent, many citizens turned to matters of personal identity and social justice. The 1960s witnessed a resurgence of ethnic pride and movements of racial, gender, and sexual rights and liberation.

While Italian Americans or other European ethnics gravitated to a language of cultural pluralism, the postwar movements for social justice forged a new social vision—multiculturalism.[4] Although both these languages of national identity champion a mosaic over a melting pot metaphor, the two should not be confused. Multiculturalists criticize pluralists for limiting social differences to white or European ethnics and to Judeo-Christians. Cultural pluralists like Horace Kallen did not include non-European ethnic and non-Christian religious cultures in the American mosaic. For Kallen and others, black culture would not be a part of the mosaic; blacks were understood as lacking their own positive culture. Instead, they presented a problem of individual integration. Europe and whiteness defined the parameters of what was considered "civilization."

Moreover, pluralists did not include differences based on gender, sexuality, or disability in the spectrum of what counts as social diversity. These identities were seen as natural: one was born a woman or a homosexual; social inferiority was understood as natural and right. For example, it was nature, not society, that was said to dictate women's social subordination to men. Women's physical and mental makeup required male protection and dominance; nature had equipped women with a limited range of capacities, making them suitable for primarily caretaking roles, not statuses that involved exercizing public authority. Women's social subordination is not a case of victimization but the workings of nature. From this perspective, the notion of a distinct women's culture makes no sense. The same was true for homosexuals. Through the 1950s and 1960s homosexuality was viewed as a natural status; homosexuals were different from heterosexuals, and this difference was a matter of psychosexual abnormality. The idea of a positive homosexual culture would have been ludicrous to most Americans. Indeed, it was roundly rejected in the political culture of the 1950s and early 1960s when proposed by the radical founder of the Mattachine Society, Harry Hay.

Finally, cultural pluralists modeled group difference after white European ethnics who voluntarily immigrated to America and wished only to find opportunity for advancement and social acceptance. By contrast, many multiculturalists model diversity after nationalist decolonizing movements in Africa, Latin America, and Asia. Viewed through a nationalist lens, differences based on race, ethnicity, gender, or disability are understood not as short-lived, but as a semipermanent basis for building distinct subcultures. Being black, Mexican American, deaf, or gay is a social status, indicating an individual's belonging to a community, Moreover, these cultural communities are valued not only as a way to gain a foothold in the American mainstream; they provide positive identities, a sense of belonging, and have their own rich, vital culture—aesthetic and literary styles, intimate values, and perhaps distinctive ways of knowing and judging. These cultural communities, multiculturalists say, are not going to melt away, but are and should be a vital part of America.

In contrast to cultural pluralists, multiculturalists imagine an America shaped in fundamental ways by these diverse groups. Cultural pluralists thought, for example, that Jews might practice their faith at home and establish their own religious associations. But they would not pressure schools to hire Jews or shape a curriculum to express their distinct values and worldview. While some Jews might want to establish their own schools, most would be expected to participate in the secular public school system; they would aim to succeed by the rules in place. But, multiculturalists ask, which or whose rules should we play by? Multicultural Jews might demand that questions of curriculum, social norms, hiring, food service, and so on be openly discussed and decided upon by consensus or majority rule. In a multicultural framework, groups that have developed their own identity and culture will feel entitled to consider the norms, social policies, and goals of institutions, including the government, in relation to their specific interests and values.

While multiculturalism has its roots in the decolonizing movements of the 1950s, it wasn't until the 1980s and the 1990s that its ideas gained a footing in the American mainstream. The battles over affirmative action, diversity training, school curricula, academic canons and disciplines, aesthetic and cultural representations, and identity politics were about which national metaphor, melting pot or mosaic, would come to define America. The battles are far from over; it seems clear, though, that the mosaic imagery of multiculturalism has secured a place in the ongoing struggle over the future of America.

A multicultural America, no matter how incomplete and contested, creates a favorable environment for outsider groups, including gays, to make their case for rights, respect, and social change. Unlike melting pot models, which tolerate differences on the condition that they would eventually be surrendered in return for national integration, multiculturalism values differences as a sustaining vital part of America. "One of the most striking changes of the recent past," comments Nathan Glazer, "has been the increasing acceptance of pluralism as a central American value—the acceptance of all races, both sexes, different lifestyles as being equally good and deserving of respect."[5]

Glazer alludes to a key feature of multiculturalism: its ethical impulse. Multiculturalism shapes a moral culture that imposes on its citizens an obligation to listen to different voices, to withhold judgment until various points of view are considered, and to try to negotiate disagreements through dialogue across differences. In such a culture, "absolutist" styles of ethical reasoning lose credibility.[6] Such approaches evaluate rules and behavior by consulting absolute notions of right and wrong or good and bad. Judgments that homosexuality is wrong because it's unnatural, abnormal, or sinful illustrate absolutist reasoning. In a multicultural cosmopolitan culture, such reasoning will be challenged as parochial, as reflecting a world that primarily values social sameness. As many of us view social life through a multicultural lens, we appreciate that people hold different and sometimes contradictory ideas about what makes a good life, about the right way to live, and about what a good society should look like. As respect for diversity becomes a chief moral value and obligation, "pragmatic" ethical styles gain considerable prominence. Moral pragmatism considers the context of action, the beliefs and values of the agent, and the possible social consequences of the action. Pragmatists favor loose ethical guidelines instead of fixed principles or imperatives to guide behavior; they will be more or less comfortable with navigating a social environment in which there is considerable moral uncertainty and cultural variation and conflict; to use political metaphors, if the confrontational tensions of the Cold War capture something of the spirit of moral absolutists, peaceful coexistence is the ethos of pragmatists.

Many of the gains made by the gay movement in the past decade or so have been made possible by this multicultural refashioning of American culture. Appealing to cosmopolitan norms of respect for social diversity and dialogue across differences, the gay movement has been particularly effective in discrediting blatantly homophobic, discriminatory practices. So long as gays have been able to persuade citizens of their essential humanity, tolerance and a life beyond the closet have been made possible. However, as we've seen, tolerance is not equality. Gays and lesbians still lack equal respect and rights; we lack equal opportunities and equal representation and participation in public life. And we have a long way to go in convincing the public that there is a distinct gay culture that merits respect and inclusion into the mosaic landscape of a multicultural America.

Our fate is not entirely in our own hands. It is in no small degree tied to the fate of other outsider groups. And the future of nonwhites, women, the disabled, and gender benders is very much dependent on whether a multicultural ideal triumphs and how it's put into practice.

The so-called culture wars have proven fierce and divisive because there is much at stake. Advocates of a multicultural America imagine a "decentering" (not a disuniting) of America. They raise challenging questions: Who has authority and why? Who has wealth and why? What cultural values and norms stand for America and who says so? Multiculturalists challenge the monopolization of positions of institutional power by specific groups (whites, men, heterosexual, and the abled); they challenge the association of cultural prestige with the practices, traits, values, and styles of particular statuses—for example, the masculinization of government authority or the whitening of the corporate hierarchy. True, some women and some people of color might make it into the ranks of senators or CEOs or the military brass, but men and whites overwhelmingly dominate in these sectors; CEOs and generals and U.S. senators are still almost seamlessly associated in the public mind with masculinity, whiteness, and heterosexuality. A multicultural America remains an ideal.

Blacks, women, the disabled, Latinos, and Asians, (and gays to a considerably lesser extent) may have equal rights, but, with regard to who exercises institutional power and who defines what is culturally valued, America remains dominated by those who are, roughly speaking, white, Christian, rich, abled, straight, and male. Equal citizenship is about more than equal legal rights. It is also about who gets to define the norms and ideals of the good citizen. In movies, television, newspapers, literature, art, and academia, and in our schools, corporations, unions, and churches, images of the good citizen are created. Certain traits and ways of thinking and acting are considered ideal; that is, attractive, reasonable, responsible, mature, and associated with authority and power. When our advertisements consistently project whites as models or icons of beauty, a statement is being made about the ideal citizen; when our heroes and most powerful public figures are overwhelmingly men and white, statements are being made about the ideal citizen; when our principals, union leaders, university presidents, and athletic coaches are always "abled," statements are being made about the ideal citizen.

So, while outsiders like blacks, Latinos, Asians, women, the disabled, and gays are today rights-bearing citizens, positions of power and the behaviors, styles, and standards that mark cultural prestige are still undeniably dominated by statuses other than these. The ideal citizen, the citizen we most deeply respect, trust, and honor, is still white, male, abled, and straight. There is today surely more tolerance of difference; many outsiders are now "at the table," but they are there only as guests, playing by the rules of the hosts. America is a long way from realizing, even approximating, a multicultural ideal. Equality for gays and real equality for women, nonwhites, the disabled, and others are inextricably linked. Justice for gays is inseparable from social justice in America—and today that means making a truly multicultural America.

APPENDIX

Film	Year	Box Office Gross
1. *Advise and Consent*	1962	45th top money-maker of 1962 ($2,000,000)
2. *The Children's Hour*	1961	48th top money-maker of 1962 ($1,800,000)
3. *The Group*	1966	37th top money-maker of 1966 ($3,000,000)
4. *Midnight Cowboy*	1969	16th top money-maker of 1970 ($4,036,491)
5. *Pawnbroker*	1965	42nd top money-maker of 1965 ($2,500,000)
6. *All That Jazz*	1979	16th top money-maker of 1980 ($20,000,000)
7. *Anderson Tapes*	1971	17th top money-maker of 1971 ($5,000,000)

Film	Year	Box Office Gross
8. *Blazing Saddles*	1973	6th top money-maker of 1974 ($16,500,000)
9. *Boys in the Band*	1970	25th top money-maker of 1970 ($3,216,380)
10. *Car Wash*	1976	49th top money-maker of 1976 ($4,190,000)
11. *Dog Day Afternoon*	1975	7th top money-maker of 1976 ($19,800,000)
12. *Five Easy Pieces*	1970	31st top money-maker of 1970 ($2,637,000)
13. *Julia*	1977	Box office bomb, ($1,000,000)
14. *Looking for Mr. Goodbar*	1977	31st top money-maker of 1977 ($9,087,240)
15. *Manhattan*	1979	19th top money-maker of 1979 ($16,908,439)
16. *Next Stop, Greenwich Village*	1976	109th top money-maker of ($1,061,000)
17. *Ode to Billy Joe*	1976	15th top money-maker of 1976 ($10,400,000)
18. *American Gigolo*	1980	28th top money-maker of 1980 ($11,500,000)
19. *Cruising*	1980	49th top money-maker of 1980 ($6,990,890)
20. *Desert Hearts*	1985	145th top money-maker of 1986 ($1,233,637)

Film	Year	Box Office Gross
21. *Making Love*	1982	53rd top money-maker of 1982 ($6,100,000)
22. *Personal Best*	1982	102nd top money-maker of 1982 ($3,000,000)
23. *Silkwood*	1983	23rd top money-maker of 1984 ($17,800,000)
24. *St. Elmo's Fire*	1985	24th top money-maker of 1985 ($16,343,197)
25. *Sudden Impact*	1983	10th top money-maker of 1984 ($34,600,000)
26. *Torch Song Trilogy*	1988	111th top money-maker of 1989 ($2,500,000)
27. *Ace Ventura: Pet Detective*	1994	15th top money-maker of 1994 ($72,217,396)
28. *Basic Instinct*	1992	8th top money-maker of 1992 ($53,000,000)
29. *Billy Bathgate*	1991	84th top money-maker of 1991 ($7,000,000)
30. *Boys on the Side*	1994	76th top money-maker of 1995 ($23,440,188)
31. *Chasing Amy*	1997	121st top money-maker of 1997 ($12,027,147)
32. *Falling Down*	1993	35th top money-maker of 1993 ($40,903,593)
33. *Father of the Bride*	1991	30th top money-maker of 1991 ($19,000,000)

Film	Year	Box Office Gross
34. *Go Fish*	1994	180th top money-maker of 1994 ($2,408,311)
35. *Higher Learning*	1995	39th top money-maker of 1995 ($38,290,723)
36. *In and Out*	1997	9th top money-maker of 1998 ($63,826,569) (preliminary gross)
37. *Jeffrey*	1995	184th top money-maker of 1995 ($3,487,767)
38. *Kiss Me, Guido*	1998	Not available
39. *Longtime Companion*	1990	131st top money-maker of 1990 ($2,200,000)
40. *Mo' Money*	1992	39th top money-maker of 1992 ($19,200,000)
41. *My Best Friend's Wedding*	1997	6th top money-maker of 1997 ($126,713,608)
42. *My Own Private Idaho*	1991	137th top money-maker of 1991 ($2,550,000)
43. *The Object of My Affection*	1998	Not available
44. *Philadelphia*	1993	14th top money-maker of 1994 ($76,878,958)
45. *Set It Off*	1996	44th top money-maker of 1996 ($34,325,720)

Film	Year	Box Office Gross
46. *The Incredibly True Adventure of Two Girls in Love*	1995	213th top money-maker of 1995 ($1,977,544)
47. *Threesome*	1994	100th top money-maker of 1994 ($14,815,317)
48. *As Good as It Gets*	1997	Not available

NOTES

INTRODUCTION

1. Daniel Mendelsohn, "Queerer Than Folk," *New York*, March 5, 2001, p. 35.
2. Jesse Green, "The New Gay Movement," *New York*, March 5, 2001, p. 27.
3. Simon Dumenco, "They're Here, They're Queer, We're Used to It," *New York*, March 5, 2001, pp. 29–31.
4. Throughout this book, I will often use the term *gay* to refer to both men and women. Further, terms such as *homosexual, gay,* or *lesbian* refer to homosexually oriented individuals or individuals for whom homosexuality is an integral part of their sexual orientation. I do not assume that homosexuality is necessarily self-defining or a core identity. Some individuals may fashion an identity based on their homosexuality; others view it as simply a desire or behavior.
5. Michelangelo Signorile, *Life Outside: The Signorile Report on Gay Men: Sex, Drugs, Muscles, and the Passages of Life* (New York: HarperCollins, 1997), p. xv.
6. Bruce Bawer, *A Place at the Table: The Gay Individual in American Society* (New York: Simon and Schuster, 1993), p. 33.
7. Ibid.
8. Ibid., p. 48.
9. Andrew Sullivan, *Virtually Normal: An Argument about Homosexuality* (New York: Vintage, 1996), p. 130.
10. Ibid., p. 163.
11. Ibid., p. 130.
12. Ibid.

13. Daniel Harris, *The Rise and Fall of Gay Culture* (New York: Ballantine, 1997), p. 7.
14. Urvashi Vaid, *Virtual Equality: The Mainstreaming of Gay and Lesbian Liberation* (New York: Doubleday, 1995), p. 5.
15. Ibid., p. 7.
16. Michael Warner, *The Trouble with Normal: Sex, Politics, and the Ethics of Queer Life* (Cambridge, Mass.: Harvard University Press, 2000), pp. 128–29.
17. My ideas about identity have benefited from the sociological views of Erving Goffman, in particular *The Presentation of the Self in Everyday Life* (Garden City, N.Y.: Doubleday, 1959) and *Stigma: Notes on the Management of Spoiled Identity* (Englewood Cliffs, N.J.: Prentice-Hall, 1963). I have also drawn considerably from poststructural approaches that emphasize the relational and performative character of identity. In this regard, see Judith Butler, *Gender Trouble: Gender and the Subversion of Identity* (New York: Routledge, 1990), and Diana Fuss, *Essentially Speaking: Feminism, Nature, and Difference* (New York: Routledge, 1990), and "Inside/Out," in *Inside/Out: Lesbian Theories, Gay Theories*, ed. Diana Fuss (New York: Routledge, 1991). The work of historians and social scientists has been crucial in recent discussions of sexual identity. For a sampling of this work, see Jeffrey Weeks, *Coming Out: Homosexual Politics in Britain from the Nineteenth Century to the Present* (London: Quartet, 1977), and *Sexuality and Its Discontents* (London: Routledge, 1985); John D'Emilio, *Sexual Politics, Sexual Communities: The Making of a Homosexual Minority in the United States, 1940–1970* (Chicago: University of Chicago Press, 1983); Lillian Faderman, *Odd Girls and Twilight Lovers: A History of Lesbian Life in Twentieth-Century America* (New York: Columbia University Press, 1991); George Chauncey, *Gay New York: Gender, Urban Culture, and the Making of the Gay Male World, 1890–1940* (New York: Basic Books, 1994); Kenneth Plummer, *Sexual Stigma: An Interactionist Account* (London: Routledge, 1975); Kristin Esterberg, *Lesbian and Bisexual Identities: Constructing Communities, Constructing Selves* (Philadelphia: Temple University Press, 1997); Arlene Stein, *Sex and Sensibility: Stories of a Lesbian Generation* (Berkeley: University of California Press, 1997); Joshua Gamson, *Freaks Talk Back: Tabloid Talk Shows and Sexual Nonconformity* (Chicago: University of Chicago Press, 1998); and Viviane Namaste, *Invisible Lives: The Erasure of Transsexual and Transgendered People* (Chicago: University of Chicago Press, 2000).
18. In thinking about heterosexual dominance, I've drawn considerably from gay liberationism and lesbian feminism. Key texts include Dennis Altman, *Homosexual Oppression and Liberation* (New York: Avon Books, 1971); Nancy Myron and Charlotte Bunch, eds. *Lesbianism and the Women's Movement* (Baltimore: Diana Press, 1975); Karla Jay and Allen Young, eds., *Out of the*

Closets: Voices of Gay Liberationism (New York: New York University Press, 1992 [1972]); and Mark Blasius and Shane Phelan, eds., *We Are Everywhere: A Historical Sourcebook of Gay and Lesbian Politics* (New York: Routledge, 1997). Among the key works inspired by these traditions are Adrienne Rich, "Compulsory Heterosexuality and Lesbian Existence," *Signs* 5 (Summer 1980): 631–60; Michael Warner, "Fear of a Queer Planet," *Social Text* 9 (1991): 3–17; Eve Sedgwick, *Epistemology of the Closet* (Berkeley: University of California Press, 1990); and, in the British context, Stevie Jackson, *Heterosexuality in Question* (London: Sage, 1999). In the past few years there has emerged an empirical literature that speaks to the ways compulsory heterosexuality operates in different institutions and societies. See Mary Louise Adams, *The Trouble with Normal: Postwar Youth and the Making of Heterosexuality* (Toronto: University of Toronto Press, 1997); Karen Dubinsky, *Improper Advances: Rape and Heterosexual Conflict in Ontario, 1880–1929* (Chicago: University of Chicago Press, 1993); Debbie Epstein and Richard Johnson, *Schooling Sexualities* (Buckingham: Open University Press, 1998); Chrys Ingraham, *White Weddings: Romancing Heterosexuality in Popular Culture* (New York: Routledge, 1999); Mairtin Mac An Ghaill, *The Making of Men: Masculinities, Sexualities, and Schooling* (Buckingham: Open University Press, 1994); Anna Marie Smith,"The Good Homosexual and the Dangerous Queer: Resisting the 'New Homophobia,'" in *New Sexual Agendas*, ed. Lynn Segal (New York: New York University Press, 1997); D. Steinberg, D. Epstein, and R. Johnson, eds., *Border Patrols: Policing the Boundaries of Heterosexuality* (London: Cassell, 1997); and Lisa Duggan, "The Social Enforcement of Heterosexuality and Lesbian Resistance," in *Class, Race, and Sex: The Dynamics of Control*, ed. Amy Swerdlow and Hannah Lessinger (Boston: G. K. Hall, 1983), 75–92.

19. In thinking about lesbian and gay politics beyond questions of rights and equality, my ideas have been sharpened by the work of Michel Foucault, *The History of Sexuality, Vol. 1: An Introduction* (New York: Vintage, 1980); Gayle Rubin, "Thinking Sex: Notes for a Radical Theory of the Politics of Sexuality," in *Pleasure and Danger: Exploring Female Sexuality*, ed. Carole Vance (Boston: Routledge, 1984); Pat Califia, *Public Sex: The Culture of Radical Sex* (Pittsburgh: Cleis, 1994); Sedgwick, *Epistemology of the Closet*; Vaid, *Virtual Equality*; Combahee River Collective, "A Black Feminist Statement," in *All the Women Are White, All the Blacks Are Men, But Some of Us Are Brave: Black Women's Studies*, ed. Gloria Hull, Patricia Bell Scott, and Barbara Smith (Old Westbury, N.Y.: Feminist Press, 1982); Shane Phelan, *Getting Specific: Postmodern Lesbian Politics* (Minneapolis: University of Minnesota Press, 1994); Diane Richardson, "Constructing Sexual Citizenship: Theorizing Sexual Rights," *Critical Social Policy* 20 (2000):

100–35; Jeffrey Weeks, "The Sexual Citizen," in *Love and Eroticism*, ed. Mike Featherstone (London: Sage, 1999), pp. 35–52.

CHAPTER 1

1. Consider this description of the world of a middle-class lesbian living in the late 1920s and 1930s: "During the 1920s and 1930s Boyer Reinstein was an active lesbian within a community of lesbian friends. She had few, if any, negative feelings about being a lesbian, and she was 'out' to her immediate family. . . . Yet, she did not publicly disclose being gay. She was always discreet." The author, Elizabeth Kennedy, cautions against using the concept of the closet to depict Reinstein's social world. "I am afraid using the term 'closet' to refer to the culture of the 1920s and 1930s might be anachronistic." Elizabeth Kennedy, "'But We Would Never Talk about It': The Structures of Lesbian Discretion in South Dakota, 1928–1933," in *Inventing Lesbian Cultures in America,* ed. Ellen Lewin (Boston: Beacon Press, 1996). Similarly, George Chauncey describes a working-class gay culture in which gays and straights openly mingle in saloons, cafeterias, rent parties, and speakeasies. The gay world before World War I is said to be very different from the era inaugurated by the Stonewall rebellions. For example, the language and concept of "coming out of the closet" was foreign to this gay world. "Gay people in the prewar years . . . did not speak of coming out of what we call the gay closet but rather of coming out into what they called homosexual society or the gay world, a world neither so small, nor so isolated, nor . . . so hidden as closet implies." George Chauncey, *Gay New York: Gender, Urban Culture, and the Making of the Gay Male World, 1890–1940* (New York: Basic Books, 1994).
2. For descriptions of homosexual life in the 1950s and 1960s, *The Mattachine Review* and *The Ladder*, respectively published by the Mattachine Society and the Daughters of Bilitis, are superb sources. For examples of personal testimony, see Peter Nardi, David Sanders, and Judd Marmor, eds., *Growing up before Stonewall: Life Stories of Some Gay Men* (New York: Routledge, 1994); Donald Vining, *A Gay Diary*, 5 vols. (New York: Pepys Press, 1979–93); Martin Duberman, *Cures: A Gay Man's Odyssey* (New York: Dutton, 1991); Robert Reinhart, *A History of Shadows: A Novel* (Boston: Alyson, 1986); Audre Lorde, *Zami: A New Spelling of My Name* (New York: Crossing Press, 1982); Andrea Weiss and Greta Schiller, *Before Stonewall: The Making of the Gay and Lesbian Community* (New York: Naiad Press, 1988); Jonathan Ned Katz, *Gay American History* (New York: Meridian, 1976) and *Gay/Lesbian Almanac* (New York: Harper and Row, 1983); and Eric Marcus, *Making History: The Struggle for Gay and Lesbian Equal Rights: An Oral History* (New York: HarperCollins, 1992). For informative popular and academic work of

the time, see Daniel Webster Cory [psuedonym Edward Sagarin], *The Homosexual in America* (New York: Peter Nevill, 1951); Evelyn Hooker, "Male Homosexuals and Their Worlds," in *Sexual Inversion*, ed. J. Marmor (New York: Basic Books, 1965); Martin Hoffman, *The Gay World* (New York: Basic Books, 1968); Del Martin and Phyllis Lyon, *Lesbian/Woman* (San Francisco: Bantam, 1972); Sidney Abbott and Barbara Love, *Sappho Was a Right-On Woman: A Liberated View of Lesbianism* (New York: Stein and Day, 1972); John Gagnon and William Simon, "The Lesbians: A Preliminary Overview," in *Sexual Deviance*, ed. William Simon and John Gagnon (New York: Harper and Row, 1967). For some current scholarly perspectives on gay life in the immediate postwar years, see John D'Emilio, *Sexual Politics, Sexual Communities: The Making of a Homosexual Minority in the United States, 1940–1970* (Chicago: University of Chicago Press, 1983); Lillian Faderman, *Odd Girls* and *Twilight Lovers: A History of Lesbian Life in Twentieth-Century America* (New York: Columbia University Press, 1991); Elizabeth Kennedy and Madeline Davis, *Boots of Leather, Slippers of Gold: The History of a Lesbian Community* (New York: Routledge, 1993); Leila J. Rupp, "'Imagine My Surprise': Women's Relationships in Mid-Twentieth-Century America," in *Hidden from History*, ed. M. Duberman, M. Vicinus and G. Chauncey Jr. (New York: Meridian, 1990); Rochella Thorpe, "'A House where Queers Go': African-American Lesbian Nightlife in Detroit, 1940–1975," in *Inventing Lesbian Cultures in America*, ed. Ellen Lewin (Boston: Beacon Press, 1996); and Marc Stein, *City of Sisterly and Brotherly Loves: Lesbian and Gay Philadelphia, 1945–72* (Chicago: University of Chicago Press, 2000).

3. Allan Berube, *Coming Out under Fire: The History of Gay Men and Women in World War Two* (New York: Macmillan, 1990), p. 271.
4. To understand the social context of the 1950s as a time of both change and anxiety, especially regarding gender and intimate life, I have drawn on the following: Wini Breines, *Young, White, and Miserable: Growing up Female in the Fifties* (Boston: Beacon Press, 1992); Stephanie Coontz, *The Way We Never Were: American Families and the Nostalgia Trap* (New York: Basic Books, 1992); Barbara Ehrenreich, *Hearts of Men: American Dreams and the Flight from Commitment* (Garden City, N.Y.: Anchor Books, 1983); Elaine Tyler May, *Homeward Bound: American Families in the Cold War Era* (New York: Basic Books, 1988); Jessica Weiss, *To Have and to Hold: Marriage, the Baby Boom, and Social Change* (Chicago: University of Chicago Press, 2000); Cynthia Enloe, *The Morning after: Sexual Politics and the End of the Cold War* (Berkeley: University of California Press, 1993); and Robert Corber, *In the Name of National Security: Hitchcock, Homophobia, and the Political Construction of Gender in Postwar America* (Durham, N.C.: Duke University Press, 1993).

5. On the making of the closet in the 1950s, see John D'Emilio, "The Homosexual Menace: The Politics of Sexuality in Cold War America," in *Making Trouble: Essays on Gay History, Politics, and the University* (New York: Routledge, 1992), and *Sexual Politics, Sexual Communities*; Allan Berube and John D'Emilio, "The Military and Lesbians during the McCarthy Years," *Signs* 9 (Summer 1984): 759–75; Barbara Epstein, "Anti-Communism, Homophobia, and the Construction of Masculinity in the Postwar U.S." *Critical Sociology* 20 (1994): 21–44; Faderman, *Odd Girls*; Robert Corber, *Homosexuality in Cold War America: Resistance and the Crisis of Masculinity* (Durham, N.C.: Duke University Press, 1997); and Gerard Sullivan, "Political Opportunism and the Harassment of Homosexuals in Florida, 1952–1965," *Journal of Homosexuality* 37 (1999): 57–81.
6. Chauncey, *Gay New York*, p. 6; William Eskridge Jr., *Gaylaw: Challenging the Apartheid of the Closet* (Cambridge, Mass.: Harvard University Press, 1999), p. 13; Paul Monette, *Becoming a Man: Half a Life Story* (New York: HarperCollins, 1992), p. 2; Joseph Beam, "Leaving the Shadows Behind," in *In the Life: A Black Gay Anthology*, ed. Joseph Beam (Boston: Alyson, 1986), p. 16.
7. Monette, *Becoming a Man*, p. 1.
8. In his memoir, Mel White, the former ghostwriter for Billy Graham and Jerry Falwell, movingly describes his experience of isolation: "I was isolated, not by bars or guards in uniforms, but by fear. I was surrounded by my loving family and close friends, but there was no way to explain to them my desperate, lonely feelings even when we were together. I wasn't tortured by leather straps or cattle prods, but my guilt and fear kept me in constant torment. . . . I was starving for the kind of human intimacy that would satisfy my longing, end my loneliness." White says that this isolation made him "feel like an alien who had been abandoned on a strange planet. . . . Living rooms and dining rooms, restaurants and lobbies, became foreign, unfriendly places. [I grew] weary of pretending to be someone I was not, tired of hiding my feelings. . . . My once lively spirit was shriveling like a raisin in the sun. . . . Desperation and loneliness surged. . . . I felt trapped and terrified." Mel White, *Stranger at the Gate: To Be Gay and Christian in America* (New York: Plume, 1995), pp. 123, 177–78.
9. Allan Berube describes the closet as a "system of lies, denials, disguises, and double entendres—that had enabled them to express some of their homosexuality by pretending it didn't exist and hiding it from view." Berube, *Coming Out under Fire*, p. 271.
10. My research suggests that the category of the closet initially appeared in the writing of gay liberationists. The earliest reference I've found was an "editorial" statement in the short-lived newspaper *Come Out!* in 1969. By the early

1970s the concept of the closet was widely circulating in liberationist writings; e.g., Signo Canceris, "From the Closet," *Fag Rag* 4 (January 1973); Bruce Gilbert "Coming Out, "*Fag Rag* 23/24 (1976); Morgan Pinney, "Out of Your Closets," *Gay Sunshine* 1 (October 1970); Ian Young, "Closet Wrecking," *Gay Sunshine* 28 (Spring 1976); Jennifer Woodhul, "Darers Go First," *The Furies* 1 (June/July 1972); and Allen Young, "Out of the Closets, into the Streets," in *Out of the Closets*, ed. Karla Jay and Allen Young. The closet underscored a condition of oppression. Gays were not merely discriminated against but dominated. And the closet was not a product of individual ignorance or prejudice but a social system of heterosexual domination. The core institutions and culture of America were said to be organized to enforce the norm and ideal of heterosexuality. In short, the closet underscored the way a system of compulsory heterosexuality creates a separate and oppressed homosexual existence. By arguing that the very organization of American society compels homosexuals to live socially isolated, inauthentic lives, the category of the closet served both as a way to understand gay life and as a critique of America.

By the mid-1970s, as liberationism gave way to a politics of minority rights, the concept of the closet was in wide use. However, its meaning began to change. Within the minority rights discourse that triumphed in the late 1970s, the closet was viewed as an act of concealment in response to actual or anticipated prejudice; it was seen as a matter of individual choice. By the late 1970s and 1980s, some gays were arguing that America had become a much more tolerant nation; the risks of coming out were greatly diminished. Being in or out of the closet was now seen as an individual choice rather than an adjustment to heterosexual domination. In fact, gays began to feel considerable pressure to come out, as many came to believe that visibility was both more possible and a key to challenging prejudice. For example, David Goodstein, the owner and editor of *The Advocate* from roughly the mid-1970s through the mid-1980s, gravitated to a view of the closet as almost self-imposed, as a product of "low self-esteem" or "cowardice." "I truly believe that there is no reason for you to be closeted and hide who you are" (*The Advocate*, 1983, p. 6). Goodstein blamed social intolerance in part on the cowardice of those who choose to be closeted. "I take a dim view of staying in the closet. . . . What brings up my irritation at this time . . . is the price we uncloseted gay people pay for the cowardice and stupidity of our [closeted] brothers and sisters" ("Opening Spaces," *The Advocate*, 1981, p. 6).

I have stated my preference for a liberationist approach. If the concept of the closet is to help us to understand changes in gay life, it should be used in a way that indicates more than an act of concealment. In this regard, the liberationist idea of the closet as a condition of social oppression is persuasive.

Explaining gay subordination, at least from the 1950s through the 1980s, as a product of individual prejudice or ignorance makes it hard, if not impossible, to understand its socially patterned character. It was not simply that gays were disadvantaged in one institution or only by isolated acts of discrimination or disrespect, but gay subordination occurred across institutions and culture. Heterosexual privilege was aggressively enforced by the state, cultural practices, daily acts of harassment and violence, and by institutions such as marriage, the wedding industry, and a dense network of laws covering taxes, family, immigration, military policy, and so on. At least during the heyday of the closet, the social risks of exposure were so great that it is naive to speak of the closet as an individual choice. In short, the concept of the closet helps us to understand the way heterosexuality functioned as an "institution" or a "system" that oppressed gay people.

A liberationist approach requires, however, some modification. In particular, the closet should be approached as a product of historically specific social dynamics; in particular, a culture of homosexual pollution and state repression. Furthermore, liberationists tend to read heterosexual domination as so closely and deeply intertwined with a whole system of gender, racial, economic, and political domination that America is viewed as irredeemably repressive. Such totalizing views are not credible.

11. Class is absent from much of queer social analysis. There are theoretical and rhetorical appeals to the importance of class, but little social research that addresses class patterns of concealment and coming out, gay and lesbian identification, and workplace dynamics. I have made use of the following work: Nicola Field, *Over the Rainbow: Money, Class, and Homophobia* (London: Pluto Press, 1995); Steve Valocchi, "The Class-Inflected Nature of Gay Identity," *Social Problems* 46 (1999): 207–44; Katie Gilmartin, "We Weren't Bar People: Middle Class Identities and Cultural Space," *Gay and Lesbian Quarterly* 3 (1996): 1–5; Roger Lancaster, *Life Is Hard: Machismo, Danger, and the Intimacy of Power in Nicaragua* (Berkeley: University of California Press, 1992); and David Evans, *Sexual Citizenship: The Material Construction of Sexualities* (London: Routledge, 1993). Joshua Gamson's *Freaks Talk Back: Tabloid Talk Shows and Sexual Nonconformity* (Chicago: University of Chicago Press, 1998) and Chrys Ingraham's *White Weddings: Romancing Heterosexuality in Popular Culture* (New York: Routledge, 1999) weave class into an analysis of sexual identities in interesting ways. Lillian Faderman's *Odd Girls, Twilight Lovers* and Kennedy and Davis's *Boots of Leather, Slippers of Gold* are indispensable sources for understanding the role of class in early postwar lesbian life.
12. Like class, race figures prominently in theoretical statements and in personal testimonies but is lacking when it comes to empirical research. There is an

abundance of personal testimonies or interpretive statements; e.g., Cherríe Moraga and Gloria Anzaldúa, eds., *This Bridge Called My Back: Writings by Radical Women of Color* (New York: Kitchen Table, 1981); Joseph Beam, ed., *In the Life: A Black Gay Anthology* (Boston: Alyson, 1986); Essex Hemphill, ed., *Brother to Brother: New Writings by Black Gay Men* (Boston: Alyson, 1991); Keith Boykin, *One More River to Cross: Black and Gay in America* (New York: Anchor Books, 1996); Carla Trujillo, ed., *Chicana Lesbians: The Girls Our Mothers Warned Us About* (Berkeley: Third Woman Press, 1991); Juanita Ramos, ed., *Companeras: Latina Lesbians* (New York: Latina Lesbian History Project, 1987); Russell Leong, ed., *Asian American Sexualities* (New York: Routledge, 1996). There has also developed a tradition of literary-critical studies of racialized gay identities; e.g., Arthur Flannigan-Saint-Augin, "Black Gay Male Discourse: Reading Race and Sexuality between the Lines," in *American Sexual Politics: Sex, Gender, and Race since the Civil War*, ed. John Fout and Maura Shaw Tantillo (Chicago: University of Chicago Press, 1993); Phillip Brian Harper, "Eloquence and Epitaph: AIDS, Homophobia, and Problematics of Black Masculinity," in *Are We Not Men? Masculine Anxiety and the Problem of African-American Identity* (New York: Oxford University Press, 1996); Isaac Julien and Kobena Mercer, "True Confessions: A Discourse on Images of Black Male Sexuality," in *Male Order: Unwrapping Masculinity*, ed. R. Chapman and J. Rutherford (London: Lawrence and Wishart, 1988); Ann duCille, "Blues Notes on Black Sexuality: Sex and the Texts of Jessie Fauset and Nella Larsen," in *American Sexual Politics: Sex, Gender, and Race since the Civil War*, ed. Fout and Tantillo; Mason Stokes, *The Color of Sex: Whiteness, Heterosexuality, and the Fictions of White Supremacy* (Durham, N.C.: Duke University Press, 2000). There is very little historical, empirical, or ethnographic research on race and gay identities. Regarding patterns of concealment, coming out, and sexual identification among African Americans, I've drawn from the following: Cathy Cohen, *The Boundaries of Blackness: AIDS and the Breakdown of Black Politics* (Chicago: University of Chicago Press, 1999); William Hawkesworth, *One of the Children: Gay Black Men in Harlem* (Berkeley: University of California Press, 1996); John Peterson, "Black Men and Their Same-Sex Desires and Behaviors," in *Gay Culture in America: Essays from the Field*, ed. Gilbert Herdt (Boston: Beacon Press, 1992); Rochella Thorpe, "'A House where Queers Go'"; "African-American Lesbian Nightlife in Detroit, 1940–1975" in *Inventing Lesbian Culture in America* (Boston: Beacon Press, 1996); Kevin Mumford, "Homosex Changes: Race, Cultural Geography, and the Emergence of the Gay," *American Quarterly* 48 (1996): 220–31; and Lisa Walker, *Looking like What You Are: Sexual Style, Race, and Lesbian Identity* (New York: New York University Press, 2001).

13. Marlon Riggs, "Black Macho Revisited: Reflections of a SNAP! Queen," in

Brother to Brother: New Writings by Black Gay Men, ed. Essex Hemphill (Boston: Alyson, 1991) p. 254.

14. See Joseph Beam, "Brother to Brother: Words from the Heart," in *In the Life*, ed. Joseph Beam Cf. Essex Hemphill, "Introduction," Charles Nero, "Toward a Black Gay Aesthetic," Ron Simmons, "Some Thoughts on the Challenges Facing Black Gay Intellectuals," and Joseph Beam, "Making Ourselves from Scratch," in *Brother to Brother: New Writings by Black Gay Men*, ed. Essex Hemphill; Barbara Smith and Beverly Smith, "Across the Kitchen Table: A Sister-to-Sister Dialogue,"in *This Bridge Called My Back,* ed. Moraga and Anzaldúa; bell hooks, "Reflections on Homophobia and Black Communities," *Out/Look* 1 (1988): 22–25; Cheryl Clarke, "The Failure to Transform: Homophobia in the Black Community," in *Home Girls: A Black Feminist Anthology*, ed. Barbara Smith (New York: Kitchen Table, 1983); and Jackie Goldsby, "What It Means to Be Colored Me," *Out/Look* 9 (Summer 1990): 8–17.
15. Hawkesworth, *One of the Children.*
16. Cohen, *The Boundaries of Blackness*, pp. 91–95.
17. There is a substantial theoretical and research literature on the role of gender in shaping patterns of sexual identification and dynamics of the closet and coming out. The literature of gay liberationism and lesbian feminism is crucial. On the tradition of lesbian feminism, see Nancy Myron and Charlotte Bunch, eds., *Lesbianism and the Women's Movement.* (Baltimore: Diana Press, 1975). For gay liberationism, see Karla Jay and Allen Young, eds., *Out of the Closets: Voices of Gay Liberationism*, (New York: New York University Press, 1992 [1972]). For more recent theoretical and empirical statements, see Judith Butler, *Gender Trouble: Feminism and the Subversion of Gender* (New York: Routledge, 1990); Biddy Martin, "Sexualities without Genders and Other Queer Utopias," *Diacritics* 24 (Summer 1994): 104–21; Chrys Ingraham, "The Heterosexual Imaginary: Feminist Sociology and Theories of Gender," in *Queer Theory/Sociology*, ed. Steven Seidman (Cambridge: Blackwell, 1996); Peggy Reeves Sanday, *Fraternity Gang Rape: Sex, Brotherhood, and Privilege on Campus* (New York: New York University, 1990); Christine Williams and Arlene Stein, eds., S*exuality and Gender* (Malden, Mass.: Blackwell, 2002); and Kath Weston, *Render Me, Gender Me: Lesbians Talk Sex, Class, Color, Nation, Studmuffins* (New York: Columbia University Press, 1996).

    It is interesting to note that the term *the closet* was initially developed in liberationist texts, which, though a mixed-gender movement, was shaped considerably by men. By contrast, the chief architects of lesbian feminism such as Charlotte Bunch, Rita Mae Brown, Ti Grace Atkinson, the Furies Collective, and New York Radicalesbians did not place the concept of the closet at the center of their thinking and politics. To the extent that being a lesbian was understood as a political act of resistance to male dominance and compulsory heterosexuality, it was the struggle against sexism and the development of a women-centered culture that was the political focus. With the decline of lesbian feminism, along with the gradual development of a gender-integrated gay movement, the closet and issues of coming out became more prominent in lesbian writing as well.

18. For a wonderful illustration of the thickness of gender codes in contemporary America, see Deirdre McCloskey's description of gender passing in her memoir, *Crossing* (Chicago: University of Chicago Press, 1999), pp. 160–62.
19. For approaches to the closet that emphasize dynamics of knowledge/ignorance, presence/absence and its haunting power, see Sedgwick, *The Epistemology of the Closet*; Diana Fuss, "Inside/Out," in *Inside/Out: Lesbian Theories, Gay Theories* (New York: Routledge, 1991); Michael Moon, "Flaming Closets," in *Out in Culture: Gay, Lesbian, and Queer Essays on Popular Culture*, ed. Corey Creekmur and Alexander Doty (Durham, N.C.: Duke University Press, 1995); and Lee Edelman, "Tearooms and Sympathy, or, The Epistemology of the Water Closet," in *The Lesbian and Gay Studies Reader*, ed. Henry Abelove, Michele Aina Barale, and David Halperin (New York: Routledge, 1993).

CHAPTER 2

1. For sociological overviews of American gay life in the 1970s and 1980s, see Dennis Altman, *The Homosexualization of America* (Boston: Beacon Press, 1982); Joseph Harry and William Devall, *The Social Organization of Gay Males* (New York: Praeger, 1978); Laud Humphries, "Exodus and Identity: The Merging Gay Culture," in *Gay Men*, ed. Martin Levine (New York: Harper and Row, 1979); John Lee, "The Gay Connection," *Urban Life* 8 (1979): 175–98; Lillian Faderman, *Odd Girls and Twilight Lovers: A History of Lesbian Life in Twentieth-Century America* (New York: Columbia University Press, 1991); Martin Levine, "Gay Macho," Ph.D. diss., New York University, 1986; Stephen Murray, *American Gay* (Chicago: University of Chicago Press, 1996); Esther Newton, *Cherry Grove* (Boston: Beacon Press, 1993); Barbara Ponse, *Identity in the Lesbian World* (Westport, Conn.: Greenwood, 1978); Carol Warren, *Identity and Community in the Gay World* (New York: Wiley, 1974); Deborah Wolfe, *The Lesbian Community* (Berkeley: University of California Press, 1979); and Karla Jay and Allen Young, *The Gay Report: Lesbians and Gay Men Speak out about Sexual Experiences and Lifestyles* (New York: Summit Books, 1979). Arlene Stein's *Sex and Sensibility: Stories of a Lesbian Generation* (Berkeley: University of California, 1997) offers much insight into lesbian-feminist culture.

2. For helpful overviews of various aspects of American gay life in the 1990s, see Christopher Carrington, *No Place like Home: Relationships and Family Life among Lesbians and Gay Men* (Chicago: University of Chicago Press, 1999); Peter Nardi, *Gay Men's Friendships: Invisible Communities* (Chicago: University of Chicago Press, 1999); Michelangelo Signorile, *Life Outside: The Signorile Report on Gay Men: Sex, Drugs, Muscles, and the Passages of Life* (New York: HarperCollins, 1997); Daniel Harris, *The Rise and Fall of Gay Culture* (New York: Ballantine, 1997); Suzanna Danuta Walters, *All the Rage: The Story of Gay Visibility* (Chicago: University of Chicago Press, 2001); Michael Bronski, *The Pleasure Principle: Sex, Backlash, and the Struggle for Gay Freedom* (New York: St. Martin's Press, 1998); Kristin Esterberg, *Lesbian and Bisexual Identities: Constructing Communities, Constructing Selves* (Philadelphia: Temple University Press, 1997); and Frederick Lynch, "Nonghetto Gays: An Ethnography of Suburban Homosexuals," in *Gay Culture in America: Essays from the Field*, ed. Gilbert Herdt (Boston: Beacon Press, 1992).
3. If the conditions of the closet are declining, at least as one noteworthy trend, why is the language of the closet so pervasive today? In part, the explanation is social. While many gays have fashioned postcloseted lives in their private social worlds—for example, they may be out to friends, may share a home with partners, and may be open to some kin and work colleagues—this "routinization" of gay life is often *not* present in key institutions. In many of our schools, families, and churches, in the military, and in many workplaces, there is still little or no institutional protection and support for lesbians and gay men. A language of the closet still resonates with an experience of institutional subordination, even though informal or interpersonal tolerance is increasingly replacing silence and invisibility in these institutions.

   The explanation is also political. As the gay movement has gained a foothold in mainstream America, the language of the closet remains a compelling moral and political rhetoric. To describe an America in which many of its citizens are forced to live isolated and fearful lives contradicts a national culture that champions individual rights and self-realization. The language of the closet aims to ensure that anti-gay discrimination remains a compelling public issue.

   Moreover, in the struggle for rights and respect, an institutionalized gay world has evolved. Many individuals now choose to organize their lives around a gay identity for reasons that have less to do with surviving discrimination than with being integrated into a subculture that celebrates their identity, provides a strong sense of community, and often secures their livelihood and status. For many of these subculturally integrated individuals, especially the elite who shape the official narratives and politics of the gay world, the experience of the closet was formative in their coming of age. Their life story—and the story they tell about being gay in America—is often told as a heroic struggle against the dark years of the closet. Accordingly, for personal, sociological, and political reasons, many gay Americans have a considerable investment in the language of the closet.

4. In 1996–97 two research assistants (Chet Meeks and Francie Traschen) and myself interviewed thirty individuals who identified as lesbian, gay, or bisexual. As other social researchers have argued, a representative sample of homosexually identified individuals is not possible. I sought a sample population that was diverse in terms of gender, race, and class.

   My aim was to interview individuals who have not organized their lives around a gay subculture. I assumed that "subcultural" gays would likely be more self-accepting and public. I sought individuals who would be closeted or at least have long closeted histories.

   The interview was divided into three parts. The first obtained demographic information. The second part focused on concealment decisions at work, with friends and family, and in daily life. The third part addressed disclosure practices and reactions, life outside the closet.

   Of the thirty respondents, sixteen were men, fourteen were women; twenty-two were white, eight were either black or Latino; eleven could be classified as working or lower middle class, nineteen as middle class; eight respondents were aged twenty-five or younger, thirteen were under forty, and nine were older than forty.

5. Researchers have documented that many youth who came of age in the late 1980s and 1990s felt compelled to conceal their homosexuality as a condition of integration into family, peer, and school communities. Indeed, given their social, economic, and legal dependence on the family and school, their need to manage their identity is potentially fateful in a way recalling closeted homosexuals. Yet, while an easy accommodation to being gay is often blocked by dependence on the family and schools, which are among the least tolerant institutions, self-acceptance often occurs anyway. This is a generation that matured in a context of unprecedented gay visibility and integration. Arguably, a relatively accelerated process of self-acceptance in the context of the aggressive homophobia of many families and schools is crucial to grasping the potentially explosive psychic and social texture of life for many gay youth today. For helpful analyses, see Gilbert Herdt and Andrew Boxer, "Introduction: Culture, History, and Life Course of Gay Men," in *Gay Culture in America: Essays from the Field* (Boston: Beacon Press, 1992); Gilbert Herdt and Andrew Boxer, *Children of Horizons: How Gay and Lesbian Teens Are Leading a New Way out of the Closet* (Boston: Beacon Press, 1993); George Smith, "The Ideology of Fag: The School Experience of Gay Students," *The Sociological Quarterly* 39 (1998): 309–35; Melinda Miceli, "Recognizing All

the Differences: Gay Youth and Public Education in America Today," Ph.D. diss, State University of New York, Albany, 1998; Robert Owens, *Queer Kids* (Binghamton, N.Y.: Harrington Park, 1998); and G. Unks, ed., *The Gay Teen: Educational Practice and Theory for Lesbian, Gay, and Bisexual Adolescents* (New York: Routledge, 1995).

6. Miceli, "Recognizing All the Differences."
7. Much of the best research assumes a homophobic, repressive workplace. While this research often speaks to a condition defined by the pervasive reality of the closet, it is still relevant. See Jeffrey Escoffier, "The Political Economy of the Closet: Notes towards an Economic History of Gay and Lesbian Life before Stonewall," in *Homo Economics: Capitalism, Community, and Lesbian and Gay Life*, ed. Amy Gluckman and Betsy Reed (New York: Routledge, 1997); Beth Schneider, "Coming Out at Work: Bridging the Private/Public Gap," *Work and Occupations* 13 (1987): 463–87; and James Woods with Jay Lucas, *The Corporate Closet: The Professional Lives of Gay Men in America* (New York: Free Press, 1993). Some recent research speaks to a more varied, often less homophobic, repressive work environment; it also analyzes the way normative heterosexuality works through sexualizing gender; e.g., Debbie Epstein, "Keeping Them in Their Place: Hetero/sexist Harassment, Gender, and the Enforcement of Heterosexuality," in *Sex, Sensibility, and the Gendered Body*, ed. Janet Holland and Lisa Adkins (New York: St. Martin's Press, 1996); and Anne Witz, Susan Halford, and Mike Savage, "Organized Bodies: Gender, Sexuality, and Embodiment in Contemporary Organizations," in *Sexualizing the Social: Power and the Organization of Sexuality*, ed. Lisa Adkins and Vicki Merchant (New York: St. Martin's Press, 1996).
8. Merle Miller, *On Being Different* (New York: Random House, 1971); Martin Duberman, *Cures: A Gay Man's Odyssey* (New York: Penguin, 1991); Julia Penelope and Susan Wolfe, eds., *The Original Coming Out Stories,* 2nd ed. (Calif.: Crossing Press, 1989).
9. For perspectives that understand coming-out narratives as both personal and political, see Robert McRuer, "Boys' Own Stories and New Spellings of My Name: Coming Out and Other Myths of Queer Positionality," in *Eroticism and Containment*, ed. C. Siegal and A. Kibbey (New York: Routledge, 1996); Bonnie Zimmerman, "The Politics of Transliteration: Lesbian Personal Narratives," *Signs* 9 (Summer 1984): 663–82; and Ken Plummer, *Telling Sexual Stories* (London: Routledge, 1995).
10. Paul Monette, *Becoming a Man: Half a Life Story* (New York: HarperCollins, 1992).
11. Coming-out stories were at the center of many memoirs and novels published between the 1960s and the 1980s. While coming-out stories remain promi-

nent today, in many contemporary novels themes addressing ordinary life concerns such as relations with family, friends, and lovers, or illness and aging, have taken the place of coming-out themes. Perhaps no writer better exemplifies this shift away from coming-out stories than David Leavitt. His first novel, *The Lost Language of Cranes,* was very much a classic coming-out story. In his subsequent work (e.g., *Equal Affections*, *Arkansas*, *The Page Turner*, and *Martin Bauman)* the coming-out theme is a minor, barely noticeable motif. Postcloseted narrative themes are at the center of the novels of, to name some prominent male writers, Michael Cunningham, Stephen McCauley, Chistopher Bram, and younger writers such as Scott Heim, K. M. Soehnlein, and C. Bard Cole.

12. One example is the gay male party circuit discussed in Signorile, *Life Outside.*
13. On the idea of homosexual signs, see Harold Beaver, "Homosexual Signs," *Critical Inquiry* (Fall 1981): 99–119. A performative understanding of identity has contributed to a recent emphasis on signifying practices; e.g., Esterberg, *Lesbian and Bisexual Identities*; Arlene Stein, *Sex and Sensibility: Stories of a Lesbian Generation* (Berkeley: University of California Press, 1997); George Chauncey, *Gay New York: Gender, Urban Culture, and the Making of the Gay Male World, 1890–1940* (New York: Basic Books, 1994).
14. Other writers have also argued that many gays today, especially those born after 1970, have much more latitude in deciding the place of being gay in their sense of identity, and that many are choosing to view it as a thread rather than as a core self-definition. For example, see Gamson, *Freaks Talk Back*; Stein, *Sex and Sensibility*; Signorile, *Life Outside*; Paula Kamen, *Her Way: Young Women Remake the Sexual Revolution* (New York: New York University Press, 2000), p. 154. This theme is central to an unpublished dissertation by Debbie Donovan, "Identity beyond the Community: The Making of Suburban Lesbian Friendship Networks," Ph.D diss., State University of New York, Albany, 1999.

CHAPTER 3

1. See Kath Weston, *Families We Choose: Lesbians, Gays, Kinship* (New York: Columbia University Press, 1991). Also see Jeffrey Weeks, Brian Heaphy, and Catherine Donovan, *Same Sex Intimacies: Families of Choice and Other Life Experiments* (New York: Routledge, 2001); Christopher Carrington, *No Place like Home: Relationships and Family Life among Lesbians and Gay Men* (Chicago: University of Chicago Press, 1999); Ellen Lewin, *Recognizing Ourselves: Ceremonies of Lesbian and Gay Commitment* (New York: Columbia University Press, 1998).
2. Cf. Gilbert Herdt and Bruce Koff, *Something to Tell You: The Road Families Travel when a Child Is Gay* (New York: Columbia University Press, 1999). See

also Gilbert Herdt and Andrew Boxer, *Children of Horizons: How Gay and Lesbian Teens Are Leading a New Way out of the Closet* (Boston: Beacon Press, 1993); Alice Hom, "Stories from the Homefront: Perspectives of Asian-American Parents with Lesbian Daughters and Gay Sons," in *Asian American Sexualities,* ed. Russell Leong, (New York: Routledge, 1996).

3. On the politics of lesbian and gay families, see Judith Stacey, *In the Name of the Family: Rethinking Family Values in the Postmodern Age* (Boston: Beacon Press, 1996) and (with Elizabeth Davenport), "Queer Families Quack Back," in *Handbook of Lesbian and Gay Studies,* ed. Diane Richardson and Steven Seidman (London: Sage, 2002); Valerie Lehr, *Queer Family Values: Debunking the Myth of the Nuclear Family* (Philadelphia: Temple University Press, 1999); and Richard Mohr, *A More Perfect Union* (Boston: Beacon Press, 1994).
4. Regarding the politics of homosexuality within the church, see Saul Olyan and Martha Nussbaum, eds., *Sexual Orientation and Human Rights in American Religious Discourse* (New York: Oxford University Press, 1998); Gary Comstock and Susan Henking, eds., *Que(e)rying Religion: A Critical Anthology* (New York: Continuum, 1999); Didi Herman, *The Antigay Agenda: Orthodox Vision and the Christian Right* (Chicago: University of Chicago Press, 1997); Keith Hartman, *The Battle over Homosexuality* (New Brunswick, N.J.: Rutgers University Press, 1996); and Michele Dillon, *Catholic Identity: Balancing Reason, Faith, and Power* (Cambridge: Cambridge University Press, 1999).
5. Clyde Wilcox and Robin Wolpert, "Gay Rights in the Public Sphere: Public Opinion on Gay and Lesbian Equality," in *The Politics of Gay Rights,* ed. Craig Rimmerman, Kenneth Wald, and Clyde Wilcox (Chicago: University of Chicago Press, 2000).
6. The appearance of literature advising straight America on what it means to be gay and how best to accommodate is indicative of the changed status of lesbians and gay men. A good deal of this advice literature is directed to straight parents; e.g., see Mary Borhek, *Coming Out to Parents: A Two-Way Survival Guide for Lesbians and Gay Men and Their Parents* (Cleveland, Ohio: Pilgrim, 1993); Betty Fairchild and Nancy Hayward, *Now That You Know: What Every Parent Should Know about Homosexuality* (New York: Harcourt Brace Jovanovich, 1989); Eric Marcus, *Is It a Choice? Answers to the Most Frequently Asked Questions about Gay and Lesbian People* (San Francisco: Harper, 1999); Robert Bernstein, *Straight Parents, Gay Children: Inspiring Families to Live Honestly and with Greater Understanding* (New York: St. Martin's Press, 1997); David Switzer, *Coming Out as Parents: You and Your Homosexual Child* (Louisville, Ky.: Westminster John Knox Press, 1996); Carolyn Griffin et al., *Beyond Acceptance: Parents of Lesbians and Gays Talk about Their Experiences* (New York: Thunder's Mouth Press, 1997).

7. There is little research on the formation of heterosexual identities and on variations and changes in patterns of straight identification. I've drawn from the following historical research: Jonathan Ned Katz, *The Invention of Heterosexuality* (New York: Dutton, 1995); George Chauncey, *Gay New York: Gender, Urban Culture, and the Making of the Gay Male World, 1890–1940* (New York: Basic Books, 1994); Kevin White, *The First Sexual Revolution: The Emergence of Male Heterosexuality in America* (New York: New York University Press, 1993). I've also profited from the following sociological work: Mary Louise Adams, *The Trouble with Normal: Postwar Youth and the Making of Heterosexuality* (Toronto: University of Toronto Press, 1997); Karen Dubinsky, *Improper Advances: Rape and Heterosexual Conflict in Ontario, 1880–1929* (Chicago: University of Chicago Press, 1996); Debbie Epstein and Richard Johnson, *Schooling Sexualities* (Buckingham: Open University Press, 1998); Chrys Ingraham, *White Weddings: Romancing Heterosexuality in Popular Culture* (New York: Routledge, 1999); Mairtin Mac An Ghaill, *The Making of Men: Masculinities, Sexualities, and Schooling* (Buckingham: Open University Press, 1994).

CHAPTER 4

1. See Suzanna Danuta Walters, *All the Rage: The Story of Gay Visibility in America* (Chicago: University of Chicago Press, 2001).
2. It's not entirely arbitrary that my focus is film. Scholars have emphasized the social role that medical-psychiatric and sexological discourses played in the making of a homophobic culture in the 1950s and early 1960s; e.g., John D'Emilio, *Sexual Politics, Sexual Communities: The Making of a Sexual Minority in the United States, 1940–1970* (Chicago: University of Chicago Press, 1983); Lillian Faderman, *Odd Girls and Twilight Lovers: A History of Lesbian Life in Twentieth-Century America* (New York: Columbia University Press, 1991); Janice Irvine, *Disorders of Desire: Sex and Gender in Modern American Sexology* (Philadelphia: Temple University Press, 1990); and Jennifer Terry, *An American Obsession: Science, Medicine, and Homosexuality in Modern Society* (Chicago: University of Chicago Press 1999). My sense is that films and popular culture in general have played a similarly key role in the social construction of the homosexual from the 1970s through the present. Also, insofar as nonpolluting images of gay identity are especially prominent in commercial film in the 1990s, this is a useful site for analyzing the sociopolitical logic of gay normalization.

   In 1998, I analyzed forty-eight films. Several criteria guided this research. First, reflecting the focus of the study, only films produced in the United States and intended for American consumption were included.

Second, I considered primarily "mainstream" films. These were defined as commercially successful films as measured by box office sales (see the appendix). I have assumed that commercial success lends plausibility to the claim that the sexual meanings in these films is at least tolerable and perhaps resonant with a substantial segment of America. I do not assume, however, that normalizing representations in films are necessarily indicative of trends in all cultural and institutional spheres. At the same time, normalizing trends in television, academic disciplines, law, and business and governmental policy make plausible the claim that normalization is one defining social trend in contemporary America. Finally, while normalizing representations may be indicative of empirical trends, they also function normatively, defining appropriate or expected beliefs and attitudes. Third, I considered only films that featured explicitly lesbian or gay male characters. I disregarded films in which homosexuality was implied. While queer cultural analysis has often brilliantly analyzed symbolically coded forms of homosexuality, my aim is not to do a queer reading of film but to trace social logics of normative heterosexuality. For queer approaches to film, see D. A. Miller, "Anal Rope," and Judith Mayne, "A Parallax View of Lesbian Authorship," in *Inside/Out: Lesbian Theories, Gay Theories*, ed. Diana Fuss (New York: Routledge, 1991); Alexander Doty, *Making Things Perfectly Queer: Interpreting Mass Culture* (Minneapolis: University of Minnesota Press, 1993) Teresa de Lauretis, "Film and the Visible," in *How Do I Look? Queer Film and Video*, ed. *Bad Object-Choices* (Seattle, Wash.: Bay Press, 1991); Chris Straayer, *Deviant Eyes, Deviant Bodies: Sexual Reorientation in Film and Video* (New York: Columbia University Press, 1996); Robert Corber, *Homosexuality in Cold War America: Resistance and the Crisis of Masculinity*, (Durham, N.C.: Duke University Press, 1997); and Ellis Hanson, ed., *Out Takes: Essays on Queer Theory and Film* (Durham, N.C.: Duke University Press, 1999).

This research strategy still posed methodological problems. There are well over a thousand movies that meet the above criteria. I decided against a random sample in part because film collections are spotty and archival access presented impossible demands. I wanted, moreover, to make sure that "breakthrough" films (e.g., *The Children's Hour*) or commercial hits (e.g., *Philadelphia, My Best Friend's Wedding)* were included. Finally, films were selected that included underrepresented segments of the gay population, such as lesbians or persons of color.

3. For example, researchers have begun to document changes in images of gay people in popular culture. See Suzanna Walters, *All the Rage*; Joshua Gamson, *Freaks Talk Back: Tabloid Talk Shows and Sexual Nonconformity* (Chicago: University of Chicago Press, 1998); Steven Capsuto, *Alternate Channels: The Uncensored Story of Gay and Lesbian Images on Radio and Television* (New

York: Ballantine Books, 2000); Alexandra Chasin, *Selling Out: The Gay and Lesbian Movement Goes to Market* (New York: St. Martin's Press, 2000); and Lisa Bennett, "Fifty Years of Prejudice in the Media," *The Gay and Lesbian Review* (Spring 2000): 30–35.

4. Jeni Loftus, "America's Liberalization in Attitudes toward Homosexuality, 1973 to 1998," *American Sociological Review* 66 (October 2001): 762–82; and Alan Yang, "The Polls—Trends, Attitudes toward Homosexuality," *Public Opinion Quarterly* 61 (1997): 477–507.
5. Bennett, "Fifty Years of Prejudice in the Media."
6. Ibid.
7. There is a considerable literature documenting the various stereotypical, polluting images of homosexuality in films through the 1980s. See Vito Russo, *The Celluloid Closet: Homosexuality in the Movies*, 2nd ed. (New York: Harper and Row, 1987); Fred Fejes and Kevin Petrich, "Invisibility, Homophobia, and Heterosexism: Lesbians, Gays, and the Media," *Critical Studies in Mass Communication* (December 1993): 396–422; Larry Gross, "Out of the Mainstream: Sexual Minorities and the Mass Media," in *Remote Control: Television, Audiences, and Cultural Power*, ed. Ellen Seiter (New York: Routledge, 1989); Richard Dyer, *Gays and Film* (New York: Zoetrope, 1984); Martha Gever, John Greyson, and Pratibha Parmar, eds., *Queer Looks: Perspectives on Lesbian and Gay Film and Video* (New York: Routledge, 1993); Parker Tyler, *Screening the Sexes: Homosexuality in the Movies* (New York: Holt, Rinehart, and Winston, 1972); Andrea Weiss, *Vampires and Violets: Lesbians in Film* (New York: Penguin, 1992); and Phillip Brian Harper, "Walk-on Parts and Speaking Subjects: Screen Representations of Black Gay Men," in *Black Male: Representations of Masculinity in Contemporary American Art*, ed. Thelma Golden (New York: Whitney Museum of American Art, 1994).
8. On the notion of social death, see Orlando Patterson, *Slavery and Social Death: A Comparative Study* (Cambridge, Mass.: Harvard University Press, 1982).
9. Indicative of the growing intolerance of public homophobic expressions is the public reaction to Jerry Falwell's statement on the *700 Club* TV show on September 13, 2001. To recap the gist of his remarks, Falwell linked the terrorist attack of September 11, 2001 to, in part, the growing tolerance of lesbians and gay men. "I really believe that the pagans, and the abortionists, and the feminists, and the gays and the lesbians who are actively trying to make that an alternative lifestyle . . . helped to make this happen." His host, Pat Robertson, responded, "Well, I totally concur." So swift and critical was the public reaction, including from the Bush administration, that Falwell soon appeared on *Good Morning America* to issue a public apology.
10. Regarding the absence of lesbians in popular culture or the notion of the

ephemeral character of lesbian identity, see Rhonda Berenstin, "Where the Girls Are: Riding the New Wave of Lesbian Feature Films," *GLQ* 3 (1996): 125–37; Edith Becker, Michelle Citron, Julia Lesage, and Ruby Rich, "Lesbians and Film," in *Out in Culture: Gay, Lesbian, and Queer Essays on Popular Culture*, ed. Corey Creekmur and Alexander Doty (Durham: Duke University Press, 1995); Weiss, *Vampires and Violets*; Tamsin Wilton, ed., *Immortal, Invisible: Lesbians and the Moving Image* (New York: Routledge, 1996).

11. Diana Fuss, "Introduction," in *Inside/Out: Lesbian Theories, Gay Theories,* ed. Diana Fuss (New York: Routledge, 1991); Eve Sedgwick, *The Epistemology of the Closet,* (Berkeley: University of California Press, 1990).
12. For perspectives on the sexual changes of the 1970s and after, see John D'Emilio and Estelle Freedman, *Intimate Matters: A History of Sexuality in America* (New York: Harper and Row, 1988); Steven Seidman, *Romantic Longings: Love in America, 1830–1980* (New York: Routledge, 1991); and *Embattled Eros: Sexual Ethics and Politics in Contemporary America* (New York: Routledge, 1992); Beth Bailey, *Sex in the Heartland.* (Cambridge, Mass.: Harvard University Press); Lynn Segal, *Straight Sex: Rethinking the Politics of Pleasure* (Berkeley: University of California Press, 1994); and Paula Kamen, *Her Way: Young Women Remake the Sexual Revolution* (New York: New York University Press, 2000).

CHAPTER 5

1. There was a notable exception to this cultural invisibility: pulp fiction. See Ian Young, "How Gay Paperbacks Changed America," and Michael Bronski, "Fictions about Pulp," in *Gay and Lesbian Review* 6 (November/December 2001).
2. See Jeff Escoffier, "The Political Economy of the Closet: Notes toward an Economic History of Gay and Lesbian Life before Stonewall," in *Homo Economics,* ed. Amy Gluckman and Betsy Reed (New York: Routledge, 1997); and Elizabeth Kennedy and Madeline Davis, *Boots of Leather, Slippers of Gold* (New York: Routledge, 1993).
3. John D'Emilio and Estelle Freedman, *Intimate Matters: A History of Sexuality in America* (New York: Harper and Row, 1988); Steven Seidman, *Romantic Longings: Love in America, 1830–1980* (New York: Routledge, 1991); Jonathan Ned Katz, "The Age of Sodomitical Sin, 1607–1740," in *Gay/Lesbian Almanac: A New Documentary* (New York: Harper and Row, 1983); Karen Lystra, *Searching the Heart: Women, Men, and Romantic Love in Nineteenth-Century America* (New York: Oxford University Press, 1989); and Peter Gay, *The Bourgeois Experience: Victoria to Freud, Vol. 1: Education of the Senses* (New York: Oxford University Press, 1984).

4. See Jonathan Ned Katz, *The Invention of Heterosexuality* (New York: Dutton, 1995) and *Love Stories: Sex between Men before Homosexuality* (Chicago: University of Chicago Press, 2001); and Seidman, *Romantic Longings.*
5. William Eskridge Jr., *Gaylaw: Challenging the Apartheid of the Closet* (Cambridge, Mass.: Harvard University Press, 1999), p. 1.
6. See Eskridge, *Gaylaw*; Jonathan Goldberg, ed., *Reclaiming Sodom* (New York: Routledge, 1994); and Katz, "The Age of Sodomitical Sin," and *Love Stories.*
7. See Katz, *Love Stories.*
8. See D'Emilio and Freedman, *Intimate Matters*, p. 133; Steven Marcus, *The Other Victorians* (New York: Basic Books, 1964); Walter Kendrick, *The Secret Museum* (New York: Viking, 1987); and Gay, *The Bourgeois Experience.*
9. Linda Hirshman and Jane Larson, *Hard Bargains: The Politics of Sex* (New York: Oxford University Press, 1998), p. 134.
10. Ibid., p. 165.
11. D'Emilio and Freedman, *Intimate Matters*, p. 147; Mary Gordon, *Woman's Body, Woman's Rights: A Social History of Birth Control* (New York: Grossman, 1967); Rosiland Petchesky, *Abortion and Women's Choice: The State, Sexuality, and Reproductive Freedom* (Boston: Northeastern University Press, 1984), ch. 2; James Mohr, *Abortion in America: The Origins and Evolution of National Policy* (New York: Oxford University Press, 1978); and Janet Brodie, *Contraception and Abortion in Nineteenth-Century America* (Ithaca, N.Y.: Cornell University Press, 1994).
12. Kristin Luker, "Sex, Hygiene, and the State: The Double-Edged Sword of Social Reform," *Theory and Society* 27 (1998): 615. See also Ruth Rosen, *The Lost Sisterhood: Prostitution in America, 1900–1918* (Baltimore: Johns Hopkins University Press, 1982); and David Pivar, *Purity Crusade: Sexual Morality and Social Control, 1868–1900* (Westport, Conn.: Greenwood, 1973).
13. D'Emilio and Freedman, *Intimate Matters*, pp. 157–59.
14. Hirshman and Larson, *Hard Bargains*, p. 172.
15. Ibid., p. 135.
16. George Chauncey, *Gay New York: Gender, Urban Culture, and the Making of the Gay Male World, 1890–1940* (New York: Basic Books, 1994). In a similar vein, Allan Berube notes that prior to World War II gays were not officially excluded from military service. "Traditionally, the military had never officially excluded or discharged homosexuals from its ranks. From the days following the Revolutionary War, the Army and Navy had targeted the act of sodomy . . . not homosexual persons, as criminals. . . . But in World War Two a dramatic change occurred. . . . Psychiatrists . . . developed new screening procedures to discover and disqualify homosexual men." Berube, *Coming Out under Fire: The History of Gay Men and Women in World War Two* (New York: Macmillan, 1990), p. 2.

17. Ibid.
18. See Hirshman and Larson, *Hard Bargains*, pp. 185–91.
19. Jana Singer, "The Privatization of Family Law," *Wisconsin Law Review* (1992): 1444–45.
20. D'Emilio and Freedman, *Intimate Matters*, p. 287.
21. See David Richards, *Women, Gays, and the Constitution* (Chicago: University of Chicago Press, 1998), p. 246.
22. Eskridge, *Gaylaw*, ch. 1.
23. Chauncey, *Gay New York*, p. 9.
24. Eskridge, *Gaylaw*, p. 98; cf. Chauncey, *Gay New York*, ch. 12; John D'Emilio, *Sexual Politics, Sexual Communities: The Making of a Homosexual Minority in the United States, 1940–1970* (Chicago: University of Chicago Press, 1983) and "The Homosexual Menace: The Politics of Sexuality in Cold War America," in *Making Trouble: Essays on Gay History, Politics, and the University* (New York: Routledge, 1992).
25. Eskridge, *Gaylaw*, p. 18.
26. For overviews of liberationist politics, see Stephen Engel, *The Unfinished Revolution: Social Movement Theory and the Gay and Lesbian Movement* (Cambridge: Cambridge University Press, 2001); Barry Adam, *The Rise of the Gay and Lesbian Movement* (New York: Twayne Publishers, 1995); Steven Epstein, "Gay and Lesbian Movements in the United States: Dilemmas of Identity, Diversity, and Political Strategy," in *The Global Emergence of Gay and Lesbian Politics: National Imprints of a Worldwide Movement*, ed. Barry Adam, Jan Willem Duyvendak, and Andre Krouwel (Philadelphia: Temple University Press, 1999); Toby Marotta, *The Politics of Homosexuality* (New York: Houghton Mifflin, 1981); Laud Humphreys, *Out of the Closets: The Sociology of Homosexual Liberation* (Englewood Cliffs, N.J.: Prentice Hall, 1972); Martin Duberman, *Stonewall* (New York: Dutton, 1993); Alice Echols, *Daring to Be Bad: Radical Feminism in America, 1967–1975* (Minneapolis: University of Minnesota Press, 1989); Verta Taylor and Leila Rupp, "Women's Culture and Lesbian Feminist Activism: A Reconsideration of Cultural Feminism," *Signs* 19 (Fall 1993): 32–61; Terence Kissack, "Freaking Fag Revolutionaries: New York's Gay Liberation Front, 1969–1971," *Radical History Review* 62 (1995): 104–34.
27. Stuart Byron, "The Closet Syndrome," in *Out of the Closets: Voices of Gay Liberationism*, ed. Karla Jay and Allen Young (New York: New York University Press, 1992 [1972]), p. 58. Cf. Judy Grahn, "Lesbians as Bogeywomen," *Women* 1 (Summer 1970): 36–38; and Carl Wittman, "A Gay Manifesto," and Karla Jay and Allen Young, "Out of the Closets, into the Streets," in *Out of the Closets*, ed. Jay and Young.
28. See the essays by the Red Butterfly Collective, Wittman, Jay and Young,

Third World Gay Revolution and Gay Liberation Front (Chicago), Woman-Identified Woman, and Martha Shelley, in Jay and Young, eds., *Out of the Closets.*

29. On the renewal of gay liberationist politics, see Urvashi Vaid, *Virtual Equality: The Mainstreaming of Gay and Lesbian Liberation* (New York: Doubleday, 1995); Michael Warner, *Fear of a Queer Planet* (Minneapolis: University of Minnesota Press, 1993); Michael Fraser, "Identity and Representation as Challenges to Social Movement Theory: A Case Study of Queer Nation," in *Mainstream(s) and Margins: Cultural Politics in the 90s*, eds. Michael Morgan and Susan Leggett (Westport, Conn.: Greenwood Press, 1966); Douglas Crimp and Adam Rolston, *AIDS Demo Graphics* (Seattle, Wash.: Bay Press, 1990).
30. For overviews of the rights-oriented gay politics of the 1980s and 1990s, see the essays collected in Craig Rimmerman, Kenneth Wald, and Clyde Wilcox, eds., *The Politics of Gay Rights* (Chicago: University of Chicago Press, 2000); Chris Bull and John Gallagher, *Perfect Enemies: The Religious Right, the Gay Movement, and the Politics of the 1990s* (New York: Crown Publishers, 1998); David Deitcher, ed., *The Question of Equality: Lesbian and Gay Politics since Stonewall* (New York: Scribner, 1995); David Rayside, *On the Fringe: Gays and Lesbians in Politics* (Ithaca, N.Y.: Cornell University Press, 1998); James Button, Barbara Rienzo, and Kenneth Wald, *Private Lives, Public Conflicts: Battles over Gay Rights in American Communities* (Washington, D.C.: Congressional Quarterly Press, 1997).
31. For example, Bruce Bawer, *A Place at the Table: The Gay Individual in American Society* (New York: Simon and Schuster, 1993), p. 47.
32. See, for example, D'Emilio, *Sexual Politics, Sexual Communities*; Toby Marotta, *The Politics of Homosexuality* (New York: Houghton Mifflin, 1981).
33. "Editorial," *Mattachine Review* 8 (November 1962): 2.
34. For an overview of gains and losses through the mid-1990s, see National Gay and Lesbian Task Force Policy Institute, *Capital Gains and Losses: A State by State Review of Gay, Lesbian, Bisexual, and Transgender, and HIV/AIDS-related Legislation in 1997* (Washington, D.C.: NGLTRF Policy Institute, 1997); see also Jean Reith Schroedel and Pamela Fiber, "Lesbian and Gay Policy Priorities: Commonality and Difference," and James Button et al., "The Politics of Gay Rights at the Local and State Level," in *The Politics of Gay Rights*, ed. Craig Rimmerman et al. (Chicago: University of Chicago Press, 2000).
35. Eskridge, *Gaylaw*, p. 139.
36. Ibid., p. 124.
37. See Suzanna Danuta Walters, *All the Rage: The Story of Gay Visibili' America* (Chicago: University of Chicago Press, 2001), p. 9.

38. Gregory Lewis and Jonathan Edelson, "DOMA and ENDA: Congress Votes on Gay Rights," in *The Politics of Gay Rights*, ed. Rimmerman, et al., p. 195.
39. Researchers have documented a dramatic and unexpected shift in moral attitudes in the mid-1990s. See Jeni Loftus, "America's Liberalization in Attitudes toward Homosexuality, 1973 to 1998," *American Sociological Review* 66 (October 2001): 762–82; Alan Yang, "The Polls—Trends, Attitudes toward Homosexuality," *Public Opinion Quarterly* 61 (1997): 477–507; Simon Dumenco, "They're Here, They're Queer, We're Used to It," *New York*, March 5, 2001, pp. 29–31.
40. Lewis and Edelson, "DOMA and ENDA"; Loftus, "America's Liberalization in Attitudes Towards Homosexuality"; Yang, "The Polls."
41. Quoted in Eskridge and Hunter, *Sexuality, Gender, and the Law*, p. 46.
42. On nationalism and sexual identity, see Jacqui Alexander, "Not Just (Any) Body Can Be a Citizen: The Politics of Law, Sexuality, and Postcoloniality in Trinidad and Tobago and the Bahamas," *Feminist Review* 48 (Fall 1994): 5–23; George Mosse, *Nationalisms and Sexualities: Middle-Class Moralities and Sexual Norms in Modern Europe* (Madison: University of Wisconsin Press, 1985); Richard Herrell, "Sin, Sickness, Crime: Queer Desire and the American State," *Identities* 2 (3): 273–300; Jyoti Puri, "Nationalism Has a Lot to Do with It! Unraveling Questions of Nationalism and Transnationalism in Lesbian/Gay Studies," in *Handbook of Lesbian and Gay Studies*, ed. Diane Richardson and Steven Seidman (London: Sage, 2002); Lauren Berlant and Elizabeth Freeman, "Queer Nationality," in *Fear of a Queer Planet*; Carl Stychin, *A Nation by Rights: National Cultures, Sexual Identity Politics, and the Discourse of Rights* (Philadelphia: Temple University Press, 1998).
43. Benedict Anderson, *Imagined Communities* (New York: Verso, 1983); Liah Greenfeld, *Nationalism: Five Roads to Modernity* (Cambridge, Mass.: Harvard University Press, 1992); Lynn Spillman, *Nation and Commemoration: Creating National Identities in the United States and Australia* (Cambridge: Cambridge University Press, 1997).
44. For example, Chrys Ingraham, *White Weddings*.
45. Cf. Anna Marie Smith, "The Politicization of Marriage in Contemporary American Public Policy: The Defense of Marriage Act and the Personal Responsibility Act," *Citizenship Studies* 5 (November 2001): 303–20; Don Westervelt, "Defending Marriage and Country," *Constellations* 8 (March 2001): 106–126; Richard Mohr, *A More Perfect Union: Why Straight America Must Stand up for Gay Rights* (Boston: Beacon Press, 1994).
46. See William Eskridge Jr., *The Case for Same-Sex Marriage: From Sexual Liberty to Civilized Commitment* (New York: Free Press, 1996) and *Equality Practice: Civil Unions and the Future of Gay Rights* (New York: Routledge, 2002).

47. A number of scholars have recently made similar arguments. Cf. Cheshire Calhoun, *Feminism, the Family, and the Politics of the Closet* (New York: Oxford University Press, 2000); Eskridge, *Equality Practice*; Morris Kaplan, *Sexual Justice: Democratic Citizenship and the Politics of Desire* (New York: Routledge, 1997).
48. Andrew Sullivan, *Virtually Normal: An Argument about Homosexuality* (New York: Vintage, 1996).
49. Ibid., p. 216.
50. Ibid., p. 170.
51. Ibid., p. 216.
52. Ibid., p. 185.
53. On the way race organizes social institutions and culture, see Michael Omi and Howard Winant, *Racial Transformation in the United States from the 1960s to the 1980s* (New York: Routledge, 1986); Joe Feagin and Hernan Vera, *White Racism* (New York: Routledge, 1995); Melvin Oliver and Thomas Shapiro, *Black Wealth/White Wealth: A New Perspective on Racial Inequality* (New York: Routledge, 1995). On gender as organizing social structure, see R. W. Connell, *Gender and Power: Society, the Person, and Sexual Politics* (Cambridge: Polity Press, 1987); Cynthia Epstein, *Deceptive Distinctions: Sex, Gender, and the Social Order* (New Haven, Conn.: Yale University Press, 1988); and Catherine MacKinnon, *Towards a Feminist Theory of the State* (Cambridge, Mass.: Harvard University Press, 1989).
54. Regarding the intersection of gender norms and heterosexual dominance, see class gay liberationist and lesbian-feminist writing (see "Introduction," note 18 and chapter 1, note 17).
55. Vaid, *Virtual Equality*, p. 183.
56. For the defense of gay marriage, see Thomas Stoddard, "Why Gay People Should Seek the Right to Marry," in *Lesbians, Gay Men, and the Law*, ed. William Rubenstein (New York: New Press, 1993); Sullivan, *Virtually Normal*; Nan Hunter, "Marriage, Law, and Gender: A Feminist Inquiry," *Law and Sexuality* 9 (1991); and Mohr, *A More Perfect Union*. For arguments against gay marriage, see Paula Ettelbrick, "Since When Is Marriage a Path to Liberation?" in *Lesbians, Gay Men, and the Law*, ed. Rubenstein; Nancy Polikoff, "We Will Get What We Ask For: Why Legalizing Gay and Lesbian Marriage Will Not 'Dismantle the Legal Structure of Gender in Every Marriage,'" *Virginia Law Review* 79 (1993): 1535–50; and Michael Warner, *The Trouble with Normal: Sex, Politics, and the Ethics of Queer Life* (Cambridge, Mass.: Harvard University Press, 2000).
57. For similar arguments, see Calhoun, *Feminism, the Family, and the Politics of the Closet*, and Eskridge, *Equality Practice*.
58. Virtually all researchers document a considerable weakening of "traditional"

gender roles in the organization of heterosexual families since the 1960s. There is much less agreement regarding the extent and meaning of this change and the role of factors such as women's earning power and children in shaping the gendered character of heterosexual intimacy. For some recent overviews of this research, see the work of the following sociologists: Suzanne Bianchi et al., "Is Anyone Doing the Housework? Trends in the Gender Division of Household Labor," *Social Forces* 79 (December 2000): 191–228; Scott Coltrane, *Gender and Families* (Thousand Oaks, Calif.: Pine Forge Press, 1998) and *Family Man: Fatherhood, Housework, and Gender Equity* (New York: Oxford University Press, 1996); and Linda Waite, ed., *The Ties That Bind: Perspectives on Marriage and Cohabitation* (New York: Aldine de Gruyter, 2000).

59. See Jeffrey Weeks, Brian Heaphy, and Catherine Donovan, *Same Sex Intimacies: Families of Choice and Other Life Experiments* (New York: Routledge, 2001); Christopher Carrington, *No Place like Home: Relationships and Family Life among Lesbians and Gay Men* (Chicago: University of Chicago Press, 1999); and Ellen Lewin, *Recognizing Ourselves: Ceremonies of Lesbian and Gay Commitment* (New York: Columbia University Press, 1998).
60. I have drawn considerably here on arguments developed by Eskridge in *Equality Practice*. The historian Nancy Cott has also commented on the historical weakening of the "normalizing" and normative status of marriage. "It could be contended, then, that by the 1980s the states and the nation had let go their grip on the institution of marriage along with their previous understanding of it. States' willingness to prosecute marital rape and wife abuse formed the most recent items in a trail of evidence, including the unchaining of morality from formal monogamy, the demise of the fiction of marital unity, and the institution of no-fault divorce. State legislatures and courts . . . resuscitated their much earlier willingness to treat couples 'living together' as if they were married, at least in economic terms. The families of unmarried couples are treated as families in courts. Parents' rights over children do not diminish . . . just because of birth out of wedlock." Cott speaks of a "public willingness to see marriage-like relationships as marriage" (p. 212). Despite what Cott calls the "disestablishment" between marriage and the state, the 1990s has seen a renewal of the preeminence of marriage in the face of new challenges such as extending marriage to gays or the "flaunting" of the uncoupling of marriage and monogamy in the Clinton-Lewinsky affair. See Nancy Cott, *Public Vows: A History of Marriage and the Nation* (Cambridge, Mass.: Harvard University Press, 2000), ch. 9.
61. For persuasive arguments to uncouple a range of basic material benefits from marriage, see Calhoun, *Feminism, the Family, and the Politics of the Closet*; Will Kymlicka, "Rethinking the Family," *Philosophy and Public Affairs* 20 (1991): 77–97; and Warner, *The Trouble with Normal.*

EPILOGUE

1. Nathan Glazer, *We Are All Multiculturalists Now* (Cambridge, Mass.: Harvard University Press, 1997).
2. For example, Ronald Takaki, *A Different Mirror: A History of Multicultural America* (New York: Little, Brown, 1993).
3. Desmond King, *Making Americans: Immigration, Race, and the Origins of the Diverse Democracy* (Cambridge, Mass.: Harvard University Press, 2000), p. 124.
4. My concept of multiculturalism has been influenced by the following work: David Hollinger, *Postethnic America: Beyond Multiculturalism* (New York: Basic Books, 1995); Will Kymlicka, *Multicultural Citizenship* (New York: Oxford University Press, 1995); Christopher Newfield and Avery Gordon, "Multuculturalism's Unfinished Business," in C. Newfield and A. Gordon, *Mapping Multiculturalism* (Minneapolis: University of Minnesota Press, 1996); Iris Marion Young, *Justice and the Politics of Difference* (Princeton, N.J.: Princeton University Press, 1990); and Charles Taylor, *Multiculturalism and the Politics of Recognition* (Princeton, N.J.: Princeton University Press, 1992).
5. Glazer, *We Are All Multiculturalists Now*, p. 79.
6. See Alan Wolfe, *One Nation, after All* (New York: Viking, 1998), p. 298.

INDEX